MADE IN KOREA

CHUNG JU YUNG AND
THE RISE OF HYUNDAI

RICHARD M. STEERS

ROUTLEDGE New York • London

Published in 1999 by
Routledge
29 West 35th Street
New York, NY 10001

Published in Great Britain by
Routledge
11 New Fetter Lane
London EC4P 4EE

Printed in the United States of America on acid-free paper.
Text Design by Cynthia Dunne

10   9   8   7   6   5   4   3   2

Library of Congress Cataloging-in-Publication Data

Steers, Richard M.
    Made in Korea : Chung Ju Yung and the rise of Hyundai / Richard M. Steers.
        p.   cm.
    Includes bibliographical references and index.
    ISBN 0-415-92050-7
    1. Chŏng, Chu-yŏng, 1915– 2. Hyŏndae Group. 3. Conglomerate
corporations—Korea (South)   4. Businesspeople—Korea (South)—
Biography.   I. Title.
HD2908.Z75H977   1999
338.7'6292'095195—dc21

98-30135
CIP

Dedicated
with sincere appreciation and admiration
to the men and women of Korea,
who sacrificed so much and worked
so diligently to create a better future
for their children.

CONTENTS

PREFACE

What differentiates highly successful companies from their more poorly performing competitors? What are the defining characteristics of successful entrepreneurial ventures? And how do companies sustain their competitive edge over the long term? Books focusing on the topic of competitive strategy are legion, filling the shelves of local bookstores. Advice to readers about how to win in the marketplace is common. Recent books on such notable American entrepreneurs as Bill Gates, Phil Knight, Warren Buffet, Sam Walton, and others stand as testimony to our collective interest in Wall Street winners. What is lacking in this literature, however, is substantive analyses of *global* entrepreneurs. While books abound on American corporate heroes, we know very little about business leaders from other parts of the world and how they built their companies. What are the keys to *their* success? They, too, are winners. They, too, are fierce competitors—frequently against our own companies. Without an awareness and understanding of these entrepreneurs from around the world, Westerners are doomed to set forth and compete empty-handed in the new global marketplace.

This book is about one such global entrepreneur: Chung Ju Yung, founder of South Korea's Hyundai Business Group. It tells the story of how Chung built one of today's truly great companies through a combination of tenacity, timing, political skills, and a business strategy that competitors understood only after it was too late. In each of his ventures, he exhibited a sheer determination to succeed, regardless of the difficulties. He referred to this unyielding drive as the *enterprising spirit*, and he worked tirelessly to instill this spirit in all of his 200,000 employees. It became the hallmark of Hyundai's success story.

Chung rose from poverty to become one of the world's richest billionaires, yet he lives in a simple two-story house in downtown Seoul. He started what has become one of the world's most successful global construction companies, and in the process built several of today's architectural wonders. He entered the shipbuilding business with no experience and went on to create the world's largest shipyard. He began making automobiles when foreign experts unanimously predicted he would fail. He convinced the International Olympic Committee to select Korea over Japan as the site for the highly successful 1988 Olympics. He was the first Korean businessman to travel to North Korea, China, and the former Soviet Union in search of both improved political relations and trade. And, much like H. Ross Perot, he ran for president in his native land because he strongly believed that he could play a role in building a stronger, more prosperous Korea. Indeed, many experts argue that had he won the 1992 election, Korea might not be in the difficult economic straits it is in today.

There is nothing usual about Chung Ju Yung. At the same time, there is nothing unusual about him. Chung repeatedly tells visitors that he is a simple man who had the good sense to recognize and capitalize on opportunities when they presented themselves. He always stayed close to his workers, preferring their company to that of the global executive elite. Hard work, creativity, and a capacity never to give up—this is the essence of Chung's life. It is his business philosophy. In fact, Chung's life is filled with lessons for would-be entrepreneurs who are committed to creating a better world. Such is the focus of this book.

What can we learn from the example of Hyundai and its leader? The deeper I got into the subject, the more firmly I became convinced that entrepreneurship is a global phenomenon, not a Western one, and that would-be players in the global economy ignore an understanding of successful "foreign" entrepreneurs only at their peril. And to understand global entrepreneurs, it is necessary to develop an appreciation of the cultures from which they emerged. Indeed, in the case of Korea, like so many other countries, it is virtually impossible to understand what makes entrepreneurs tick without knowing how they think, where they came from, what is important to them, and how they view their nation's destiny. Country and company are difficult concepts to disentangle for Korean entrepreneurs. In fact, little effort is expended in trying. If the company succeeds, so does the country, and vice versa. Winning is a national triumph; losing is a national disgrace. Chung Ju Yung understood this better than most, giving him a signal advantage over his competitors. To the extent that Westerners can learn these simple lessons, entrepreneurial success in the global marketplace can be significantly enhanced.

This is my third book about business enterprise in Korea. My first book, co-authored with Gerardo R. Ungson of the University of Oregon and Yoo Keun Shin of Seoul National University, was entitled *The Chaebol: Korea's New Industrial Might* (Harper & Row, 1989). This book attempted to summarize what was known at the time about the Korean business groups and the reasons behind their success. My next book, with Gerardo R. Ungson of the University of Oregon and Seung-Ho Park of Rutgers University, was entitled *Korean Enterprise: The Quest for Globalization* (Harvard Business School Press, 1997). This second book examined seven key challenges facing Korean companies as they attempted to evolve from national companies doing business internationally into truly global firms. Obviously, many of these firms never made it, as evidenced by the catastrophic economic crash of November 1997. Many Korean firms are now paying the price for failing to understand the fundamental economic and strategic precepts underlying globalization.

In this third book, I have focused on one Korean company to better understand how it grew and why it became so successful. I selected Hyundai because it is Korea's largest business group and because its founder, Chung Ju Yung, is nothing short of a national hero. He is widely admired and sometimes feared, not unlike Bill Gates or Phil Knight in the United States. Above all, though, he is widely respected—even revered by some—for helping to lead Korea out of the poverty and misery that followed the Korean War and into a sort of economic promised land, which became known in the 1980s and 1990s as the "miracle on the Han River." Although the "miracle" may be temporarily on hold, the long-term future of Korea remains bright according to most knowledgeable international economists, and there are still lessons to be learned.

The information for this book was derived from several sources. In recent years there has been a significant increase in the number of authoritative books focusing on Korea and its economic development. These include Alice Amsden's *Asia's Next Giant: South Korea and Late Industrialization*; Mark Clifford's *Troubled Tiger: Businessmen, Bureaucrats, and Generals in South Korea*; Kae Chung, Hak Chong Lee, and Ku Hyun Jung's *Korean Management: Global Strategy and Cultural Transformation*; Myung Hun Kang's *The Korean Business Conglomerate*; Chong Soon Kim's *The Culture of Korean Industry*; Eun Mee Kim's *Big Business, Strong State*; Linsu Kim's *Imitation to Innovation: The Dynamics of Korea's Technogical Learning*; Richard Pound's *Five Rings Over Korea*; Ray Weisenborn's *Korea's Amazing Century*; and Simon Winchester's *Korea: A Walk Through the Land of Miracles*. (Citations for these books are provided in the selected references section in the back of this book.) These books constitute a solid reference base upon which to begin the study of Korean enterprise.

Newspapers and business magazines from the United States, Europe, and Korea also provided considerable information. Of particular note here are *The Economist, Fortune, Business Week, Business Korea, Wall Street Journal, Los Angeles Times, International Herald Tribune, Korea Herald*, and *Chosun Ilbo*, all of which feature frequent and authoritative reporting on events in Korea. In addition, Hyundai made available numerous documents and reports covering the firm's long history. Most of these were translated from Korean for the purposes of this book. The company also arranged for site visits to various industrial facilities at my request. And the Korea Foundation continued its tradition of excellence in providing valuable source materials on Korean history and culture.

Additional information was collected through numerous interviews with people both inside the Hyundai organization and out. Hyundai executives were particularly helpful. Despite initial concerns about the objectivity of these sources, I was pleasantly surprised to find that most of the executives exhibited an uncommon level of candor and forthrightness in the interviews. The interviews were held privately, and everyone involved was given the option to remain anonymous, although few chose to do so. Identical questions were asked of several people in an effort to verify the quality of information that was secured. Interview data were also checked against published sources where possible, again to ensure accuracy. Interviews were also conducted with representatives from other companies, universities, and governmental agencies to provide additional perspectives on the events under study. Throughout, triangulation was used to the extent possible to cross-verify the facts and figures reported in this book.

Among those interviewed were several members of the Chung family, including the Honorary Chairman himself. I am particularly indebted to the family for their openness and access throughout this project. This is a family that understands the value of scholarship. In particular, I wish to thank Chung Ju Yung, Chung Se Yung, Chung Mong Koo, Chung Mong Joon, and Chung Mong Yoon for spending time with me on this project. This book would not have been possible without their willingness to cooperate in a manner not frequently seen with many global executives. I am most appreciative of their efforts on behalf of this project.

At the same time, I owe a special debt of gratitude to Park Se Yong, President of Hyundai Corporation; Kim Young Hwan, President of Hyundai Electronics Industries; Lee Young Il, Vice President of the Hyundai Public Relations Office; and Shyn Dong Soo, former Executive Vice President of

Hyundai Semiconductor America, for their continued support throughout this project. Each worked tirelessly on my behalf to provide relevant data and access to high-level personnel for interviews and discussions. They were ably assisted by Park Il Kwon and Kim Sang Nyun, who made the schedules work and were always available when help was needed. I respect their contributions and value their friendship.

As noted, research on this book was facilitated by a series of interviews with Hyundai executives and managers, who provided invaluable information. They include (in alphabetical order): Bae Jong Ho, Director, Hyundai Precision and Industry Company; Chae Soo Sam, President and CEO, Diamond Ad Ltd.; Chang Dong-Kook, Senior Executive Vice President, Hyundai Electronics Industries Company; Cho Choong Hooy, Executive Vice President, Hyundai Heavy Industries; Cho Kyu Chung, Vice President for Corporate Planning and Coordination, Hyundai Electronics Industries; Cho Song Rhee, Senior Manager, Hyundai Precision and Industry Company; Cho Sung Yong, General Manager, Hyundai Institute for Human Resources Development; Cho Yang Rae, President, Hyundai Motor Service Company; Choi Dae Jin, Director, Hyundai Pipe Company; Choi Har Kyung, Senior Vice President, Hyundai Electronics Industries; Chon Sung Won, advisor, Hyundai Motor Company; Chung Chai Kwan, Executive Vice President, Hyundai Corporation; Chung Soon-Won, Senior Director of Research, Hyundai Research Institute; Eum Yong Ki, President, Hyundai Livart; Han Sang-Joon, Vice President, Hyundai Motor Company; Han Yong Gyoo, Technical Marketing, Hyundai Electronics Industries; Jim Hartman, former President, Hyundai Semiconductor America; Hong Sung Wha, General Manager, Global Education Team, Hyundai Institute for Human Resource Development; Hwang Inseok, Senior Vice President, Hyundai Electronics Industries; Ju Shoong Ehl, President, Hyundai Semiconductor America; Juhn Myung Hun, President and CEO, Hyundai Motor America; Jung Chang Woo, General Manager, Hyundai Oil Refinery; Kim Choong Yong, Managing Director, Hyundai Motor Company; Kim Choong Yub, Vice President, Hyundai Petrochemical Company; Kim Dong Jin, President, Hyundai Space and Aircraft Company; Kim Hai Shik, Director, Polymer Production, Hyundai Petrochemical Company; Kim Ho Yung, Vice President, Hyundai Electronics Industries; Kim Jong Suk, former Vice President, Hyundai Precision and Industry Company; Kim Jong Keun, Director, Hyundai Institute for Human Resources Development; Kim Joo Yong, President and CEO, Korea Industrial Development Company; Kim Joong-Woong, President and CEO, Hyundai Research Institute; Kim Jung Kook, President, Hyundai Heavy Industries; Kim Kyung Hyun, Vice President, Hyundai Heavy Industries; Kim Kwang Myung, President and CEO, Hyundai Engineering & Construction Company; Kim Sang

Myung, Vice President for Corporate Planning, Hyundai Corporation; Kim
Seung Nyun, Assistant to the Group Chairman, Hyundai Business Group;
Kim Taik Ho, President, Hyundai Information Technology Company; Kim
Yung Ho, General Manager, Hyundai Engineering & Construction Com-
pany; Kwak Tae Yeub, Senior Executive Vice President, Hyundai Oil Refin-
ery; Kwon Ae Ja, Director, Welfare Department, Hyundai Engineering and
Construction Company; Kwon, Soo Shik, President, Hyundai Pipe Company;
Lee Byung Kyu, Director General, Asan Social Welfare Foundation; Lee Ik
Chi, President, Hyundai Securities, Ltd.; Lee Jun-Ho, Senior Research Fel-
low, Hyundai Research Institute; Lee Nae Heun, President and CEO,
Hyundai Engineering and Construction Company; Lee Woo-Sun, Secretary
to the Group Chairman, Hyundai Business Group; Lee Young Kyu, Section
Chief, Hyundai Public Relations Office; Lee Youn-Jae, Executive Vice Pres-
ident, Hyundai Heavy Industries; Min Kye Shik, Executive Vice President,
Hyundai Heavy Industries; Min Wang-Sik, General Manager, Hyundai
Motor Company; Park Byung Jae, Vice Chairman, Hyundai Motor Company;
Park Chan Jong, Director, Sales-Marketing, LED Division, Hyundai Elec-
tronics Industries; Park Chong Sup, President and CEO, Hyundai Electron-
ics America; Park Jeong In, President and CEO, Hyundai Precision and
Industry Company; Park Seung Kyun, Senior Vice President, Hyundai
Heavy Industries; Roger A. Richards, Senior English Instructor, Hyundai
Institute for Human Resources Development; Song Ji-Hun, Section Chief,
Hyundai Public Relations Office; Suh Tae Hwan, Executive Director, Inter-
national Division, Hyundai Securities Company; Yang Yong-Seok, Public
Relations Staff, Asan Medical Center; and Yoo Chul Jin, former President and
CEO, Hyundai Precision & Industry Company.

In addition, I should like to recognize several colleagues and friends who
also made substantive contributions to my research on this subject. They
include (again in alphabetical order): Alice Amsden, Professor of Political
Economy, MIT; Cho Dong Sung, Professor of Management, Seoul National
University; Kae Chung, Professor of Management, Old Dominion Univer-
sity; Joseph Ha, Vice President, Nike; Martin Hart-Landsberg, Professor of
Economics, Lewis and Clark College; David Holley, *Los Angeles Times*; Hong
Il-Sik, President, Korea University; Hong Keum Pyo, Shinhan Accounting
Corporation; Huh Wan Koo, Chairman, Sungsan Group; Hwang Eui-gak,
Professor of Economics, Korea University; Kim Byung Soo, President, Yonsei
University; Kim Jin-won, Director, Korea Representative Office, State of
Oregon; Kim Jooup, Associate Professor of Management, Chungbuk
National University; Kim Joungwon, President, Korea Foundation; Kim Kee
Young, Vice President, Yonsei University; Kim Linsu, Professor of Manage-
ment, Korea University; Kim Wan-Gyoo, Director, Industrial Development

Board for Northern Ireland-Korea Office; Louis Kraar, Board of Editors, *Fortune*; Kwak Soo-Il, Professor of Management, Seoul National University; Lee Byungnam, Executive Director, LG Academy; Lee Chang Kyu, Economic Editor, *Joong-Ang Ilbo*; Lee Hak-Chong, Professor of Management, Yonsei University; Lee Hong Kyu, Assistant Secretary to the President, Republic of Korea; Sang Lee, Professor of Management, University of Nebraska; Lee Chong Suk, Executive Director, LG Group; Nam Sanghoon, Assistant Professor of Management, University of Victoria; Park Oh Soo, Professor of Management, Seoul National University; Seung-Ho Park, Associate Professor of Management, Rutgers University; Park Ungsuh, President, Samsung Economic Research Institute; Helena Phua, *International Herald Tribune*; Rhee Song Nae, Northwest Christian College; Rhew Ki-won, President, PacInfo; Ryu Han Sup, Chairman, Shinsegae Group; Shim Won Shul, Assistant Professor of Management, Hanyang University; Shin Yoo-Keun, Professor of Management, Seoul National University; John Sohn, Executive Deputy Chairman, Federation of Korean Industries; Sung Ki Bum, President, Holt Social Services; Horace Underwood, Dean, Yonsei University; Gerardo R. Ungson, Professor of Management, University of Oregon; and Yoon Suk Chul, Professor of Management, Seoul National University.

I would like to recognize the Charles H. Lundquist College of Business at the University of Oregon for its continued support and encouragement of my research on Korean enterprise. The University of Oregon has long been committed to international research and education and has been a supportive partner throughout this project. I am deeply indebted to Sam Cho, my research assistant on this project, both for his friendship and his tireless commitment to making this project a reality. Similarly, I want to thank Melissa Rosati of Routledge for her patience, encouragement, and expertise to help bring this project to fruition. Finally, I would like to express a special debt of gratitude to my family for their continued support and encouragement throughout this project. To my mother Pat, my wife Sheila, and my daughter Kathleen, I offer a special thanks that can only come from the heart.

Richard M. Steers
Eugene, Oregon

SHARED DESTINIES:
KOREA AND CHUNG JU YUNG

"To my way of thinking, there may be miracles in religion but not in politics or economics....[W]e succeeded because our people devoted their enterprising spirits. They used the force of their minds. Conviction creates indomitable efforts. This is the key to miracles....Man's potential is limitless."

—CHUNG JU YUNG[1]

I n 1970, Chung Ju Yung decided that he would enter the shipbuilding business.* At the time, his company, the Hyundai Business Group, was South Korea's largest construction company. It was also just beginning to assemble a small number of cars for the local market under a licensing agreement with Ford Motor Company. But although Chung's company was successful by Korean standards, it was minuscule compared to its American and Japanese rivals. Few Western executives had ever heard of the fledgling company, and fewer still wanted to do business with it. Korean companies were widely seen as manufacturers of shoddy products based on antiquated technology, and doing business with them was thought to be a risky proposition at best. But Chung was undeterred: shipbuilding would be his next major venture. Never mind that he had never built a rowboat, let alone a large, oceangoing carrier. Never mind that he didn't even own a shipyard. He had made up his mind.

To Chung, the logic for Hyundai to enter the shipbuilding business was obvious. At the time, his company was working hard to expand its construction

---

* Following Korean custom, Chung's family name is listed first, followed by his given names. This is the reverse of the Western practice of listing one's given names first, followed by one's family name. The Korean custom will be followed throughout this book.

business overseas. With the experience he had gained as Korea's largest contractor, Chung was convinced he could compete successfully in the construction business abroad, especially in the oil-rich Middle East. As he saw it, if Hyundai was going to construct harbors, ports, housing, and other facilities in overseas locations like Iran, Bahrain, Kuwait, and Saudi Arabia, it might as well also make the ships that served those ports. Why give the business to someone else?

With this vision in mind, Chung approached several Japanese companies in search of assistance, but only one Japanese firm—Mitsubishi Heavy Industries—would even talk with the Korean upstart. Japan, after all, built the biggest and best ships in the world and saw no reason to foster competition from an underdeveloped nation. After months of painful negotiation, Mitsubishi finally made an offer to Hyundai. They would assist the Korean firm in building ships as long as Hyundai's shipyard capacity was limited to relatively small 50,000 dead weight ton (DWT) vessels and as long as Mitsubishi retained sole management rights to oversee all projects. As Chung saw it, Mitsubishi's offer was reminiscent of Japan's painful colonial rule over Korea. Their real intent was to block Korean ship builders from competing in the larger and more lucrative 500,000 DWT ship market.[2] Chung rejected Mitsubishi's offer out of hand as a ploy to keep him from becoming a global player in this market. He wanted to be a leader, not a follower.

Unsuccessful in the Pacific, Chung and his brother traveled to Europe in March 1971 in search of technology and financing. Before they left, however, Chung had already laid the groundwork for his shipbuilding empire. Taking advantage of the Korean government's development policy aimed at stimulating heavy industry, Chung bought land for his shipyard in the port city of Ulsan, 250 miles southeast of Seoul. Then he signed up the British engineering firm of Appledore and Scott Lithgow to provide engineering, administration, and marketing support for the new venture. The terms were very favorable to Hyundai: $1.7 million for the technology and 0.5 percent as a commission on future sales. What Chung needed now was $63 million in financing to get the project started.

Hyundai could raise only $10 million, which was matched with another $10 million by a Korean government eager to see the venture succeed. Chung now needed to raise the remaining $43 million—more than the total assets of Hyundai at the time. Meeting with bankers in Switzerland and France, Chung repeatedly heard the same refrain: How can we make a shipbuilding loan to a company that has never even built a row boat? Chung's proposal was ridiculed as the unrealistic vision of a Third World dreamer. Next, Chung flew to London. As he recalled later, "The British were my last chance, and I was determined to make the most of it."[3] Chung outlined his grand design to representatives of Barclays Bank. Chung wanted a loan to build the shipyard, as well as several ships. After listening patiently, Barclays replied that no Korean company had ever built large ships and that Korean firms did not even possess the technology to do so. "I insisted, however, that we could build one," Chung replied.[4]

The Barclays representative then cited Korea's own shipbuilding association's conclusion that the country was incapable of building ships of such a size. Chung again had a reply:

> Don't you know that the person who thinks a job is possible is the one who is going to get it done? If other Korean shipbuilders thought that the venture was feasible, they would all be vying to undertake it. But it's precisely because they don't think it is possible that they aren't even trying. It's only obvious that they gave you that kind of evaluation. I think the project is possible and, because of this, I am going to do everything possible to make it come true.[5]

Barclays Bank finally agreed to listen to a recommendation from Hyundai's engineering partner, Appledore. However, Appledore's chairman remained unconvinced that Hyundai could find buyers for the kind of ships it wanted to build, even if it got the loan and actually completed construction. When Chung heard this, he sensed victory. In a meeting with Appledore executives, Chung pulled a Korean 500 won note out of his wallet and invited his colleagues to examine the bill. On the reverse side of the bill was a reproduction of Korea's famous turtle ship, the world's first ironclad vessel, built in 1592 by the Korean navy to successfully fend off a Japanese invasion. "Korea built ironclad vessels in the 16th century," Chung observed wryly. "You can't possibly compare Korea with the U.K., which only began making such ships in the 19th century....Once we get started, our enormous potential ability will emerge."[6] The point was made, and Appledore agreed to support Hyundai's efforts.

Only one more hurdle remained. For Barclays to make the loan, Britain's Export Credit Guarantee Department had to insure the loan with an export credit guarantee. For this to happen, Hyundai would have to prove that it had buyers for its ships. Toward this end, Appledore introduced Chung to a ship-broker who, in turn, introduced him to George Livanos, a wealthy Greek shipping tycoon. Chung showed Livanos drawings of both his proposed shipyard and a 260,000 DWT oil tanker he hoped to build there. Impressed with Chung's audacity and commitment, Livanos agreed to purchase two such tankers, called VLCCs (for "very large crude carrier"), for $31 million each, with an initial $2 million down.

With this agreement in hand, Barclays finally agreed to form a European consortium of banks to lend Hyundai $50,570,000 for the venture. At the age of 57, with no experience or technology and very little of his own capital, Chung was now in the shipbuilding business. All he needed now was a ship-yard.[7]

CONFUCIAN TIGER

Many stories like this one are told about Chung Ju Yung, the billionaire founder of Korea's largest company. Most of these stories have a common theme. They tell how an upstart entrepreneur from a Third World nation repeatedly made outrageous promises to secure contracts and business op-portunities and then proceeded to make good on his commitments. They also tell about undaunted courage and perseverance in the face of adversity. Chung was born in rural poverty but grew up to become one of the world's wealthiest businessmen. He contracted to build two supertankers before he even broke ground on a shipyard and would go on to build the world's largest shipbuilding facility. He built an automobile plant that had an annual pro-duction capacity ten times larger than Korea's entire domestic car market and that would go on to become one of the world's largest automobile companies. He became the world's largest contractor in the lucrative Middle East within a year of entering the market. He started an electronics company that quickly became a technology leader in a highly competitive global industry. He became Korea's biggest farmer by reclaiming land from the Yellow Sea for rice cultivation. He led Korea's successful campaign to secure the 1988 Olympics. He became the first Korean businessman to open dialogues with the Soviet Union, China, and even North Korea at a time when such efforts were not even supported by his own government. And he tried, albeit unsuc-cessfully, to become Korea's first democratically elected civilian president.

"Unbelievable audacity." "Unyielding determination." "Cunning strate-gist." These are but a few of the ways that Chung and his company have been described over the years. Indeed, Harvard economist Michael Porter compares Chung's business style with "the shoot-'em-up cowboys of the American West."[8] According to Porter, Chung and several of his Korean com-petitors "rush into industries and are prepared to make huge investments in equipment and plants in advance of any substantial orders."[9] It is a phenom-enon that few Westerners can fully comprehend, let alone emulate. It is entrepreneurship at its finest, and no one did it better than Chung Ju Yung.

When Chung officially retired as chairman of Hyundai in 1991 at the age of 77, group sales surpassed $51 billion, accounting for 16 percent of Korea's total gross national product (GNP). Hyundai exports, at $9 billion, repre-sented 12 percent of Korea's foreign trade. Corporate assets totaled more than $30 billion. The company was actively engaged in producing and managing countless different product lines and services that included construction, automobiles, shipbuilding, electronics, petrochemicals, oil refining, offshore oil rigs, banking and investments, wood products, aluminum, industrial robots, merchant marine, engineering services, high-rise apartment complexes, department stores, hotels, and advertising. Had these figures been made public at the time—in deference to Chairman Chung's desire for privacy, they were not—Hyundai would have been ranked as the eleventh largest firm in the *Fortune* International 500.

Today, Hyundai remains a world leader. Group sales for 1997 surpassed $90 billion, making the company larger than all but a handful of U.S. and Japanese firms.[10] Hyundai currently employs 200,000 people worldwide working for more than 50 group companies in Korea and 113 subsidiary companies in 53 countries. Overseas sales alone surpassed $17 billion, or about 12 percent of Korea's entire exports for 1997. Despite recent economic downturns and political upheavals at home and increased competition abroad, Hyundai continues to prosper.

Today, Chung Ju Yung is widely recognized as one of the world's most successful entrepreneurs. His net worth in 1997 was estimated at $6 billion, making him one of the ten wealthiest men in Asia and among the thirty wealthiest people in the world.[11] His wealth surpassed that of all but a dozen Americans.[12] In 1995, *Time* magazine identified him as one of the top six business leaders in Asia who were most responsible for the region's striking economic achievements during the past fifty years.[13]

BECOMING A GLOBAL PLAYER: KOREA IN THE 1990s

Chung Ju Yung's meteoric rise from rags to riches is paralleled closely by Korea's emergence as a key player in the global economy. Indeed, the two worked their way to prosperity hand in hand, along with several other successful Korean firms—and in record time, too. Back in December 1985, *Business Week* sounded an alarm to the West. Printed across its front cover in boldface type was this warning: "The Koreans Are Coming."[14] For most Americans at the time, the prevailing view of Korea was based largely on watching reruns of the *M*A*S*H* television series. Korea was considered an underdeveloped nation with few prospects for the future. Many believed that Korea's capital, Seoul, still lacked paved streets and other fundamental amenities. Few Westerners had ever thought of Korea as a major industrial power, let alone a global competitor. In 1985, the prevailing fear focused on whether Korea would flood the American market with cheap cars and poorly made televisions and VCRs, much as the Japanese had in an earlier time.

Only a short decade later, in July 1995, *Business Week* again featured Korea on its cover. This time, however, the headline read, "Korea Headed for High Tech's Top Tier."[15] In just ten years, Korea had moved from an ignominious Third World producer of second-rate goods to an industry leader in such high-tech products as DRAM (dynamic random access memory) memory chips and liquid-crystal-display (LCD) panels. Korea was reaching for the top of the technology ladder in record time and was achieving heights that few thought possible just a few years before. No other country had accomplished what Korea had in such a short period of time. It had redefined the meaning of global entrepreneurship.

To understand just how far Korea had come by the end of 1997, consider the following:[16]

▶ South Korea ranked as the world's eleventh largest economy. It was a world leader in shipbuilding, steel production, consumer electronics, semi-conductors, construction, and personal computers.

▶ Korea produced close to 3 million automobiles and exported over 1 million of these, making it the fifth largest car-exporting nation in the world.

▶ Korea's per capita income had risen from $94 per year in 1960 to over $10,000. Some economists estimated that this income would reach $42,000 by the year 2010.

▶ Korean exports had grown from $33 million in 1960 to $130 billion.

▶ Life expectancy had soared from 47 years in 1955 to 71.

▶ Korea ranked as the United States' eighth largest trading partner. Korean firms exported $25 billion worth of goods to the United States. At the same time, U.S. firms exported over $30 billion in goods and services to Korea. Korea was the sixth largest market for overall U.S. exports and the fourth largest market for U.S. agricultural exports.

▶ Korean firms invested about $2 billion in developing their U.S. operations. To date, Korean firms have invested over $20 billion to establish overseas production bases. U.S. firms currently have more than $3 billion in direct investment in Korea.

▶ Korea's gross domestic product (GDP) growth rate was 7.1 percent.

▶ Total gross national product (GNP) for South Korea was expected to rise from $490 billion in 1997 to over $2 trillion in 2010.

By any measure, Korea in 1997 represented an economic success story. It is often referred to as the "Miracle on the Han River," after the river that flows through its capital city. Korea's rise from the ashes of war and occupation to the pinnacle of success across a wide spectrum of advanced products and services has been considered no less than an economic miracle and an inspiration for many newly industrializing countries. Many saw its recent acceptance for membership in the Organization for Economic Cooperation and Development (OECD) as testimony to how this former impoverished country has emerged as a new global economic and political force.

Hyundai's Chung Ju Yung provided his own assessment of why Korea was able to accomplish so much in such a short period of time:

> To my way of thinking, there may be miracles in religion but not in politics or economics. What economists call a 'miracle' is in reality a lame excuse for the realization that something that contradicts one's favorite economic theory has actually been accomplished. Theoretically or scientifically, we [Koreans] have accomplished the impossible. In fact, we succeeded because our people devoted their enterprising spirits. They used the force of their minds. Conviction creates indomitable efforts. This is the key to miracles....Man's potential is limitless.[17]

Chung did not believe in miracles. He believed in hard work combined with ingenuity and innovation. He believed in discovering and capitalizing on opportunities before his opponents could act. In this way, he built a career, a business empire, and a personal fortune.

Unfortunately, however, progress is seldom linear or even predictable. Throughout history, great accomplishments have frequently been followed by significant setbacks. Achievements seem to reach a plateau, only to rise again at a later date. Such was the case in the West with the Great Depression of the 1930s, as well as the serious economic recession of the late 1980s. Banks failed. Companies failed. Massive layoffs ensued, as did economic restructuring. Following such travails, most Western economies, including those of the United States and Great Britain, returned stronger than ever and better positioned to compete in the emerging global economy. Beginning in late 1997, it became Asia's turn. One by one, Asia's great economies, from Indonesia and Thailand to Japan and South Korea, began to falter. The pattern was hauntingly familiar: bankruptcies, layoffs, and bailouts. Government leaders and policy makers seemed incapable of stemming the slide.

In the case of Korea, the fall was swift and sure. It began with a surprise announcement by the government in late November 1997 that the country was in financial trouble and required outside support. Overnight, Korea's economy went into a tailspin. The economic crisis was initially prompted by several major corporate bankruptcies. Korean banks were found to have made over $50 billion in bad, and probably unrecoverable, loans. Many corporations had borrowed well beyond their means of repayment for massive projects that often made little sense in terms of economic development. Accusations of corporate greed flourished, countered by accusations of union greed. Labor unions seemed intent on demanding ever-increasing wages and benefits that far outstripped any productivity gains. A weak government vacillated and proved either unwilling or unable to take concrete actions to curb either business or labor. International markets began to repudiate the Korean currency (the *won*), which fell to half its value within weeks. The Korean stock market also fell precipitously, as did Korea's foreign reserves. Consumer prices and Korea's trade imbalance with other nations both increased significantly. As a result, massive layoffs were initiated by companies that had lost the capacity to pay their bills. More bankruptcies ensued, as did more layoffs. In the end, the Korean government was forced to seek a record $57 billion bailout from the International Monetary Fund.[18] And as the economy unraveled, voters were about to go to the polls to elect a new president. Becoming Korea's new leader would prove to be a daunting responsibility indeed.

But this book is not about Korea's recent economic crisis. Instead, it is a study of global entrepreneurship. It focuses on the life and contributions of Chairman Chung as he rose from poverty and obscurity to wealth and fame. It tells the story of how he built his company. Even so, many of the lessons of Chung's life may be pertinent to the decisions faced by today's policy makers. When Chung published his autobiography in 1991, he chose the audacious title *Ordeals, But No Failures*.[19] It was an immediate best-seller in Korea. In his book, Chung told many stories about his early life and later success. Throughout, he asserted that although he had confronted numerous challenges, he had steadfastly refused to be beaten. He possessed a will to succeed that drove him to avoid failure. Throughout his career, he drove his employees tirelessly to refuse to give up. In many ways, this theme characterizes modern Korea. Currently, Korea is experiencing a major economic ordeal, clearly the most serious it has faced since the Korean War. As Chung's book title implies, however, most informed Korea watchers believe that this is only a temporary setback. Koreans are used to coping with crises, economic and otherwise. In the end, however, they will emerge stronger and more agile in the global marketplace. It is an optimism born of experience.

ENTREPRENEURSHIP AND ECONOMIC GROWTH

Throughout history, entrepreneurship like that exemplified by Chung Ju Yung and his company has been a defining characteristic of any great society. It represents the principal engine of growth that transforms a people or culture from an underdeveloped land characterized by poverty and despair into a modern, dynamic—and prosperous—nation capable of holding its own in the global environment. The nation-building consequences of genuine entrepreneurial behavior can be seen throughout history, from the ancient civilizations of Greece, Rome, and Byzantium to the more modern examples of contemporary Japan, Germany, and the United States.

In the West, we have been inundated with stories of the great American entrepreneurs: Bill Gates of Microsoft, Phil Knight of Nike, Steven Jobs of Apple, Sam Walton of Wal-Mart, Michael Dell of Dell Computers, Warren Buffett of Berkshire Hathaway, and so on. What we frequently fail to understand, however, is that entrepreneurial behavior is a global phenomenon. Throughout the world we find world-class entrepreneurs, including Japan's Akio Morita of SONY, Taiwan's Stan Shih of Acer Computer, Thailand's Dhanin Chearavanont of the CP Group, Britain's Richard Branson of the Virgin Atlantic Group, Germany's Dietman Hopp of SAP, France's Bernard Arnault of Louis Vuitton and Givenchy, Mexico's Carlos Helu of Grupo Carso, Hong Kong's Lee Shau Kee of Henderson Land, and South Africa's Albert Koopman of Cashbuild. Though perhaps less familiar than their U.S. counterparts, these entrepreneurs exhibit the same characteristic flair to create value through innovation, to develop new products or services, and to create markets where none existed before. It is because of such individuals that the global economy advances.

Entrepreneurship is the creation of value through innovation. Wherever it is practiced throughout the world, it typically involves the same interrelated functions:[20] identification of a new economic opportunity, such as a new product, service, production process, or market; evaluation of the profitability of the new opportunity; access to sufficient financial resources to implement the new concept; access to appropriate physical resources and technologies; access to trained personnel capable of producing or delivering the new product or service; a predictable, and preferably mutually beneficial, relationship with government; and access to suitable suppliers and purchasers. These functions in open and competitive markets typically lead to innovative products and services becoming widely available at competitive prices. They also create wealth for individuals and societies. Although some view this as creeping materialism or even exploitation, others see it as economic development and an inevitable sign of progress. Either way, it is this entrepreneurial spirit that is largely responsible for most of our advancement along the economic highway.

For this reason, it is important to understand the motivations and drives of successful entrepreneurs. It is also instructive to learn how such motivations have been put into practice to accomplish great works. The more we can learn about the craft of great entrepreneurs, the more we can teach others so they can succeed in their own endeavors. This book is about one such entrepreneur, his company, and his country. It tells the story of South Korea's remarkable transformation from a poverty-ridden agrarian country of little global consequence into one of the world's most advanced nations—all within the span of several decades. It also tells the story of a Korean company that in no small way was responsible for this transformation. Countries and companies both prosper when political and economic principles mandate cooperative efforts, and nowhere is this more true than in the case of South Korea. It is a lesson well worth serious study by developing and developed countries alike.

In the case of Korea in general and Hyundai in particular, the emergent conditions that fostered entrepreneurial behavior came together under the regime of Major General Park Chung Hee, who assumed near dictatorial control over the country in 1961. For the next eighteen years, Park ruled with one goal in mind: the economic development of Korea. Park offered government financing; access to technology, education, and training for workers; and protected markets to entrepreneurs willing to take their chances. In return, he tolerated no failures. These conditions perfectly suited Chung Ju Yung's goals and aspirations for his fledgling company. Chung was a man with big dreams, countless ideas, and infinite drive. And, like Park, he tolerated no failures.

Chung and Park were kindred spirits, both committed to Korea's national prosperity and both possessed of an enterprising spirit that drove them to their respective destinies. Without either of these men, Korea would not be the developed and prosperous nation that it is today. Without strong government leaders like Park, who had a specific economic game plan and demanded widespread adherence to it, and without entrepreneurs like Chung, who had a corporate game plan and demanded widespread adherence to it, Korea would have remained an agrarian nation of farmers and beggars subsisting on handouts from the superpowers. It would have spent decades trying sincerely but ineffectively to pull itself up by its own broken bootstraps. But these two leaders, Park and Chung, worked hand in hand to rebuild their homeland. And in this pursuit they had a secret weapon: the tireless resolve and fanatical dedication of the Korean people, who would make any sacrifice for the benefit of future generations.

In many ways, the story of Hyundai's success over the past fifty years is the story of Korea's success over the same period. The company and the country grew and developed together through a cooperative effort—sometimes friendly, sometimes hostile. Throughout, Hyundai required the assistance of the Korean government, just as the government required the assistance of Hyundai and other Korean companies. Westerners, with their widespread mistrust of close business–government relations, have a difficult time understanding this effort in co-prosperity, but in the case of South Korea such a relationship succeeded. The government created the opportunities, technology, and financing for companies like Hyundai. The companies, in turn, provided the entrepreneurial genius and drive to construct concrete realities out of government dreams.

Korea is blessed with many entrepreneurs, but this book focuses specifically on the growth and development of the Hyundai Business Group and its founder. It examines how Chung Ju Yung was able to emerge from poverty to create one of the world's largest and richest companies. It examines how Korea and Koreans prospered as a result. And, perhaps most important, it examines what Westerners can learn from the example of Chung and Hyundai that can be applied to their own entrepreneurial pursuits. If there is a fundamental lesson in this book, it is that, although entrepreneurial endeavors may be influenced by cultural differences, their origins and consequences remain global in scope. Every nation has entrepreneurs. They may navigate using different cultural road maps, but each strives in his or her own unique way to achieve innovative excellence and to cross the finish line before the competition. In this endeavor, the lessons of Hyundai are universally applicable.

KOREA'S ENTREPRENEURIAL HERITAGE

"Contemporary Koreans think they have escaped history and tradition in the dizzying pace of an energetic twentieth century. Meanwhile, they move in ways that would be inexplicable without investigations of a much longer period....To grasp modern Korea we will first need a tour through previous centuries...to make the point that you can forget about history but history will not forget about you."

—BRUCE CUMINGS, HISTORIAN, NORTHWESTERN UNIVERSITY[1]

South Korea, officially the Republic of Korea, occupies the southern half of the Korean peninsula, as shown in Figure 2-1. It is approximately 300 miles long and 185 miles wide and covers a land mass of 39,000 square miles, about the size of the state of Indiana. Its coastline is 819 miles long; its highest point, Mount Halla on Cheju Island, is 6,398 feet high. Beijing, China, is 500 miles to the west, and Japan is 150 miles to the southeast. Its only land boundary is with the Communist-led Democratic People's Republic of Korea to the north. Almost 80 percent of Korea consists of rugged mountains, leaving only 20 percent of the land to be used for agriculture and living. This difficult terrain has helped Koreans defend themselves throughout their history from various invaders and has helped preserve traditional Korean culture. At the same time, this uninviting landscape has made both commerce and agriculture very difficult. The Koreans have always had to struggle to survive.

The current population of South Korea is 45 million people, approximately 80 percent of whom live in urban areas. Korea's capital, Seoul, with over 11 million people, is one of the most modern and dynamic cities in Asia. It is the

Figure 2-1　*Map of the Korean Peninsula*

commercial and political center of the country, housing Korea's National Assembly as well as the headquarters for all of Korea's major firms. A modern subway system, built for the 1988 Olympics, eases some of the commuting burden on people who work downtown, where streets are routinely heavily congested with automobile traffic. Downtown Seoul contains some of the most impressive high-rise buildings in the world—most designed by Korean architects. These include the Daehan Life Insurance Company building, one of the tallest commercial buildings in the world; the award-winning twin towers of the LG Group headquarters on Yoido Island; and the World Trade Center in Yongdong, the envy of most nations. Numerous other high-rise buildings are currently under construction in the prosperous new Kangnam section of Seoul on the south side of the Han River.

Visitors to Korea are repeatedly struck with the vibrancy of the entire country. Korean cities like Seoul, Pusan, and Taegu, among others, are commercial centers first and foremost—cities where manufacturing, investments, and trade thrive. To the outsider, Koreans seem to conduct business around the clock. In contrast to many Westerners, who typically work to live, Koreans definitely live to work. From the wealthy conglomerates to the countless shop owners to the impoverished street vendors, everyone is buying, selling, trading, negotiating, and making deals late into the night. In fact, it has always been this way in Korea. Despite repeated assertions in the West that Koreans have historically lacked an entrepreneurial drive, nothing could be further from the truth. Korea has always been an entrepreneurial nation, although these efforts frequently have been smothered by foreign invasions and occupations. During periods of true independence, the Korean people have repeatedly shown themselves to be among the world's foremost innovators, inventors, and traders. This is amply demonstrated by even a cursory look at Korean history, a requisite starting place for understanding Korea's cultural influences on contemporary business practices.

Korea's recorded history spans five thousand years, a fact that is hard for many Westerners to comprehend. It is a history of struggle, conflict, and change.[2] Following centuries of existence in the shadow of stronger neighbors to the north and east, and after continual invasions and conflicts with the Chinese and Japanese, the Mongols and Manchus, the Russians and Americans, it is indeed surprising that Korea is still called the "Land of the Morning Calm." Its history is characterized by adaptation and innovation. From earliest times, Koreans learned from the Chinese and, in turn, taught the Japanese. Even so, Korea is not a miniature China or Japan. Throughout the ages and in the face of almost continual intrusion and attack, Korea has retained its own uniqueness, identity, and culture.

MYTHICAL BEGINNINGS

Korea's earliest history is shrouded in mystery. As the American historian James Gale correctly points out, Korea "takes its beginnings in the misty ages of the past that elude all attempts at close investigation, ages that lie somewhere between that of man and those of angels and spirit beings, joining heaven on the one hand and earth on the other."[3] An ancient text describes Korea's beginning as follows:

> In those days there lived a she-bear and a tigress in the same cave. They prayed to Hwanung [the son of the divine creator who had descended from heaven] to be blessed with incarnation as human beings. Hwanung took pity on them and gave each a bunch of mugwort and twenty pieces of garlic, saying, 'If you eat this holy food and do not see the sunlight for one hundred days, you will become human beings.' The she-bear and the tigress took the food and ate it, and retired into the cave. In twenty-one days the bear, who had faithfully observed Hwanung's instructions, became a woman. But the tigress, who had disobeyed, remained in her original form. The bear-woman could find no husband, however, so she prayed under the sandalwood tree to be blessed with a child. Hwanung heard her prayers and married her. She conceived and bore a son who was called Tan'gun Wanggom, the King of Sandalwood.[4]

As the saga continues, after Tan'gun grew up, he consolidated the various primitive tribes into a single kingdom, which he purportedly ruled from 2333 B.C.E. to 1122 B.C.E. Then, Kija, a decedent of the mythical Shang rulers of China, is said to have arrived and established himself as ruler, whereupon Tan'gun resumed his spirit form and returned to the heavens. It is important to remember that similarly improbable stories of the creation can be found in most religions and cultures around the world today. Moreover, modern-day archaeological studies clearly demonstrate that people inhabited the peninsula as early as 4270 B.C.E. and that in 108 B.C.E. the Han Empire of China conquered what is now Korea, thereby reinforcing the myth of Kija, the Chinese invader (see Table 2-1).

Beyond its story value, the myth of Tan'gun and the founding of ancient Korea provides some insight into the cultural motivations of the Korean people that persist to this day. The she-bear was rewarded for following the directives of superiors, while the tigress was penalized for demonstrating independence. Koreans believe strongly that there is a natural order of things that individuals breach at their own peril. Nature and people must live in harmony, and there is a divine structure underlying this relationship. Indeed, Korea's oldest religion, shamanism, emerges from this set of beliefs. Shamanism derives its

TABLE 2-1

TIMELINE OF EARLY KOREAN HISTORY AND CULTURAL DEVELOPMENTS

DATE	EVENT
2333–1122 B.C.E.	Tan'gun Period. Mythical Tan'gun said to consolidate various Korean tribes into a single kingdom.
1122–450 B.C.E.	Kija Period. Mythical Kija arrives from China and establishes himself as ruler over Korea.
450–108 B.C.E.	Emergence of Tribal Leagues (Puyo, Mahan, Chinhan, Pyonhan).
108 B.C.E.	China's Han rulers conquer Korea.
57	Three Kingdoms Period begins (Koguryo, Paekche, and Silla).
634	World's first astronomical observatory built.
668	Unified Silla Period begins; Kyong-ju becomes capital.
706	World's first wood block printing completed.
751	Sokkuram Buddhist cave shrine completed, containing one of the world's largest statues of Buddha carved from a single block of white granite.
751	Pulgaksa Temple built as Korea's center for Buddhism.
771	Emille Bell cast.
935	Koryo dynasty begins.
958	Civil service examinations introduced for selecting government officials.
1234	Invention of movable metal type to print books, over 200 years before Europeans.
1251	First complete wood block printing of Buddhist scriptures.
1392	Yi (or Choson) dynasty begins; capital moved to Seoul.
1429	First public handbook on farming methods published.
1434	Invention of first water clock, or clepsydra. Construction of first sundial for public use.
1438	Royal Astronomical Observatory begins collecing systematic meteorological data. Records compiled for over 400 years.

DATE	EVENT
1440	World's first public opinion poll completed.
1442	Invention of the rain gauge for the scientific study of agriculture, 200 years before Europeans developed similar technology.
1443	Korean alphabet (hangul) developed.
1445	First systematic study of medicine published.
1446	First book to teach people how to read and write in Korean published.
1458	First comprehensive history of Korea begun.
1592	Japanese invasion defeated by Admiral Yi's use of ironclad vessels, almost 300 years prior to Western usage.
1627	First Europeans (Dutch) land in Korea; taken captive.
1866	*U.S.S. Sherman* invades Korean waters; sunk by Koreans.
1882	Korea signs trade treaties with the West.
1910	Japan officially annexes Korea with the approval of Western nations.

name from the Tungus word *shaman*, meaning sorcerer. It teaches that spirits control all forces of nature and that followers must put their faith in ghosts, fate, and magic. As with the ancient—and also contemporary—Chinese practice of *feng shui*, many Koreans today decry shamanism but nonetheless continue to heed its practices—just to be on the safe side.

Nowhere is the existence of shamanism more prevalent than in the contemporary company-sponsored kosa. A *kosa* is a shamanistic ritual in which food and prayers are offered to certain deities in the hope of securing prosperity and good health for the firm and its employees.[5] Many companies today routinely conduct ceremonies that are designed to placate the company deities. As Laurel Kendall observed in her study of the use of rituals in contemporary Korea:

> When a company opens an office or when a restaurant relocates, the group offers a kosa led by the director or manager. I once saw men set up kosa offerings in the foyer of the Garden Tower Apartments, where a cement company had just opened an office on one of the upper floors. The man in business dress who was arranging the pig's head told me that the kosa would benefit both his company and everyone else in the building.[6]

CREATING A NATION: THE SILLA DYNASTY

During the occupation of Korea by China's early Han rulers, efforts were made to integrate the Korean people into Chinese society. These efforts proved largely unsuccessful. After the fall of the Han dynasty around the first century, the Koguryo, one of Korea's principal tribal states, began to form an alliance with various nomadic tribes in southeastern Manchuria. By the fourth century, Koguryo had developed into a sizable kingdom with a centralized government built around a hereditary military aristocracy. While this development was occurring in the north, two kingdoms were emerging in the south, the Paekche and the Silla (also spelled, and pronounced, "Shilla"). This became known in Korean history as the Three Kingdoms period and lasted until the year 668. Despite continued warfare, culture and science flourished. In 634, for example, Silla's Queen Sondok, the first female ruler in Korean history, built the world's first astronomical observatory, called Ch'omsongdae, which still stands today.

Between 598 and 647, China launched four major invasions against Koguryo in an effort to regain control in the region. All of these efforts met with failure. Finally, the T'ang emperor of China allied himself with the king of Silla and attacked Paekche in preparation for another attack against Koguryo. By 660, Paekche had been conquered, and by 668 the two allies had conquered Koguryo. The Unified Silla period had begun. After their victory, however, the Chinese attempted to establish administrative control over all of Korea, thereby challenging the new Silla rulers. Silla responded by forming an alliance with the defeated Koguryo and ultimately forcing the Chinese out of Korea. This victory, in 735, is considered by most Asian scholars to be the beginning of Korea as a unified nation. The Silla dynasty was born.

The Silla period was characterized by continual internecine warfare, but also by significant cultural and scientific achievements. The rulers established their capital in Kyong-ju, a beautifully wooded city that survives today as a major tourist destination near the industrial city of Ulsan, a modern-day Hyundai stronghold. In the eighth century, history records, Kyong-ju had 170,000 houses, suggesting a population of between one-half and three-quarters of a million inhabitants.[7] The Emille Bell, cast in bronze in Kyong-ju in 771, was the largest of its kind throughout Asia and could be heard from forty miles away. Commerce with Japan increased significantly during this period. Indeed, Korea became the principal thoroughfare for the transport of Chinese goods and ideas to Japan. Korean monks staffed Japan's first Buddhist monastery, and Koreans tutored some of Japan's most celebrated princes. Korean immigrants brought Chinese medicine and characters to Japan, and by 815 almost one-third of all Japanese noblemen were of Korean descent.[8]

Buddhism, originally introduced in Korea in the fourth century, flourished and was adopted as the official state religion. The magnificent Pulguksa Temple was constructed in Kyong-ju as the state center for Buddhism. About the same time, the Sokkuram grotto shrine, containing one of the world's largest statues of Buddha carved out of a single block of white granite, was built. Both can be seen by tourists today. From the sixth to the sixteenth centuries, Buddhism dominated Korean culture, religion, and social behavior. Buddhism not only promised salvation but also provided answers to many questions about birth, rebirth, and the causes and cures of pain. It taught that society must concentrate its efforts on suppressing human desires in order for pain and suffering to disappear. It also promoted the state and the well-being of the people and served as a useful social control mechanism that reinforced aristocratic rule throughout the land.[9]

Chinese civilization flowered throughout the region during the Silla dynasty. Art and architecture, poetry and literature, the written Chinese language, and the Confucian principles of bureaucracy and organization were all introduced. In terms of cultural development, it was indeed a renaissance period. The Silla dynasty was also a period of aristocratic supremacy. A highly stratified hierarchy based on birth was formed, with members of the royalty and other aristocracy monopolizing all high offices. As greed and internal rivalries intensified during the ninth century, the foundations of the dynasty began to crack. Lower echelons that were excluded from power felt alienated. Prominent among this group was the increasingly wealthy merchant class, the predecessors of Korea's current-day entrepreneurs. The merchant class, who had done much to build the wealth of the region, felt marginalized by aristocratic indifference. The resulting chaos led to an insurrection that ultimately brought the downfall of the Silla dynasty and the emergence of the new Koryo dynasty beginning in 935.

KORYO AND THE RISE OF CONFUCIANISM

The new Koryo dynasty was to last 450 years and would stimulate further advancement of Korean culture. Among the important events of this period, three are particularly relevant for an understanding of contemporary entrepreneurial behavior in Korea: the rise of Confucianism, the development of new technologies, and the willingness of Koreans to take on adversaries much larger and more powerful than themselves.

During this period, Confucianism began to overtake Buddhism as the preeminent model of behavior in society. In 958, the new Korean rulers introduced competitive civil service examinations as a means of filling the highest offices with those members of the ruling class who were most competent in

Chinese literature and the Confucian classics. Once one was selected, however, advancement depended primarily on social status and seniority. Order, respect, and one's place in the social and organizational hierarchy were critical determinants of acceptable behavior. Confucian beliefs, developed during this period, continue to play a major role in everyday life in modern Korea. To this day, every child is taught the natural order of things according to these teachings.

Contrary to popular Western belief, Confucianism is a philosophy, not a religion. Confucius (Kong Fu Ze) was a senior civil servant in China around 500 B.C.E. Known for his wisdom and insight, Confucius promulgated a code of ethical behavior that was meant to guide interpersonal relationships in everyday life.[10] This code was summed up in the so-called five cardinal virtues.

The first cardinal virtue is *filial piety*, which requires a son to show love, respect, and absolute obedience to his father at all times. This principle is inviolate. From this principle we can see the origin of the familism that permeates Korean society to this day. One's family is vitally important because it defines who people are and where they belong in the larger society. The family looks after its own, a factor that leads to the nepotism frequently seen in Korean companies. As a part of this familism, we see, too, the special emphasis placed by the family on education and continual self-improvement as a means of aiding in the development of oneself, one's family, and one's community. Each individual has an obligation to maximize his or her contribution to the family.

The second cardinal virtue is *absolute loyalty* to one's superiors in all things. Here can be seen the origins of the strong commitment so many Korean employees feel toward their company and its leader. The president of the company traditionally embodies the essence of the company itself and, as a consequence, is to be respected and followed without question.

Third, social order is to be arranged according to *strict seniority*, with the young showing respect and obedience to the old and the old assuming responsibility for the well-being and future of the young.

Fourth, wives are duty-bound to be subservient to their husbands in all things. From this results a rather clear *sex-role differentiation* in which the role of women is defined as mother and wife and as someone who must obey the male members of the family and society.[11]

Finally, *mutual trust* between friends and colleagues must be preserved at all times. This is seen as the key to all human relationships and as a major determinant of the humanity and solidarity of the culture. Even today, maintaining harmonious relationships among close work associates is a never-ending pursuit for most Korean employees at all levels in the organization.

Business activity is based more on personal relationships and contacts than on written contracts. Reciprocity and exchange represent an important part of this process.

Confucius and his followers saw the universe—and hence society—as a hierarchically ordained system, ruled by an educated aristocratic elite. Concepts such as democracy and equality were disdained; learning and education were highly prized. Confucian society emphasized the virtues of self-discipline, hard work, diligence, and frugality. Hence, the fundamental nature of human relationships in Korea historically has not been that of interactions among equals but, rather, that of interactions between unequals. "Correct" interpersonal behavior is determined by one's gender, age, and position in society, and a breach in this social etiquette carries with it severe penalties.

From these five cardinal virtues followed several additional principles that guide behavior. Taken together, these principles help explain the environment in which Chung Ju Yung grew up and later thrived. First, it is important to recognize that Confucian principles were never intended to be universally applied. Rather, as noted, they were designed to recognize hierarchy and differences among class members. As a result, the behavioral requirements of individuals differed according to who was involved in the relationship. Among equals, certain patterns of prescribed behavior existed. This is seen today when two Koreans discover upon meeting that they attended the same high school or college. An instant bond emerges, and there is a sense of immediate camaraderie. By contrast, for people from outside this common background or clan, there is frequent hostility. Koreans can be very blunt and impolite when talking with total strangers, yet very hospitable and generous when dealing with friends or acquaintances. It is a question of belonging.[12]

Second, within one's broad circle of acquaintances, there is a clear responsibility for maintaining social harmony *(inhwa)*. As noted by Y. C. Chang, the principle of inhwa emphasizes harmony between unequals.[13] That is, it links persons of unequal rank in power, prestige, or position. Because personal relationships tend to occur only between persons of equal rank, age, or prestige, inhwa is the means of defining all other necessarily more formal relationships. It is everyone's responsibility to maintain this harmony among one's acquaintances and family members, and considerable effort is invested in doing so, including gift-giving. It is also everyone's responsibility to support others and make them happy.

Closely related to the principle of inhwa is the concept of *kibun*, a uniquely Korean characteristic that has to do with one's feeling of internal peace and harmony.[14] The word has no English equivalent but is similar in meaning to "feelings" or "mood." When one's kibun is good, everything is all right; when it is bad, one feels "like eating worms," as many Koreans say. In interpersonal relationships in Korea, it is vitally important that one does not disturb another individual's kibun. Hence, great efforts may be made not to convey bad news or news someone does not wish to hear.

Face (*ch'emyon* in Korean) is another long-standing tenet of Korean society. Simply put, "face" represents the confidence society has in one's moral character.[15] It represents one's self-image or reputation. The loss of face makes it impossible for an individual to function properly in the community. Loss of face occurs when an individual, either through his own actions or through the actions of people close to him, fails to meet essential requirements placed on him by virtue of the social position he occupies. If an individual cannot keep a commitment—however small—he loses face. Similarly, a person loses face when he or she is not treated in accordance with his or her station or position in society. Thus, a senior manager will lose face if it becomes known that a junior colleague is earning a higher salary or has been promoted ahead of him.

Finally, there is Korea's psychology of *han*. Han is a Korean abbreviation of *han't'an*, meaning unrequited resentment, bitterness, anger, or deploring.[16] Han results from Korea's long history of tragedy—invasions, wars, and catastrophes. It is a burden to be carried and is characterized by simultaneous feelings of joy and sorrow, hope and grief. As a result, many Koreans have developed an outlook of eternal optimism in the face of tragedy and a willingness to tolerate current hardships in order that future generations can enjoy a better life. Indeed, Koreans have cultivated several shamanistic rituals designed to turn sorrow and grief into joy and excitement and to release their suppressed feelings of han.

The importance of these concepts in understanding social behavior in traditional Korea cannot be overestimated. Losing face, for instance, represents a serious threat both to one's position in society and to one's feeling of self-worth and dignity. Suicides are often traced directly to such a loss. Likewise, disturbing group harmony is done only at one's own personal peril. In considering all forms of interpersonal interactions in Koreans, one must be ever sensitive to the dynamics of these characteristics as they relate to work and well-being.

At the same time that Confucianism was taking root in the Koryo dynasty, Korea also began developing as a technological and intellectual stronghold. Typography, or the use of movable wooden (and eventually metal) type to print multiple copies of one document, was invented in Korea in the early thirteenth century and used to reproduce various Buddhist texts. In 1251, the world's oldest and most comprehensive collection of Buddhist scriptures was completed. Called the *Tripitaka,* this collection consists of 163,000 pages carved on 81,258 wood blocks. It is important to note that Korea's invention of movable type and printing occurred over two hundred years before the

Europeans uncovered the same technology. Indeed, continued Western claims in encyclopedias and high school and college textbooks that German goldsmith Johann Gutenberg invented movable type in the mid-fifteenth century are not only incorrect but also reflect a widespread Eurocentrism among contemporary scholars that to this day impedes our understanding and appreciation of Asian cultures and contributions to world civilization. It is also worthy of note that Gutenberg's "discovery" was widely greeted in Europe as *schwarze Kunst*, or Black Art. Europe's ruling elite, fearing the dissemination of written materials into the hands of the masses, soon imposed strict press controls and taxes on paper. By contrast, the advent of movable type and printing was welcomed in Korea as a means of educating the public, a treasure to be shared.

Art and religious scholarship also flourished during this period. Literature became a true art form in Korea during this time. Scientists studied everything from improved agricultural methods to astronomy. The first spinning wheel is believed to have been developed in Korea in the fourteenth century. So too was the first suspension bridge, built across the Imjin River over one hundred years before the first such bridge appeared in the West.[17] Although many Westerners today express surprise at Korea's ability to develop competitive technologies, in point of fact the Koreans have done this many times before throughout their history.[18]

Finally, the Koryo dynasty is important for an understanding of contemporary Korean–Japanese relations. Toward the end of the fourteenth century, Korea was plagued by repeated attacks by Japan. Through tenacity and ingenuity, Korea was able to repel these attacks, thereby proving to itself that Japan, though bigger and more powerful, was not invincible—either in war or in commerce. Hence, as the Koryo dynasty gave way to the new Yi dynasty in 1392, its contributions to an organized society committed to achievement and innovation were well established. Perhaps the best reminder of this important era of achievement is the fact that the name for modern Korea is derived from the word *koryo* ("ko-ree-o").

CHOSON AND THE SEJONG RENAISSANCE

As is typical of most dynastic shifts, a period of war and rebellion preceded the emergence of the new Yi dynasty. A Mongol invasion and accompanying civil unrest led to the emergence of General Yi Song-gye, who first reestablished order and then proceeded to overthrow the last remnants of the Koryo dynasty and establish his own. The new ruler promptly resumed diplomatic and tributary relations with Ming China and took the ancient Chinese name for Korea, Choson, meaning "Land of the Morning Calm." Because of this, the Yi dynasty is also referred to as the Choson dynasty. To solidify control over his empire, Yi built a new walled capital city in the center of his kingdom in an area surrounded by high mountains that provided a natural defense against outside attacks. The new city was called Seoul.

Despite its militaristic origins, the Yi dynasty was marked by further cultural and economic developments. A noteworthy period of this era was that of King Sejong in the first half of the fifteenth century. King Sejong was born in 1397 and ruled Korea from 1418 to 1450. During his reign, he oversaw the development of many progressive ideas in administration, linguistics, music, science, and humanistic studies. He established the Hall of Talented Scholars (Chiphyonjon) to promote research in institutional traditions, politics, and economics. In 1443, he developed a new Korean alphabet, known as *hangul*, as a way to reflect the Korean language accurately in writing. Heretofore, Korean sounds had been forced awkwardly into traditional Chinese characters, even though Chinese was based on an entirely different linguistic system. Sejong intended this new alphabet to be used to educate the populace to read and write. Indeed, the first manuscript describing the alphabet (in 1446) was called "Correct Sounds to Teach the People" (*Hunmin Chong-um*).

Scientific research blossomed during this time, and many new inventions emerged. In 1429, the world's first handbook on farming methods (*Nongsa Chiksol*, or *Straight Talk on Farming*) was written so farmers in rural villages could learn the best methods for improving their harvests. This handbook was distributed by the world's first state-run agricultural extension service. In 1434, during Sejong's reign, the water clock, or clepsydra (*chagyongnu*), was invented. The rain gauge, or pluviometer (*ch'ugugi*), was invented in 1442 to improve weather forecasting and agricultural yields—two hundred years before its "discovery" in Europe by an Italian inventor. And the world's first sundial (*angbu ilgwi*) for public use was constructed in 1434. People were encouraged to make copies of this sundial for home use.

Medical science also prospered under King Sejong. In 1445, the world's first comprehensive medical text (*Uibang Yuch'wi*, or the "Classified Collection of Medical Prescriptions") was published. This was followed by the world's first manual on pregnancy and childbirth (*T'aesan Yorok*) that was made available to the general public.

King Sejong also contributed another innovation to world culture: the world's first public opinion poll. In the twelfth year of his reign, Sejong initiated a major effort to revise Korea's land tax system. To learn how his people viewed the new tax proposals, he surveyed over 200,000 people from throughout Korea to learn their views. The final revised tax code, considered by contemporary scholars to be one of the fairest systems of its time, was finally implemented in 1444. One wonders where else in the world during the fifteenth century were farmers, merchants, peasants, and craftsmen asked their opinion on tax reform.

Unfortunately, during the late 1500s, the Japanese initiated a new series of invasions of the Korean peninsula under Hideyoshi Toyotomi. By forming an alliance with the Chinese and conducting several ingenious naval campaigns, Korea again emerged victorious, but at great personal and economic cost. Among the innovations developed by the Koreans in response to the Japanese military threat were the first ironclad ships ever built. Western history textbooks incorrectly identify the American Civil War as the first time ironclad vessels were used in combat; in fact, however, the Koreans under Admiral Yi Sun-sin used such ships—referred to as "turtle ships," or *kobukson*, because of their shape—to defeat Hideyoshi's invasion of Korea in 1592, over 250 years before their use in the West.[19] Yi's boats were faster than those of the Japanese invaders and were rendered virtually impregnable by their armor plating. During the battle, the Koreans sank over three hundred enemy boats.

SHATTERED DREAMS: INVASION AND OCCUPATION

Less than a generation later, however, the Manchus invaded from China and occupied Korea, forcing it to pay significant tribute. Political and economic decline soon followed. For the next two hundred years, Korea limped along under Chinese influence. Then, beginning in the mid-1800s, a new opponent emerged: the West. Hostilities initially broke out with the French after Korea refused to engage in open trade. This was followed by a similar rebuff of the Germans and then the Americans. In 1866, little more than a decade after Commodore Perry's successful gunboat diplomacy led to the opening of Japan to Western markets, the American ship *U.S.S. General Sherman* was sent to Korea to force the Korean government to open up commercial relations. In defiance of Korean government edicts, the ship steamed up the Taedong River with a cargo of European goods. Its presence and concomitant show of force so infuriated the Koreans that the ship was attacked and burned, with the loss of the entire crew. Whereas the Japanese had capitulated to Western pressure following Perry's show of force, the Koreans were determined to chart their own destiny. Even so, in 1871, the United States followed up this repulse by sending two expeditionary ships in a vain effort to secure trading rights. This was quickly followed by a fleet of five U.S. warships, which again entered Korean waters in an effort to force Korea to open its markets to U.S. trade and influence. The resulting battle caused significant Korean casualties but no surrender. Finally, after repeated attacks by various international powers, Korea, realizing that it could no longer remain the "hermit kingdom," began negotiating bilateral trade treaties, first with the United States in 1882 and later with Great Britain, Germany, Russia, France, and Japan. Korea had decided that it was time to join the world community, but it was to learn shortly that it was not welcome on equal terms.

By the turn of the twentieth century, Korea began a period of rapid industrial development, brought on in part by its forced entry into the global economy. Small and medium-sized businesses flourished, especially in the textile and rubber industries, and many Korean entrepreneurs became wealthy. Department stores and publishing companies also flourished. Most of these businesses were financed by their owners' families and operated with government approval. Many, however, were risky ventures—for example, Korea's first railroad line, which was privately financed in 1898 but later driven out of business by the Japanese occupation government.

Japanese, Chinese, and Russian competition for control and influence in East Asia led to a series of armed conflicts in the region. In short order, first China and then Russia lost their influence in the region, leading to a period of Japanese supremacy. During the Russo-Japanese War in 1904, the Japanese sent troops into the Korean peninsula, and by 1905 their control of Korea was widely recognized. In the West, many saw this occupation as helping to uplift a backward people who had repeatedly proved their incapacity to defend themselves and build a modern society. As the Japanese grip on Korea tightened, various Korean ministers appealed repeatedly for help from the Western powers, but to no avail. Finally, in 1910, the Japanese formally annexed Korea. Korea was to serve as a colony of Japan, providing raw materials for Japan's emerging industries and markets for Japan's finished goods.

By all accounts, the period of Japanese occupation was a cruel one. Japan saw in Korea a colony that could be exploited in support of the Japanese industrial complex. Even so, the Japanese also built highways, railroads, ports, and communications facilities and, in doing so, contributed to a degree toward building a modern industrial infrastructure for Korea. An elaborate government bureaucracy was also established, albeit one that reported ultimately to Tokyo. As a symbol of their power, the Japanese constructed a massive capital building to serve as their new government headquarters on the grounds of the royal palace of the former Korean kings. Located in the heart of the city at the end of Seoul's major boulevard, the new structure was a way of signaling the Korean people that Japan was now the new aristocracy.*

---

* As an act of defiance, the Korean government later had the huge building demolished and restored the palace grounds to their former grandeur. Hyundai Engineering & Construction Company carried out the demolition. Several original palace buildings, long destroyed, were rebuilt using old plans, and a new museum celebrating Korean history and culture was constructed near the site.

Modern schools were built on the Japanese model, and in many ways the material well-being of many Koreans improved—but at a cost.

As part of the colonization process, efforts were made to eliminate all vestiges of a distinct Korean culture. Laws were passed forbidding all political activities. Books about Korean heroes and history were destroyed. Indeed, new books were written in which the very history of Korea was reinterpreted to put Japan in a more favorable light. Finally, the Korean language itself was outlawed; all teaching, all newspapers, and all commerce would henceforth be in Japanese. All families had to take new Japanese names. Korean traditional dress was proscribed, and anyone resisting these efforts in any way was punished severely. Japan determined on a campaign to make Korea a "little Japan," though clearly not an equal to Japan.

During the occupation, many Korean businessmen joined together to promote education and enterprise as a way of countering Japanese efforts at cultural integration. *Kukkwon hoibok,* meaning restoration of national independence, became the watchword for such efforts. Despite such resistance, however, Japan continued to increase its economic and political stranglehold over Korea. Shortly after annexation, Japan enacted what became know as the Company Law, making it illegal for Koreans to run a business without Japanese investment and requiring that Japanese hold key managerial positions in all major companies. Soon Japanese and Japanese-dominated firms controlled the majority of Korea's strategic industries, including 98 percent of the metals industry; 86 percent of textiles; 100 percent of chemicals, electricity and gas, and ceramics; 90 percent of the lumber industry; and 93 percent of food processing. It is estimated that 94 percent of Korea's entire industrial base was controlled by Japan.[20] In 1915, the occupying government closed down the Seoul Chamber of Commerce, originally founded in 1884, because of concerns that it fostered local business enterprise over Japanese business interests.

It was into this world of Korea as a Japanese colony that Chung Ju Yung was born in 1915. But even during this dark phase of Korean history, some international observers believed in a brighter future for Korea. Looking at Korea at the time, the eminent Indian philosopher Rabindranath Tagore observed with insight:

> *In the golden age of Asia*
> *Korea was one of its lamp bearers.*
> *And that lamp is waiting*
> *To be lighted once again*
> *For the illumination of the East.*[21]

LEARNING THE BUSINESS

"I've woken up early ever since I was young. I couldn't help waking up because of the expectations of what I was going to do that day. And when I went to bed, I would fall asleep thinking about what I was going to do tomorrow."

—CHUNG JU YUNG[1]

Korea in the early 1900s was a feudal society based on Confucian principles and occupied by Japan. While the Japanese military governed all important political and economic aspects of life, Confucian traditions played a major role in village life, as well as in Chung Ju Yung's subsequent life in the business world. As Chung would later observe, "The Confucian spirit is my management philosophy."[2] In fact, throughout his life Chung credited his parents with instilling in him a commitment to diligence and hard work. When he began his company, he would carry these principles with him.

In the early days, however, Chung frequently felt more oppressed than enlightened by his family life in a rural village. He would go to great lengths to escape and seek his fortune. To his friends, he demonstrated early on his high spirits and entrepreneurial skills. Someday, they concluded, he would become an important person. To his parents, Chung's early behavior more resembled that of the biblical prodigal son who put his own interests before that of his family and farm. But to Chung, he was simply seeking his destiny.

THE FARMER'S SON

Chung Ju Yung was born into this restrictive political, economic, and social environment on November 25, 1915, in the village of Asan in the Songjun

28

area of the Tongchon district. Asan is located near Korea's eastern shore, about thirty miles north of the current demilitarized zone (DMZ) in what is now North Korea. Chung's ancestors came from the Pukchong area of northern Korea, and, indeed, Chung is very proud that he can trace his lineage back sixteen generations. From Pukchong the family migrated to Myongsu, where they remained as farmers for several centuries. Chung's great grandfather later moved to Asan village in search of better land on which to farm so he could provide a better life for his family. But the land was still barren and unproductive. Chung's grandfather and his two brothers remained peasant farmers in this inhospitable rural environment.

Chung's father owned a four-acre parcel of land on which he raised rice and vegetables. Chung later recalled:

> We frequently had very difficult harvests. Survival was very difficult. As a young man, I remember wanting to go to the city to avoid extreme poverty. In those early days on the farm, you left home before dawn. You worked 15 to 16 hours a day in the field. Even if you worked very hard, you frequently didn't have enough to eat. Nobody in our village of fifty households had enough money for a doctor. If there was a major epidemic, a whole generation could be wiped out.[3]

Despite the hardships, Chung remembers his love of the early mornings and the anticipation they brought:

> I've woken up early ever since I was young. I couldn't help waking up because of the expectations of what I was going to do that day. And when I went to bed, I would fall asleep thinking about what I was going to do tomorrow. It is much like a child's anticipation of a picnic. I would fall asleep with my expectations and delights.[4]

Throughout his life, Chung would remain an early riser. There would always be something exciting to do the next day.

Chung's mother raised silkworms in the spring and summer, and she spent considerable time searching the countryside for mulberry leaves to feed to the worms. "When I see the wild mulberry trees in bloom," Chung observed, "my nose tingles as I think to myself of my mother's memory."[5] She also wove or knitted all of the family's clothes.

The extremely cold winters were frequently hard to bear. As Chung recalls:

> I wore only a thin layer of cloth, even in the winter. As I ran home with cloth-wrapped books in front of me to shield me from the wind, a cold wind would blow in through the hem of my clothes. By the time I reached home, my belly would often be red and itchy because of the cold. That was caused by lice since I wore the same clothes day and night. Then my grandmother would try to

catch the lice. When she could not see them, she told me to take off everything and get under the quilt. Then she would hang my clothes out in the snow to kill the lice. In the morning, she would flap the clothes in front of our stove to take off the chill before I put them on.[6]

Following Confucian tradition, Chung accorded his father deep respect. "My father was a model peasant in my eyes. There couldn't be a harder work-ing peasant. He never rested in summer or winter." Recounting how his father worked the land using only hand tools, Chung noted, "I can still remember the way my father tilled the field. Plough the land, pick up stones, dig the ditch, bring in the good soil, spread the fertilizer. I remember clearly the satisfied look on my father's face after opening up a new field."[7] Citing the examples of both his father and mother, Chung continued, "My parents' actions taught us to be diligent and hard-working. My father was a man of few words. I cannot recall ever receiving any praise from him when I was small. There were many instances of my being reprimanded, but I could see in his actions there was undivided love, and my mother was always kind and sup-portive of me. I was heavily influenced by their example."[8]

In March 1931, Chung graduated from Songjun Primary School. His prin-cipal studies there had been Chinese history, poetry, calligraphy, and music. Chung dreamed of becoming an elementary school teacher, but only the rich could afford the necessary advanced education.[9] Instead, he continued to help his father in the fields. For a brief time, he entered a Confucian school run by his grandfather, a strict, obstinate scholar from the village. Chung later praised his grandfather for having a profound influence on the development of his personal value system and for providing him with a "solid understand-ing of the universe and human life based on Oriental philosophy."[10] From these teachings, Chung learned the importance of perseverance: one must never give up. Indeed, throughout his career, Chung reminded his subordi-nates that a defeat or setback meant only that greater effort was required in future endeavors. Chung became convinced that he could do anything if only he tried hard enough. The "can-do" spirit that would later characterize Hyundai's success was born.

Chung was now at the end of his schooling; soon it would be time for him to go to work full time in support of his family. But he had come to detest farming and wanted a better life. "Farm life was wretched," he decided. "Though we worked our fingers to the bone, we received a pitifully small harvest because of our primitive cultivation methods....We had bad harvests two out of every three years."[11] Life had to be better elsewhere. As the eldest son, with five younger brothers and a sister to support, Chung was expected to follow in his father's footsteps and remain on the farm in Asan village. But

Chung was developing other ideas. He was developing a sense of his own destiny.

On his frequent trips to market towns to sell wood, Chung saw well-dressed people who had made money without toiling on the land. He read newspaper articles depicting adventures and opportunities around the world. In one article, he read about two new construction projects in the industrial port city of Chongjin, near the border with the Soviet Union. The article said that the projects needed as many construction workers as possible. As Chung tells it, "my heart beat faster" upon reading the news.[12] Returning home that night, he concluded that "the soil was not very fertile and did not produce enough harvest for a big family. I wanted to go to the city because our economic conditions were so bad that we could hardly eat. We would eat oatmeal late in the morning, skip lunch, eat bean porridge at night, and go to bed. I decided to go somewhere where I could eat all the rice I wanted."[13] He had found his dream: he would escape his cycle of poverty and travel to Chongjin in search of work. With a friend, he secretly began to save his money for his great adventure. "Whatever work they wanted me to do would be better than farming," Chung reasoned. "I knew how to work hard. Running away was the only thing to do. I looked up Chongjin on the map."[14]

Chung learned that Chongjin was a four-day boat ride away. He had no money for the fare, so he would have to walk. Friends told him it would take two weeks to walk the 250 miles. At the age of sixteen, Chung was apprehensive about traveling so far by himself, so he invited a friend to join him on his great adventure. On a hot July night after his family had gone to sleep, Chung crept out of his house and met up with his friend for the long journey. They took no luggage and between them had only 47 jun, less than a dollar in U.S. currency at the time.* Together, the boys climbed over the rugged mountains and hiked through the Paechun Valley, an area widely known for thieves and escaped criminals. The moonless night added to their apprehension as they persevered through the hostile territory. By dawn, they had hiked about fifteen miles and were getting hungry. Short on cash, they stopped and decided to beg for some food, but hostile villagers refused their pleas for assistance. The boys had no better luck in the next village. By now, they were starving and decided to spend 5 jun to buy three small rice cakes, which they divided among themselves. This hardly met their needs, but the boys moved on.

By nightfall, they reached the port city of Wonsan. Chung had a friend who had moved to Wonsan and was employed in a watch store. The boys immediately sought out their friend in the hope of securing something to eat and perhaps a place to stay for the night. Much to their dismay, Chung discovered

---

* One hundred jun equal 1 Korean won.

that his friend had no intention of feeding the runaways. He just wanted to talk to his old friends. The boys succeeded in getting some melons from a fruit vendor and spent the night behind an old warehouse. In the morning, they set out again for Chongjin. En route, in the town of Kowon, they walked past a railroad construction site and decided to ask for work in order to make some money to continue their journey. The construction foreman at the site asked the boys if they wanted easy work or hard labor. Since hard labor (ditch digging) paid more—45 jun per day—both asked for the more demanding jobs. The work was indeed arduous, but the boys found pride in having work—and money. At the end of the day, the boys stayed in the *hamba*, a communal dormitory where each paid 30 jun for a bed and food. But soon, Chung realized that the jobs that he and his friend had taken offered little future. As he calculated:

> If 15 jun were saved each day, 450 jun would be saved each month. Rainy days would be wasted. However, since I still had to eat and sleep on rainy days, I would suffer a loss of 30 jun. In addition, clothes and shoes wore out quickly doing hard labor. Far from saving money, I was on the brink of going into debt. We sweated for 15 or 16 hours every day from dawn after breakfast until the sky turned dark after dusk. After dinner, we would sleep soundly and wake up for another day's work the next morning. Whenever we got up, it would be work. Even so, we were satisfied that we were making a living by our own efforts and this drove us to work hard.[15]

Chung continued to work hard. About two months after leaving home, however, he received word that he had a visitor at the construction site. He rushed to the front office, only to find his father standing before him. Surprised, Chung asked his father how he had found him. His father replied that a worker from the site who knew him had passed through Asan village on his way home and told the villagers that he had met two boys from the village. Chung's father had walked almost a hundred miles to the construction site to retrieve his son. Embarrassed and disappointed, Chung and his friend were dragged home in disgrace. Chung's father told him that, as the eldest son, it was his responsibility to remain on the farm and follow in the tradition of his ancestors. Chung disagreed, but he obeyed. He had learned a valuable lesson from the experience. In addition to learning the importance of hard work—a lesson he already knew from his life on the farm—Chung had also learned to be careful about sharing information with strangers. Had he been more circumspect about his personal life around the evening campfires, he could have kept his freedom and his job. It was a lesson he would never forget. But Chung had learned something else, too. Despite the arduous work and the long hours, he had had a taste of construction work and he loved it. He had found his life's work. He wanted to build things.

On his return to Asan village, Chung immediately set about saving money to run away again. Chung had always been an avid reader, and while reading a local newspaper one evening he ran across a serialized story about a young man from a small rural village like his own who moved to Seoul in search of his fortune. The young man worked and studied hard and ultimately became a successful lawyer. The story, called "The Earth," was fiction—a classic poor-boy-makes-good story written by the noted Korean author Lee Kwang Soo—but Chung thought it was a true story. The young man in the story became his hero, and Chung decided that he too would study hard and overcome hardship. As a result of reading this story, he now set his sights on Seoul—120 miles southwest of his village and across several mountain ranges. Whereas Chongjin was a two-weeks' walk from home under the best of circumstances, Seoul was only four or five days' walk and thus presented a more realistic destination for the experienced traveler.

With two companions, Chung set out on foot for Seoul in April 1933. The journey was a disaster from the start. Early in the trip, one of his friends was spotted by his elder brother and taken home. Then, the two remaining boys were duped by a stranger who promised to get them jobs but instead absconded with all of their money. Tired, hungry, and broke, Chung and his friend were forced to travel to the nearby home of one of Chung's grandfathers in search of assistance. Unbeknownst to the boys, however, Chung's father had visited the house several days earlier in search of them and had alerted the grandfather, who promptly sent word to Chung's father to come and collect the boys. Chung had been trapped again, this time after only ten days on the road. Once again, the boys were returned to Asan village. Far from scolding his son, however, Chung's father welcomed him home. Planting season had just begun, and Chung would be a big help. "I returned home as a farmer, a farmer's son. My conscience felt guilty for having broken my father's heart. To compensate for this, I devoted myself to farm work more than at any other time. But as before, I knew some day I would leave this farming village for good."[16]

With the planting season behind him, Chung was soon ready for his next escape attempt. Through a newspaper ad, he learned that with only an elementary school education he could get a job in Seoul if he completed a six-month course in accounting. This he would do. To finance his trip, he secretly took 70 won that his father received from selling a cow and left after dark for the rail station. If walking had failed in the past, this time he would go by train. Chung bought a night rail ticket and departed for Seoul.

Upon arrival, his eyes were filled with a myriad of sights and sounds. Seoul had been Korea's capital since long before the Japanese occupation and in the 1930s was bustling with cultural and business opportunities. It was also the site of the Japanese colonial government for Korea. Chung immediately set out for the Doksu Bookkeeping School, enrolled in the accounting program, and took a room in the school dormitory. Chung quickly emerged as one of the best students in his class. Soon he would seek employment and begin a career as an accountant. He felt sure that he was now on his way.

When not studying, Chung read biographies of the world's great leaders. He could afford only a few books, so he read and reread the books in his possession. One such book was about Napoleon. Chung greatly admired Napoleon, who had risen from poverty to become the ruler of France through his indomitable spirit, tenacious mental power, gallantry, and unrivaled combative drive. Napoleon's story gave Chung strength, courage, and hope. It gave him a role model. The life of Abraham Lincoln was also an inspiration to Chung. Lincoln, too, had come from rural poverty to become a great national leader. Chung could do the same. "I became so intoxicated with these biographies that I got up very early and went to sleep very late at night. Apart from my bookkeeping studies, they formed a part of my studies as well."[17]

Two months had passed when, again, Chung's father showed up. This time his father had been able to trace him to Seoul because he had left an accounting school brochure behind. His father again argued that it was Chung's responsibility to return to the farm and take up his position as eldest son and heir. "You must worship your ancestors and take care of your younger brothers," his father admonished. Chung resolutely refused. He had only four months to go to complete his course work and would then be a respected office worker. "What is so respectable about being an office worker?" his father asked. His father then repeated that if Chung refused to return home, the family's welfare would be endangered. They might lose everything and become beggars. "Is this what Chung wants?" his father asked. Finally, Chung again yielded and agreed, once more, to return home with his father.

Chung was again welcomed back to his family. No mention was ever made of the money he had taken; they were just happy that he had returned. This time, Chung threw himself into becoming the best farmer he could. Although he still hated farming, his filial obligations seemed to overcome his disappointments. He now had a moral commitment to make the best of it. Unfortunately, nature was not on his side. After he had worked day and night in the fields for almost a year, an unexpected early frost destroyed the family crop in a single day. To Chung, this was a sign that his original intention to leave farming had been correct. For a fourth time, he began thinking of leaving. He remembered the childhood story of the tree frog that repeatedly tried to jump up into a willow tree but fell to the ground after every attempt. Still, the dedicated tree frog continued its efforts until it finally succeeded. Chung took the message. He must try again to get to Seoul.

BECOMING A RICE MERCHANT

In 1934, at age 18, Chung set out for a fourth time to seek his fortune. This time, he traveled with a friend who was trying to escape from a wife he had been forced to marry. Again, they left at night after everyone had gone to bed. This time, however, they would find fewer opportunities. A global depression had created hardships throughout Asia. Western nations increasingly erected protectionist barriers, putting a squeeze on Japan's mammoth industrial enterprises throughout much of Asia. Feeling the strain, Japan announced the creation of a "co-prosperity sphere" and marched across China and much of Southeast Asia in search of raw materials—especially oil and rubber—for its industrial production. Clouds on the horizon warned of the approach of World War II. The economic situation in Korea—still under Japanese occupation—worsened. Chung vowed he would succeed and find a better life so his father would understand why he felt compelled to run away. This was the only way for him to reconcile his Confucian past with his somewhat dubious recent behavior. He had to succeed.

Upon reaching the Seoul area, Chung got work wherever he could find it. First, he worked as a stevedore, loading and unloading ships in Inchon harbor, about thirty miles west of the capital. In later years Chung enjoyed telling stories of how primitive his life was at this time. He lived in a small room that was infested with crawling insects. Each night, they would crawl all over his body, and he would awake each morning with numerous bites. He tried everything to rid his room of the insects, but to no avail. Finally, out of desperation, he got an idea. He lifted his bed up and placed each leg in a small dish filled with water, thereby creating a liquid barrier that the insects could not cross. Thus isolated on his island, he finally got a good night's sleep. However, relief was short-lived. The next night, an insect crawled up the wall and across the ceiling to a spot above Chung and then dropped onto his sleeping body. Chung again awoke with numerous bites and decided it was time to move. But the lesson was clear: persistence usually won the day.

Returning to Seoul on foot, Chung worked for a short time as a construction laborer, carrying stones and lumber for a new building at what is now Korea University. (Ironically, in later years, Chung was invited to be on the board of trustees for this prestigious Korean university.) Next, he found work as a handyman for close to a year at a starch syrup factory. Finally, he landed a job as a delivery man at Bokheung Rice Store. This would be his first permanent job, and he became so successful at it that he stayed on to take over the company.

The way Chung got the rice delivery job is illustrative of the way he would secure huge business contracts later in life. He used pure audacity. When Chung applied for the delivery position, the store owner pointed out that all deliveries were made by bicycle and asked how well Chung could ride. "Very well," Chung replied, even though he had never before ridden a bike. During his first day of work, the inexperienced Chung set out to deliver 175 pounds of rice and beans but fell so many times that by the end of the day the bike's handlebars were completely bent out of shape and much of the rice lay ruined in the wet city streets. Undeterred, Chung later said: "I practiced riding the bicycle for four nights with a couple of hours sleep each night. I could eventually ride like a professional cyclist and rode around Seoul easily loaded with two *kama* [sacks containing about 60 kilograms each] of rice."[18] No other delivery man could carry two sacks of rice on one trip. Looking back on this episode, one observer noted: "Inexperience—even inability—could not deter him. His response showed the attitude of a man who would later order his thousands of workers to build ships, trucks and cars, diesel engines, railroad cars, steel towers, containers, computers, robots, and a host of other items from nothing."[19]

Chung's new job offered him what he had been seeking: an opportunity for advancement. The job at Bokheung paid him a modest salary but also provided him three meals and a half sack of rice per day. "For the first time, I managed to secure a good all-weather job that was becoming of me," he would later say.[20] "Delivering rice is hard work, but it is very stable," Chung noted.[21]

Soon Chung had won the confidence of his boss by arriving early each morning to clean up the store and organize the rice sacks into orderly stacks. He set up attractive product displays in the shop to attract more customers. Impressed with the young man's talents and dedication, his boss entrusted him to keep the store's accounts after only six months on the job. To accomplish this, Chung established an inventory system so that he and the owner could readily account for all stock. At last, Chung's two months' training as a bookkeeper had paid dividends. For this, Chung was paid the equivalent of the value of 18 kama of rice in one year. This was a small fortune to Chung, who proudly showed his father what he had accomplished. At last, his father understood that Chung's new life was an improvement over farming. Chung began learning the business from the inside with the help of the proprietor.

In January 1936, Chung returned to his home village to marry a young woman he had never met before; the marriage had been arranged by a matchmaker. His new sixteen-year-old bride, Byun Joong Suk, was the eldest daughter of a nearby farmer. It is rumored that Chung decided to marry her because she was too shy to meet him.[22] The newlyweds returned to Seoul and established their residence in a single rented room in a shabby little house lacking both a kitchen and running water. Even so, Byun was soon making *kimchi* (a spicy pickled cabbage), *dwenjang* (salted soybean paste), and *gochujang* (hot soybean paste) for the workers in the shop and to sell to regular customers along with the rice.

In 1937, the proprietor became seriously ill and decided to give the store to the diligent Chung instead of his own irresponsible son. After three years in the business, Chung was offered a chance to become his own boss, and he jumped at the opportunity. At the age of 22, he was now a store owner. He renamed the store the Kyungil Rice Store. Soon, all five of his brothers and his one sister moved to Seoul to live and work for their elder brother. The business flourished as Chung continued to build a reputation for honesty and punctuality. He repeatedly observed that trust was the most important characteristic for a rice dealer; it was worth more than money.

As World War II approached, the Japanese occupation forces tightened their control over Korean society. Fearing a loss of control over food and other strategic supplies, the occupation government outlawed Korean ownership of rice shops in early 1939. Chung was out of business, with no compensation for his losses. Chung, however, felt he had learned a valuable lesson: "If I put my heart and soul sincerely into whatever work I am doing, I will surely succeed."[23] For a man who had just lost his only source of livelihood, it was indeed an optimistic outlook.

THE CAR REPAIR SHOP

Chung returned to his native village and spent some of his savings to buy more land for his father's farm. By now, he knew that he was destined to be not just a businessman, but an entrepreneur. He wanted to spend his life creating new businesses. He remained in Asan village for nearly a year to consider his next business venture before returning to Seoul in 1940.

Chung needed a new business, one that was acceptable to his Japanese overlords and one that required little capital investment. He soon found the answer in the automobile repair business. Although recent laws reserved the sale of cars and car parts to Japanese owners, Koreans were allowed to repair cars and, as Chung saw it, a garage had a high value-added with a small capital investment. When a friend offered him an opportunity to buy a service garage, Chung jumped at it. Never mind that he had never owned a car before. Never mind that he had never before worked on a single engine. To Chung, it was an easy decision: he would learn the business as he went along.

It was the start of a Chung tradition that would continue for decades to come. In February, with a loan from a friendly rice mill owner, he established Ado Service Garage. So convinced was the lender of Chung's ability that he refused to accept any collateral on the 3,000 won loan. Chung would observe: "Trust is wealth. When you have trust, there's always money."[24] This trust remained constant when Chung's repair shop burned to the ground only one month after it opened in a fire that was set accidentally by a worker. The mill owner proceeded to loan Chung another 3,500 won—again unsecured—and Chung's workers built a new and better repair shop on the premises. Chung was now getting a small taste of the automobile business, and he would never forget it.

To begin Ado Service Garage, Chung used someone else's technical expertise and someone else's money. What he contributed was a business strategy that made everything work. His strategy for success in the repair business was simple: Ado Service would repair cars more quickly than the competition. Chung reasoned, correctly, that the loss of transportation represented a major inconvenience for car owners and that they would pay virtually any price for quicker repairs. "Officials, VIPs, even their wives, made such a big fuss when their cars broke down because their activities were halted....As long as we fixed their cars promptly, we were paid whatever we asked for," Chung observed.[25] Hence, whereas a certain repair might take his competition twenty days, Chung saw to it that Ado Service did it in perhaps five days—often by working through the night. He could then charge customers higher prices for the superior service. Chung was learning the important lesson of added value from the customer's viewpoint.

He was also learning how to retaliate against the Japanese occupiers in subtle yet profitable ways. Time and again, when Japanese cars were brought in for repair, Chung would remove working parts, polish them, reinstall them in the cars as new parts, and charge his Japanese customers for each part. "To be able to insist we changed everything in the catalog, I had to know a lot of parts....I made piles of money that way," Chung later recalled with glee.[26] Once again, risk taking and audacity paid off. So successful was Chung that his work force grew from an initial twenty employees when he opened Ado in 1940 to over seventy in 1943.[27]

Soon, Chung had sufficient income to invite his parents to Seoul. The extended family moved to a larger house on Donahmdong. In all, twenty family members converged on the Chung household, including his parents, two brothers and a sister, and their families. The eldest son had fulfilled his traditional responsibilities; he had become the dutiful son. He also had replaced his father as the head of the household. In his crowded home, to preserve peace in the family, Chung insisted on what he called "dinner table conversation," even though it occurred at breakfast time.[28] All twenty family members began the day by having breakfast together to discuss the events of the coming day, as well as any problems that had emerged. Harmony was maintained. These breakfasts began a tradition that Chung would continue with his own sons well into his seventies.

From the beginning of his new enterprise, local Japanese officials frowned on his efforts. For starters, Chung refused to get the necessary permits to operate a garage from the Japanese occupation government; he simply did not have the money when he started. The local Japanese police repeatedly ordered Chung to close down his shop and threatened to jail him if he did not buy the required permits. Chung responded by visiting the local police chief at the front gate of his house each morning. Chung, bearing cookies as an offering, pleaded with the chief to let his shop remain in operation. The chief refused the cookies and reiterated his warning to close the shop. Chung returned every morning at dawn for a month to ask again for the chief's support. Finally, the police chief relented and suggested that Chung build a fence around his garage so the authorities couldn't see the garage. Thereafter, he was left alone to conduct his business, which increased so much that Chung had to add a night shift to keep up with the demand.

From this incident, Chung learned that persistence and shrewdness can overcome most obstacles.[29] Over four years, he accumulated a considerable profit from his operations. In the long run, however, even his shrewdness could not protect him from Japan. In 1943, his garage was forced to merge with a local steel plant as an economy move in support of the war effort. Like the rice shop before it, Ado Service was a victim of Japanese aggression and suppression. One again, Chung would need to begin again from scratch. After a brief job as a subcontractor for a Japanese-affiliated Korean construction firm, Chung pulled out of the business just before the end of the war—and the demise of the construction firm. He took his sizable savings, now 50,000 won, and briefly returned to his home village in the north to consider his next move.

Throughout his life, Chung felt that leadership, strategy, and perseverance were at the root of successful enterprise management. He also felt that few differences existed between business enterprise and war. Both required an all-out effort to succeed against the odds, and both required that there be winners and losers. With sound strategies and command leadership, Chung planned to be a winner. He also read books about Japanese industrialists, which were readily available in Korea at the time. Chung was particularly impressed with the manner in which Japanese leaders made decisions. These leaders insisted that business plans originate at the building site and then be approved by headquarters, instead of the reverse. Headquarters might see the larger picture, the industrialists reasoned, but they would likely miss many important details that could determine the success or failure of the venture. From this, Chung learned not to delegate but, rather, to live on site during major projects. In this way, he was assured of the best of all possible outcomes.

Chung also had time to consider the role of religion in his life. Never particularly religious, he concluded that for religion to be useful, it had to serve his purpose. He frequently observed that Protestants wanted him to believe in Protestantism, Catholics in Catholicism, and Buddhists in Buddhism. But, he observed: "I believe in nothing. I would prefer to try the religion that tells me I will receive a great fortune in the present world. I can't wait for a next world that might not exist."[30] To Chung, religion was a corporate issue. Time is not just money, he frequently observed. "If you lose time, you lose not just money but life, and everything you have done in life will wash away."[31] Henceforth, Chung's goal in his future endeavors became to finish each project with the least cost and in the shortest period of time.

From his limited experience with the Ado Service Garage, Chung learned the importance of controlling his own destiny. From now on he would do things his way. In fact, throughout his career, he resisted taking over declining or bankrupt companies from others. He preferred to start his own and to instill what he considered to be proper values—*his* values—in employees from the outset. Moreover, although he recognized the need to use foreign technology and foreign advisors when entering a new field, Chung preferred to move as rapidly as possible to an exclusively Korean enterprise. Reflecting his lifelong sense of nationalism, Chung often noted that it was best "to look at your own feet in order to start anything."[32] From such values Chung developed what ultimately became known as the Hyundai spirit, a set of beliefs that are taught to every new employee from day one and reflect the deeply held values of the company founder. This Hyundai spirit is perhaps best captured in the company's orientation manual for new recruits: "An indomitable driving force, a religious belief in attaining a goal, and a commitment to personal diligence tempered with the frugality have materialized as a major part in the development of heavy industry in Korea."[33] This fatalistic optimism is perhaps best captured by the Korean term *ha-myun-doen-da*, which means "unyielding drive."

Throughout his later career, Chung insisted that he was not a capitalist: "I am merely a man who became rich from his toils....I am a farmer's son who became a successful industrialist. I am a self-made man, not in the sense that I accomplished everything by myself, but in the sense that I built a huge business enterprise from scratch only with hard work and innovative thinking."[34] Searching for a way to sum up his accomplishments late in his life,

Chung observed, "I have worked and lived with the common people, farmers, and workers."[35]

CREATING THE MOTHER COMPANY

Japan's repressive rule over Korea ended with the close of World War II. At the Yalta Summit, the Soviet Union and the principal Western powers agreed that Japanese forces north of the 38th parallel would surrender to the Soviet Union, while those south of the parallel would surrender to the Americans. This division of Korea was intended to be temporary but, once created, became a barrier that no amount of negotiation could dissolve. In the north, Kim Il Sung emerged as the leader of a new Democratic People's Republic of Korea, while in the south the United States first tried to retain some Japanese officials and later established a military government under General John Reed Hodge with U.S. personnel as executives and Koreans in subordinate positions. The Koreans were essentially treated as a conquered people. The West had learned little about Asia, and virtually nothing about Korea, during the war. It would take another devastating war before they would come to recognize the importance of this land.

With his newfound freedom from Japanese control, Chung returned to Seoul from Asan village while it was still possible and reentered the car repair business in April 1946. He named his new venture Hyundai Auto Service (see Table 3-1 for a timeline of Chung's early days).* He chose the word *Hyundai* because it meant "modern" in Korean. Chung wanted to send his customers the clear message that his was a state-of-the-art company. Most of his business involved repairing old Japanese cars left behind by retreating Japanese government officials. Gasoline was in short supply, so repairing the cars often meant converting them into charcoal-burning vehicles.

With the Japanese gone, business opportunities were rare, but Chung soon discovered that the Americans had money to spend and were building facilities to house their occupation forces. He also noticed that construction companies made far more money than auto repair garages. He determined to enter the construction business and, in May 1947, when he was 31, he started Hyundai Civil Works Company. Chung's friends advised him against this move. He had a successful car repair business, but knew nothing about construction, they reasoned. Why risk everything on such a new venture? But Chung rejected these warnings. He reasoned that much of the construction work that was available involved repairs, not unlike his auto repair work.

---

* Timelines appear throughout this book to chronicle the origin and evolution of principal business ventures or events that aided in the growth and development of Hyundai.

TABLE 3-1

TIMELINE: EARLY DAYS OF CHUNG JU YUNG

DATE	EVENT
1915	Chung Ju Yung born in Asan village (November 25).
1931	Chung graduates from primary school.
1934	Chung sets out for a fourth and final time to seek his fortune.
	Arrives in Seoul and takes odd jobs until he is hired by Bokheung Rice Store as a delivery boy.
1936	Chung marries Byun Joong Suk.
1937	Chung establishes Kyungil Rice Store.
1939	Kyungil closed by Japanese military government.
1940	Chung opens Ado Service Garage to repair cars.
1943	Ado nationalized by Japanese military government.
1946	Chung establishes Hyundai Auto Service.
1947	Hyundai Civil Works Company, cornerstone of the current Hyundai Business Group, established.
1950	Hyundai Construction Company established by merging Hyundai Motor Service and Hyundai Civil Works Company.
	Hyundai Construction receives its first major contract from the Korean government to build warehouse facilities in Pusan.
	Hyundai Commercial Transportation Company formed to ship foodstuffs throughout liberated areas of Korea.
	Hyundai Construction begins small construction projects for U.S. military.
1952	Hyundai renovates facilities and plants barley at UN cemetery in preparation for visit of President Eisenhower.

To Chung, construction represented a logical extension of his previous business. Besides, there were considerable emerging opportunities in construction, and he wanted a piece of the action. Initially, he served as a subcontractor to more established construction firms and took whatever business he could get. Within three years, however, in 1950, he had secured sufficient business from the Americans that he merged his car repair business into his construction company and renamed the enterprise the Hyundai Construction Company.

The same year Hyundai Construction was founded, the United Nations General Assembly called for the creation of a unified and independent government in Korea and appointed a temporary commission to oversee elections. However, the Soviets denied access to the northern half of the country, so elections were held only in the south. On May 10, 1948, a constituent assembly was selected to draft a new constitution and elect a new leader. On August 15, Rhee Syngman was elected South Korea's first president. In the north, Communist leader Kim Il Sung formally assumed power with the backing of the Soviet Union. Between December 1948 and June 1949, most Soviet Union and U.S. troops left Korea. The resulting vacuum and the weakness of the Rhee government created an opportunity for Kim Il Sung to launch an invasion of South Korea on June 25, 1950. The United States responded by sending troops back into Korea and, shortly thereafter, requested and received UN support for such a move. The Korean War had begun in earnest.

As North Korean troops approached Seoul—just twenty miles from the earlier DMZ—Chung abandoned his construction sites, withdrew his personal savings from the bank, and, along with his younger brother In Yung, headed south to Pusan. In Yung had an advantage over his older brother in dealing with the Americans: he spoke enough English to be understood. As luck would have it, In Yung met a young U.S. Army lieutenant named Hank MacAlister who had recently arrived from the States. MacAlister was an engineer assigned to the Commandant Section of the U.S. 8th Army headquarters, the top level of command. He was responsible for securing new bases of operations as the armies moved north and south following the course of the war. MacAlister needed someone who could interpret for him when he met with local villagers; he hired In Yung for the job. Several days later, In Yung introduced MacAlister to his older brother. At the time, Chung Ju Yung had an oxcart and five workers, and he was taking whatever work he could find, including building tent floors on U.S. Army bases.

Learning that construction would be more lucrative than interpreting, In Yung soon got himself transferred to the 8th Army's Corps of Engineers. Meanwhile, elder brother Ju Yung hounded the Korean Ministry of Transportation until they gave him a contract to construct a large warehouse near the Pusan docks. When goods began piling up in the newly constructed warehouse, Chung formed the Hyundai Commercial Transportation Company to ship foodstuffs throughout the southeast region of Korea that remained free from North Korean domination. He was now thirty-four years old and still struggling against the odds.

When the Americans recaptured Seoul on September 28, 1950, Chung and his brother immediately returned to link up with family members left behind in the capital during the turmoil and confusion of the evacuation. He then returned to Asan village to rescue his parents and other relatives who had been trapped there since the beginning of the war. With his family safely in hand, Chung reestablished himself in Seoul, although he remained ready to flee at a moment's notice. He set about trying to secure as much construction work from the 8th Army as he could get. This included a major new headquarters facility planned for Seoul. Through his contacts, he easily landed this and several other military contracts and was soon making profits of 500 to 600 percent on each job.

Chung's strategy for success was simple. He concluded that, for the Americans, money was not the issue; they had a seemingly endless supply. What the Americans wanted was guaranteed on-time performance in the middle of a chaotic, war-torn environment. Chung was determined to deliver. He set about developing and publicizing his now-famous "can-do" motto. Chung could—and would—do just about anything if the price was right. In a world where few things were predictable, Chung could be relied on; his word was indeed his bond. Establishing this reputation was not easy, however, and many times Hyundai suffered major financial losses on contracts. To construct a U.S. Air Force facility near Suwon just south of Seoul in late 1950, for example, Chung stockpiled all the required supplies for the project just as the Chinese and North Korean armies recaptured the area, forcing Chung to flee for his life. When the area was liberated a year later, Chung returned and began work on the facility. He used his own money and paid nearly twice the previous cost for new supplies. He experienced a sizable loss on the project, but he had given his word to build the facility and he did. In the process, he also bought himself enough good will from the U.S. military to guarantee him a major share of any future business. Chung understood that he was now playing a high-stakes game, and he planned to win.

In December 1952, President Dwight Eisenhower announced his intention to visit Korea in fulfillment of a campaign pledge to conclude the long war. Planning for the important visit went smoothly until, several days before his arrival, the boiler system in the old palace where Eisenhower was scheduled to stay broke down. Hyundai was called in at the eleventh hour in an effort to refurbish the facilities. They succeeded in rebuilding the boiler system, fixing the toilet facilities, and redecorating the rooms just prior to the president's arrival.

Then it was announced that President Eisenhower wanted to visit the

United Nations cemetery in Pusan to honor the soldiers who had recently died in the war effort. Army commanders scrambled. The cemetery had to look its best for the official visit. But it was the dead of winter, and the normally endless green fields of grass were now brown and unkempt. Something had to be done. Chung was again called in and asked what to do. He thought for a moment and then told his brother-in-law to buy all of the available barley (still green in the midst of winter) from a farming area near the eastern coast, haul it to Pusan, and transplant it in the cemetery field to serve as greenery. It required thirty truckloads of barley to complete the job. From a distance—and during a short visit—Eisenhower would not notice the difference. The visit went smoothly, and President Eisenhower complimented the army commanders for the care they had given to the cemetery.[36] For his work, Chung received three times what the army had originally promised him. His stock rose again in the eyes of the Americans. As Chung later recalled with pride, "From then on, all construction projects for the 8th Army were mine."[37]

Looking back, it is clear that Chung and Hyundai received a great deal of assistance and support from their U.S. military contacts. For starters, they learned how to prepare project bids in the commonly accepted international format, as required by the U.S. military procurement system. In addition, Hyundai learned about Western specifications and was required to upgrade the quality of their construction work to the level required by U.S. federal regulations. They learned about construction management and quality-control techniques. They improved because they had to in order to keep the business and stay ahead of their competitors. Finally, they were able to acquire war surplus construction equipment that allowed them to mechanize their operations.[38] These early construction experiences were like a university education for Chung, and he proved to be an exceptional student.

In the coming years, Hyundai would go on to secure much larger contracts around the world. They would diversify into a wide range of products and services. But throughout his career, Chung always saw construction as his principal love. Hyundai Construction (renamed Hyundai Engineering & Construction in 1981) became known as the "mother company." "People who become competent through work on construction sites can accomplish anything they envision in any field," he would later say.[39] Because the construction business is fiercely competitive and requires people to confront nature's challenges on a daily basis, it must be the best training ground, he reasoned. As Chung explained recently: "Hyundai construction managers are frequently given full responsibility for managing a $100 million project over a period of several years. This is the same as running a $100 million company. These people have to create something from nothing. They have to organize and manage personnel, materials, and budgets and complete the task on time. I can think of no better preparation for executive management."[40]

Henceforth, when Chung began a new venture—whether it was shipbuilding, electronics, oil refining, advertising, securities and investments, or automobiles—he would invariably appoint a Hyundai Construction executive to run it, even if the executive knew nothing about the products or services of the new venture. In later years, when Chung formed a corporate office to coordinate his many companies in the group, almost all of the members, from top executives down to drivers and custodians, came from Hyundai Construction. Indeed, until the corporate reorganization of 1998, many of the group's principal staffing functions, including personnel, employee welfare, and public relations, reported not to the group but to Hyundai Engineering & Construction. It is fondly referred to as the West Point of the group, and all aspiring managers understand that they must serve time in construction if they intend to succeed at Hyundai.

REBUILDING THE HOMELAND

"In 1960, South Korea had a per capita gross national product of $80 a year, a figure putting it on roughly the same level as Ghana and Sudan and a bit behind India. In Seoul, people were sleeping and even starving in the streets. Koreans were still numbed by the Korean War....Private cars were a novelty and electricity and running water still luxuries of the well-to-do....South Korea seemed destined to remain a perennial mendicant."

—MARK CLIFFORD, JOURNALIST[1]

By the end of the war in July 1953, Korea lay in virtual ruins. Three million people had died, and millions more were homeless. The country's dream of reunification was more remote than ever. From a commercial standpoint, the budding industrial base that had developed before the conflict was in shambles, necessitating a new beginning. In many ways, Korea seemed to be without direction or leadership. The Rhee government, preoccupied with solidifying its power base through favoritism and corruption, had become increasingly authoritarian. Korea was largely a closed agrarian economy, with about two-thirds of the working population engaged in agriculture. Three out of every five Koreans lived on farms, barely making ends meet.[2] Because of its rural poverty, few funds were available for needed industrialization efforts.

This bleak assessment of Korea's future economic prospects was shared by many international observers. One economic analyst concluded at the time: "Korea can never attain a high standard of living. There are virtually no Koreans with the technical training and experience required to take advantage of Korea's resources and effect an improvement over its rice-economy status."[3]

During most of the 1950s, the lack of an adequate economic infrastructure and capital investment precluded long-term economic development in

Korea. Between 1954 and 1959, more than 70 percent of all reconstruction projects were financed by aid from other countries, most notably the United States.[4] As a result, economic policy emphasized meeting people's immediate needs for consumer goods and easing distribution bottlenecks, rather than fostering long-term economic development. Urban sprawl and unemployment exacerbated Korea's early economic difficulties. Population growth reached 3 percent per annum after 1954. The influx of North Koreans during the Korean War only made the situation worse, with increased unemployment, higher demand for consumer goods, low capital formation, housing shortages, and greater political unrest. From 1953 to 1962, per capita GNP increased from $67 to only $87, while U.S. foreign aid increased from $194 million to $232 million.[5] Economic forecasters were unanimous in their lack of confidence in this backward country. Korea's prospects, on the whole, were exceedingly dim.

Korea also was plagued by widespread corruption.[6] Shortly after the close of the Korean War, the Rhee government secured control of 166,000 different assets that had formerly belonged to the Japanese government or to Japanese residents of Korea prior to World War II. Initially held in safekeeping since 1945 by the U.S. occupation forces, these assets included 3,500 operating plants and companies, land, infrastructure, and inventories that accounted for close to 30 percent of the nation's entire wealth. Beginning in the early 1950s, officials of Rhee's government set about selling these assets, not to the highest bidders or the most qualified entrepreneurs and managers, but to those who paid the largest bribes to the government.[7] A number of new companies were begun with this property, while several existing firms grew larger and richer by acquiring plants and property below cost. At the same time, the Rhee government (through the Commercial Bank Act of 1954) began to privatize government-held banks, again selling not to the highest bidder but to friends and supporters. And again, several major conglomerates capitalized on this government giveaway.[8] But not Chung, who remained firm in his conviction that he would keep a healthy distance between Hyundai and the Rhee government. He refused to participate in the allocation schemes. Although he required government support to take advantage of most of the available business opportunities at the time, he preferred to walk a fine line, staying on friendly—but not too friendly—terms with the government. In Chung's view, governments were not to be trusted.

BUILDING BRIDGES

Despite the Rhee government's ineffective economic development strategies, Chung Ju Yung found ways to prosper in the aftermath of the Korean

War. He turned increasingly to Korean government projects sponsored largely by foreign aid. One of his first projects involved the reconstruction of the Koryung Bridge over the Nakdong River near Taegu (see the timeline in Table 4-1). This was the largest project underwritten by the Korean government to date, and no one really understood the extent of the costs involved. It represented a major challenge for Hyundai. Chung accepted this project with gusto but soon found he was in over his head, both technically and financially. The project was far more complicated than first thought and was threatened by labor strikes and unpaid creditors. Hyundai did not have the right equipment for the project. Inflation ate away at Chung's personal savings and significantly escalated the costs of supplies. Within several months,

TABLE 4-1

TIMELINE: HYUNDAI CONSTRUCTION COMPANY'S EARLY PROJECTS

DATE	EVENT
1955	Hyundai completes its first major bridge reconstruction, the Koryung Bridge over the Nakdong River near Taegu.
1957	Hyundai selected to build five new bridges across the Han River in Seoul.
1958	Hyundai selected to construct the new U.S. Army–UN Command headquarters in Seoul.
1959	Hyundai selected to rebuild harbor facilities in Inchon.
1960	Hyundai becomes Korea's largest construction firm.
1964	Hyundai Cement facility completed in support of company's construction efforts.
1965	Pattani–Narathiwat Highway begun in Thailand, the first overseas construction project by a Korean firm.
	Hyundai initiates construction projects in Vietnam, Guam, Papua New Guinea, Alaska, and Australia.
1967	Soyang Dam project begun.
1968	Kyungbu Expressway project begun.
1970	Kyungbu Expressway completed.
1973	Soyang Dam completed.

prices had increased by over 120 percent, and Chung had to take out huge loans to complete the project. Later, he had to sell the four houses owned by himself and three of his brothers to generate sufficient cash flow to continue. In the end, on a 55 million won contract, Chung *lost* 65 million won. Nevertheless, despite his losses, Chung went on to finish the bridge in May 1955. His reputation was at stake, and he understood that could not afford to fail.

Payback came two years later, in 1957, when the Korean government awarded Hyundai a contract to build five new bridges across the Han River in Seoul to replace bridges destroyed during the war. Having learned from its past mistakes, Hyundai was ready this time with sufficient engineering technology to accomplish the task. Hyundai also had opened a heavy machinery office, which bought and then reconditioned used construction equipment. Never again, Chung promised himself, would Hyundai lack proper equipment to bid on any contract, however large. President Rhee publicly praised Hyundai's technology and construction skills in a televised ceremony marking the grand opening of the first bridge. At last, the once obscure construction company received the national recognition it thought it deserved. Hyundai made a tidy 40 percent profit on the project and soon emerged as a member of the "big five" construction firms in Korea.[9] At the age of 43, Chung was a success.

This success was soon followed by another major contract from the U.S. Army to construct a new 8th Army–United Nations Command headquarters in Seoul. In contrast to earlier work done for the army during the war, these new facilities were meant to last for decades. Then, in 1959, the U.S. Army awarded Hyundai another $2 million contract to rebuild Inchon harbor for military and commercial shipping. The docks that Hyundai worked to reconstruct were the same ones on which Chung had labored when he first came to Seoul in the 1930s. With an eye toward economy, Chung convinced the army to suspend a requirement that U.S. funds had to be spent exclusively on U.S.-made machinery and supplies. As a result, Hyundai was able to purchase local supplies, thereby reducing project costs and ensuring a 30 percent profit margin on the venture.[10]

Throughout this period, technical inexperience still plagued the company on occasion, but Chung and his colleagues improvised when necessary. On one occasion, during a paving project at Osan Air Base, specifications required the use of a batch plant to mix concrete properly. Chung had never seen a batch plant, nor did he know what it was. Not to be deterred, he sent one of his subordinates to another construction site to see what one looked like. He then drew the plans and had one made by his engineers for use on the project. On another occasion, he needed to lift a 110 ton gate into place on a huge sluice but lacked a crane big enough to lift the mammoth gate. Instead,

Chung used two 60 ton cranes in unison. It violated standard practices, but it worked.

On every project, Chung was a force to be reckoned with. He continually called his project supervisors at all hours of the day or night to ask if certain tasks had been completed. He believed in keeping his subordinates on a short leash, lest they lose their sense of immediacy. One of his favorite tactics was intentionally to give his workers less time than they needed to complete a task, thereby forcing them to improvise and innovate. He was an early believer in Parkinson's law, which stipulates that people will use as much time as they are allowed to complete a task. "Only if fire falls on their feet will people quickly attend to the work they are instructed to do," he observed.[11] Chung had no tolerance for laziness and would fire workers on the spot if he felt they were not carrying their load.

Chung also had an annoying habit of showing up on a project site unannounced, sending terror through the hearts of his workers as he barked questions and orders at anyone in sight. Once, when he was taking the train to a work site outside of Seoul, he fell asleep and missed his stop. He soon woke and exited at the next station, then hiked back to the work site. He arrived in the middle of the night but immediately set about inspecting the work and quizzing the sleepy workers and supervisors about their progress during the day. No one could believe he would visit so late. Behind his back, and sometimes even to his face, he was frequently called the "tiger," referring to his stealthy ability to appear from nowhere and pounce on the unsuspecting. When he left a construction site, workers would send an all-clear signal throughout the camp. Chung seemed to enjoy this persona; it kept his people on their toes. To him, such behavior arose not so much from a need to control as from a need to compete. As an industrial leader, he was always keenly aware that Korea had to compete with Japan and others if it was to climb out of its economic hole and succeed in its industrialization. Chung saw it as his responsibility to help achieve this national goal. To him, it was a point of honor.

One of the keys to Hyundai's early success was Chung's insistence on trying to hire only the best people available. In contrast to the widespread custom at the time, Chung based hiring decisions exclusively on individual competence, not personal connections. And, with an eye toward future international business opportunities, he emphasized the importance of hiring people who could speak English whenever possible. English-language tests were required for many jobs at Hyundai long before most Korean companies recognized the importance of being bilingual. In the early days, when jobs were scarce, government bureaucrats frequently tried to influence Chung to hire their sons. Refusing such requests could lead to considerable difficulties in securing necessary permits and approvals on various construction jobs. But Chung found a way around this by telling his brother, Chung Se Yung, who oversaw hiring at the time, to give such applicants particularly difficult English-language tests, which essentially guaranteed failure. Chung could then tell their fathers in good faith that, although he had no problem hiring their sons, the young men were simply unable to pass the company entrance examination. In a Confucian society familiar with such examinations, the government officials—who had gotten their own jobs on the basis of an examination system—would have no acceptable response.[12]

In the early days, Byun Joong Suk supported her husband's efforts by providing food for the workers.* She helped create a company cafeteria in the Hyundai building in downtown Seoul that proved to be popular among employees and was always busy. Byun was committed to serving as many Hyundai employees as possible. "I even sent *gochujang* (hot soybean paste) to overseas construction sites. I used to steam 30 bags of soybeans at that time; later it was 200," Byun noted later.[13] Eventually, Byun would set up her own soy paste factory in support of her efforts. From the beginning, Hyundai was truly a family enterprise.

By 1960, Hyundai had become Korea's largest construction firm. But while it was prospering—and while Chung was becoming well off by Korean standards—the Korean economy in general continued to falter. A World Bank economic report of the time singled out Burma and the Philippines as the two Asian countries, after Japan, most likely to industrialize successfully; Korea was at the bottom of their list of prospects.[14] Another World Bank assessment of Korea's first economic development plan, in 1961, concurred, concluding that "there can be no doubt that this development program by far exceeds the potential of the Korean economy.... It is inconceivable that exports will rise as much as projected."[15] After an in-depth investigation of Korea's future prospects, a group of U.S. State Department experts concluded that "Korea was an economic basket case that would always depend on American handouts for its existence."[16]

Rhee's government seemed incapable of managing the economy. A former cabinet member in his government noted: "Rhee was a patriot and in some sense a revolutionary but not in any sense an administrator. Rhee was born in the nineteenth century. He hadn't seen modern Korea. He spent most of his life in the U.S. in exile. He thought that if he simply appealed to the people's sense of patriotism they would follow him."[17] Koreans followed for a time, but as their poverty continued, Rhee lost his mantle of leadership for the country. Another observer of the time noted:

---

* In keeping with long-standing custom, Korean women retain their maiden names after marriage.

On the eve of the coup it was almost total chaos, economically, politically, socially. North Korea was far ahead of us. They had ten years of tough mobilized action. They worked hard and there were visible results....[F]rom the president down to the street beggar there was a mendicant mentality. The general attitude was 'we need more aid, we need more American help.' Half of our government budget relied on [American] government aid.[18]

In 1960, following a series of student revolts, Rhee was forced into exile. His departure was followed by a brief democratic experiment under President Yun Po-son, with Chang Myon as prime minister. The Chang government, though committed to democratic principles, was unable to maintain itself in power, and a military coup led by forty-three-year-old Major General Park Chung Hee assumed control in May 1961. Park would rule Korea for the next eighteen years. Although he was often viewed as a despot in the West, Park's principal motive for the takeover was not self-aggrandizement or power for its own sake. Rather, like other military officers at the time, Park was alarmed about Korea's economic misery and the resulting political instability. Many people feared that Korea would turn to communism or be too weak to resist a second invasion from the North. As one observer noted at the time:

The Korean people suffered from hunger. In the spring just before the barley harvest people had to eat pine bark. Korea was entirely dependent on U.S. assistance, but that assistance was not enough. We didn't have any capital facilities or natural resources. At the time, the whole country was completely in ruins. We didn't know when the North Koreans would attack us again. The civilian government was totally relying on U.S. assistance. They were not interested at all in developing the country's economy.[19]

THE NEW BUSINESS—GOVERNMENT PARTNERSHIP

From his first day as Korea's new leader, Park Chung Hee exhorted his countrymen to work tirelessly to help develop their nation. He frequently complained that Korea, with its 24 million people, produced less electricity than Ford Motor Company in Detroit. In his 1962 book *Our Nation's Path*, he blamed Korea's lack of economic progress on centuries of oppression, first by the ruling elite of the Yi dynasty and later by the Japanese: "Under tyranny, where an individual cannot work on his own, we cannot expect independent creativity."[20] Park emphasized the need for national cooperation led by a strong central government. Personal freedom must follow, not precede, economic freedom and stability. Confucius, after all, had said that people must first be taken care of materially before they could prosper spiritually.[21] To Park, this meant that all development "must be done with the cooperation of the authorities."[22] Confucianism offered a rationale for the supremacy of the state, for unequal relations between government and the governed. Indeed, Park's rule was marked by increasing centralization of power and a national obsession with economic growth and development. Park felt passionately that a strong democracy in Korea could succeed only if it was based on stable economic growth. His government policies placed considerable emphasis on administrative efficiency and long-range planning as the foundation for an economic renaissance for his country.

Park ruled as part of a military junta until October 16, 1962, when he was elected president of the country. He managed the state's economy through a series of five-year plans that proved to be effective both in focusing national energies on well-targeted goals and in holding government and corporate officials responsible for measurable results. Park's first five-year plan, issued in 1962, had two principal objectives: breaking Korea's vicious cycle of poverty and establishing the foundation for self-sustaining economic development (see Table 4-2). These objectives were to be met through six interrelated strategies: (1) developing greater sources of energy, (2) correcting structural

TABLE 4-2

KOREA'S FIRST FIVE-YEAR PLAN: 1962–1966

STRATEGIES	OBJECTIVES	LONG-RANGE GOAL
Develop greater sources of energy.		
Correct structural imbalances in the economy.	Break Korea's vicious cycle of poverty.	
Build basis industries and infrastructure.		Improve industrial performance, farm output, and living standards.
Rechannel idle resources into productive endeavors.	Establish a foundation for self-sustaining economic development.	
Improve Korea's balance of payments.		
Promote technological development.		

imbalances in the economy, (3) building basic industries and infrastructure, (4) rechanneling idle resources into productive endeavors, (5) improving Korea's balance of payments, and (6) promoting technology development.[23] As part of this strategy, Park implemented new government policies requiring brutally long work hours and an authoritarian system that rewarded those who cooperated and punished those who did not.[24] Park noted in 1962 that "the people of Asia today fear starvation and poverty more than the oppressive duties thrust upon them by totalitarianism."[25]

Although Park was a disciplinarian with the ability to squelch dissent firmly, he was also sufficiently pragmatic to ensure that Korean companies became increasingly competitive. His government promoted the inflow of foreign resources of all types, as well as the development of Korea's exports. His reforms included new fiscal and monetary policies aimed at increasing public and private saving, the establishment of a uniform exchange rate, and the creation of a free trade zone.[26] In 1964, to commemorate Korea's attainment of $100 million in exports, Park initiated National Export Day, celebrated on November 30 each year thereafter.[27] (Korea's exports today exceed this figure by more than eight hundred times.) Awards were given out to companies that contributed significantly to this endeavor, and national awareness of the importance of exports was heightened significantly. Everyone in the nation had to understand the importance of exports. Park also made effective use of slogans that appealed to Korean's sense of national pride. The year 1966 was declared the Year of Hard Work. This was followed by the Year of Progress in 1967 and Fight While Working, Work While Fighting in 1968. Propaganda proved to be an effective tool in Park's national drive for development.

Park's industrial policies in the cities were complemented by his innovative *Saemaul Undong* program in the rural areas. Saemaul Undong, or New Community Movement, was aimed at reducing poverty in the small farming villages throughout the country through cooperative efforts. At the time, more than 70 percent of Koreans lived on farms, and Park was intent that these people not be left behind as Korea grew and developed. Saemaul Undong created farmers' cooperatives much like those in Scandinavia. New roads were built to ease access to and from villages. New farming techniques were introduced to increase crop yields. Efforts were made to strengthen support services and enhance cultural life in the region. Evidence of the enduring success of this movement can be seen both in the numerous imitations of the program by neighboring countries and in the political strength of Korean farmers to this day.

The spectacular growth in Korea's exports from $50 million in 1962 to $1.1 billion by 1971—just nine years later—is testament to the success of Park's strategies. Domestic savings rates also increased, from 26 percent in 1962 to 60 percent in 1971. The share of raw materials exported declined from 73 percent of total exports in 1962 to only 14 percent in 1971, while exports of industrial products rose from 27 percent to 86 percent.[28] This outward-looking strategy served to expand labor-intensive manufactured exports, which increased employment opportunities and significantly improved the economic welfare of millions of Koreans.

Park's government was able to control the actions of the private sector in several ways.[29] For starters, the government became a major stockholder in all domestic banks and appointed senior bank executives. Second, the government controlled the inflow of foreign capital, the principal source of corporate loans in Korea. Third, through the Bank of Korea and the Ministry of Finance, the government also controlled interest rates for all borrowing. The rationing of bank loans gave the government considerable leverage in promoting its export growth policies. In addition to these conventional methods, other mechanisms included a system of setting export targets and the practice of holding monthly national trade promotion meetings with major company presidents—including Chung Ju Yung—which were attended by President Park himself. The president set the tone with his commitment to "nation-building by export." These sessions provided the principal forum in which the various parties could informally negotiate product mixes and levels of administrative incentives, as well as resolve any problems or conflicts in export expansion efforts.

The government's policy-making efforts were also facilitated by a strong and highly competent Economic Planning Board (EPB), whose minister was also the deputy prime minister and was accountable only to the president. The EPB was entrusted with special powers and responsibilities, including developmental planning, budgeting, foreign cooperation and investment promotion, and the preparation of Korea's five-year economic plans. Although the EPB was not directly responsible for specific industrial policies, it was responsible for macroeconomic planning. Industrial policy was designed mainly by the Ministry of Trade and Industry in consultation with the Ministry of Finance.[30] To ensure success, all plans were consistently reinforced with solid budgets and financing from various ministries. The probability of successful implementation was further enhanced by linking policy implementation with the career advancement of the government planners.

An illustration of Park's administrative prowess can be seen in his decision to develop a self-sustaining cement industry for Korea. Cement, crucial to Korea's infrastructure development, largely had to be imported from Japan and elsewhere.[31] In 1962, Park determined that Korea should cease its dependency on others for this core resource. With financial support from the

U.S. Agency for International Development (USAID), Park's government loaned monies to several companies, including Hyundai, to construct new cement plants. For Hyundai, the move into cement represented the next logical step for a company increasingly involved in construction. It was simply a case of vertical integration. Why should Hyundai be dependent on foreigners—or even other Korean companies—for such a basic ingredient in construction? Hyundai sought and received a loan of $4.25 million, with an attractive repayment plan. With U.S. companies supplying the technology, engineering, and equipment, Hyundai Cement was open for business by 1964, just in time for Hyundai's major push into the Southeast Asian construction markets. Chung called his cement brand "Tiger." Owning its own factory cut Hyundai's cement costs in half, allowing it to surge ahead in the construction business. Indeed, before long, Hyundai had mastered the technology to such an extent that it was able to build turnkey cement plants for export to Saudi Arabia and other countries. The student had once again become the teacher.

Certainly, a good part of Korea's economic success was due to the entrepreneurial skills of Korea's top business leaders, like Chung. It is no secret that Park Chung Hee was favorably disposed toward successful entrepreneurs. Business executives who were hard-driving, dynamic, and enterprising leaders of their organizations impressed Park with their commitment to nation building. Indeed, when President Park once paid a surprise visit to a Hyundai construction site, he himself was surprised to see Chairman Chung—who had slept on the site with his men—working with the crew at dawn.[32] Such commitment would always be rewarded. But President Park also could be ruthless when an entrepreneur disagreed with him or failed to follow his directives. On several occasions, he had intransigent business leaders arrested or confiscated their companies for failure to follow his orders. Therefore, Chung had to be ever vigilant not to incur the wrath of the government.

ENGINES OF GROWTH

It is unlikely that Hyundai or any other Korean company could have succeeded to the extent that it did without relying on the uniquely Korean chaebol organization design. The term *chaebol* roughly translates from Korean as "fortune cluster" or "fortune grouping." It shares the same Chinese characters as the Japanese term *zaibatsu*. In practice, a chaebol is a large, family-held business conglomerate consisting of numerous diversified companies.[33] Today, there are over fifty chaebol groups in Korea. The ten largest, in order of sales, are Hyundai, Samsung, LG (formerly Lucky-Goldstar), Daewoo, SK (formerly

Sunkyong), Ssangyong, Kia, Hanjin, Lotte, and Hanwha. LG is somewhat unusual in that it is owned by two related families.

At the risk of oversimplification, chaebols like Hyundai tend to exhibit several common characteristics (see Table 4-3). Most of these follow from the national culture in which they operate. These include tight family ownership and control over the management structure of the firm; a strong entrepreneurial orientation that drives these firms continually to pursue new business opportunities; a strong paternalistic leadership in which the directives of the chairman and other managers are to be followed without question; centralized planning and coordination, usually through a central planning office for the entire group; and close cooperation between the firm and the government. During the past decade, however, the prominence of many of these features has eroded somewhat as Hyundai and other Korean firms have evolved from national firms conducting business abroad into global firms conducting business transnationally.

MIT economist Alice Amsden argues that over the past several decades the size of the chaebols has afforded them an ability to diversify into both related and unrelated industries.[34] She notes that their broad diversification and central coordination are products of late industrialization. Korea's business groups had no technical expertise to build on in related industries or in higher quality product market niches. Thus, as with other late-industrializing countries after World War II, Korean firms had to industrialize by borrowing and improving technology that had already been developed by experienced firms from more advanced economies. For all practical purposes, low wages were the only asset available to most late industrializers that had to compete against firms from industrialized economies. Most Korean firms began their rise by combining reengineered technology and mass production with favorable labor costs.

Large diversified conglomerates are not unique to Korea. In addition to the Japanese *keiretsu* (the successor organization to the prewar *zaibatsu*), many developing nations like Taiwan, the Philippines, and Thailand have similar large industrial groupings. So, too, do developing nations in other parts of the world, like India, Brazil, Argentina, and Venezuela. And, of course, such conglomerates are found in North America, although these firms are seldom as diverse in their holdings as those found in Korea. What differentiates Korea's major conglomerates—including Hyundai—from their counterparts elsewhere in the world is neither their financial strength nor the years of experience that we see in many U.S. firms nor the commitment to the long term seen in many Japanese firms. Rather, a chief characteristic of Korean firms is their fervent commitment to entrepreneurship. Successful Korean firms will do almost anything to leapfrog over the competition as a means to

TABLE 4-3

EARLY DESIGN CHARACTERISTICS OF THE HYUNDAI BUSINESS GROUP

CHARACTERISTIC	IMPORTANCE
Family ownership and control	Guaranteed that corporate management spoke with one voice on both strategic and operational issues; reduced potential for disagreements among divergent stakeholders; allowed for the development of second-generation owner-managers.
Strong entrepreneurial orientation	Encouraged company to be first to market and continually alert for new and promising business ventures; facilitated creativity and innovation throughout the organization.
Paternalistic leadership	Minimized potential disagreements over strategic directions of the firm; assured customers (including the government) that company could deliver; provided employees with charismatic role model.
Centralized planning and coordination	Ensured tight management controls over all funding and investment decisions; allowed company to pursue numerous divergent business ventures simultaneously.
Close business—government relations	Facilitated access to government-controlled capital, foreign technologies, and export licenses.

both survival and growth. What also makes Korean chaebols different is their sheer size compared to the national economy. Indeed, Korea's ten largest chaebols account for more than half of Korea's entire GNP.

Westerners who do business in Asia frequently assume that few, if any, differences exist between the major Korean conglomerates and their Japanese counterparts. Both exist in East Asian countries and both are influenced by similar cultural and religious roots. Indeed, several of today's Korean companies were established during Japanese occupation. And both represent huge organizations that are highly diversified in their holdings. However, although a number of similarities can be identified between the two groups, it would be misleading not to recognize several distinct differences.[35] At least eight such differences can be identified.

First and foremost among these differences is the relative size of the major conglomerates in each country. The typical Japanese keiretsu is much larger than the typical Korean chaebol. At Mitsubishi, Japan's largest conglomerate, for example, there are 29 *kinyo-kai* or "President's Council" companies, each of which is a conglomerate in its own right. In addition, Mitsubishi owns 160 smaller companies and controls numerous other smaller "independent" subsidiaries. All told, Mitsubishi has 146 companies that are large enough to be listed on the Tokyo or Osaka stock exchange. Annual group sales for 1996 were $433 billion, and the group employs 400,000 people. Mitsui and Sumitomo, Japan's other giants, are not far behind in these statistics. The Hyundai Group, by contrast, consists of about 50 companies with annual group sales of less than $100 billion. Hyundai employs 200,000 people worldwide. Clearly, Japanese firms are larger by an order of magnitude than Korean firms. Even so, despite their relative size, Korean firms like Hyundai routinely generate more income per employee than their Japanese counterparts.

A second distinguishing characteristic of Korean firms is the extent of their business diversification into unrelated industries. As they grew, Korean firms were much more likely than their Japanese competitors to diversify into enterprises that were completely unrelated to their core businesses or expertise (see Table 4-4). Some companies pursued almost any business opportunity that came along, however remote. In one case, for example, a major conglomerate bought a hotel, which led it to buy a restaurant, which led it to buy a bakery—hardly its strategic competency. In another case, a conglomerate recently entered the already-crowded Korean automobile industry using expensive foreign technology when it had no prior experience or expertise in the area and little chance of making a profit. Until recently, this diversification strategy was encouraged by generous credit guarantees from a supportive government. As a result, companies often found themselves involved in operating highly diverse and frequently unrelated businesses about which they

TABLE 4-4

BUSINESS DIVERSIFICATION BY MAJOR KOREAN, JAPANESE, AND U.S. FIRMS

TYPE OF DIVERSIFICATION	KOREA	JAPAN	UNITED STATES
Related industry	6%	40%	45%
Unrelated industry	57%	7%	20%

Source: Adapted from Seong Min Yoo, "Korean Business Conglomerates: Misconceptions, Realities, and Policies," in *Korean Economy: 1995.* (Washington D.C.: Korea Economic Institute of America, 1995), p. 16.

knew very little. Growth was all that mattered. Fortunately, Hyundai has not pursued this strategy as extensively as did many of its competitors.

Third, there are differences in the nature of ownership patterns among the Korean chaebols and Japanese keiretsus. As noted, in Korea most companies are closely held by family members. Although many large business groups in Japan (especially those founded before World War II) are also family enterprises, the percentage of family shares in contemporary Japanese conglomerates is now typically much smaller. Moreover, the definition of *family* is different in Japan than in Korea. In Korea, family members are determined by blood relationships (consanguinity), whereas in Japan there are two different definitions of *family*, one based on blood relationships and one based on household or clan relationships. In most cases, it is this clan relationship, not blood, that determines inheritance and succession. Hence, in Korea, not only do family members typically own a larger share of the company, but also the determination of who is part of the family is narrower. Hence, we see a greater concentration of wealth or assets in fewer hands.

As a result of this, a fourth difference emerges, namely the increased centralization of power in the hands of the CEOs in Korea compared to Japan. Korean CEOs are seldom challenged, however politely; their decisions are absolute. This characteristic has allowed many Korean firms to move more quickly and decisively than their Japanese counterparts on many occasions since less time is spent in consensus building among people at various levels of the organization. By the same token, this centralization leaves open greater possibilities for strategic errors due to hasty decisions or decisions made without sufficient information or discussion.

Also as a result of greater family ownership of Korean enterprises, a greater proportion of top managers in Korea are family members. Hence, the percentage of professional managers who have worked their way to the top is considerably higher in Japan than in Korea. However, much of this difference can be attributed to the relative newness of the Korean companies (i.e., many of the founders are still alive, whereas many of the major Japanese companies are several hundred years old); and, as we shall see later, Korean companies are moving rapidly to enhance the number of professionally trained managers on their staff.

A sixth difference is the nature of business-government relationships. As noted, this relationship has historically had a decidedly superior-subordinate nature in Korea as opposed to Japan, although this too is changing slowly under the new government. In Japan, this relationship (especially with the Ministry of International Trade and Industry), though not equal, is at least a little less one-sided than it has been in Korea. Korean companies grew by paying very close attention to what their government wanted. Although the same can be said of many Japanese firms, others, like Honda and Sony, grew and prospered outside the traditional Japanese system. No such examples of corporate independence can be found in Korea.

Because of this, a seventh difference can be noted, namely the nature of financing. Until very recently, most borrowing for new ventures in Korea has been from government-controlled financial institutions, whereas in Japan far more borrowing is from company-affiliated banks. Indeed, most of the major keiretsu own their own banks and several own multiple banks, thereby easing credit and borrowing issues. In Korea, during the military regimes, banks were controlled by the government. Only recently have the banks been privatized, and now several of the chaebols are following the Japanese example of buying a bank or another financial institution. Still, with rare exception, the major chaebols do not own banks. This gives Japanese concerns far greater financial freedom than their Korean counterparts and allows the Japanese added financial security to focus on long-term business development instead of short-term returns on investment.

Finally, although many similarities exist in the two approaches to human resource management, several differences can also be noted. In essence, Korean firms have tended, historically, to treat employees more as a variable cost of production—much as in the United States—whereas Japanese firms treat employees more as a fixed cost of production. If employees are treated as a variable cost, management's responsibility is to minimize such costs to enhance return on investment. By contrast, treating employees as a fixed cost (or fixed asset) implies that it is important for managers to tend these resources well and to make prudent investments where appropriate. Differences here include corporate approaches to lifetime employment guarantees, training costs, bonus payments, and retirement policies. In Japan, lifetime employment was considered an entitlement until very recently, when the practice began coming into question in a declining economy. In Korea, by contrast, employment guarantees have been based historically on the assumption of continued economic growth coupled with labor laws that until very recently made layoffs nearly impossible. As will be seen later, however, the approach to human resources taken by Korean firms is currently undergoing a major transition that will have an impact on its efforts to compete successfully in the global marketplace.

Thus, despite a number of similarities across the two cultures, clear differences must be recognized that influence both the day-to-day operations and the long-term strategic planning carried out by major corporations in Korea and Japan.

LEARNING THE HARD WAY

As Chung once observed, "I have always worked surrounded by risk and tension. The lion's share of any business expansion lies in innovation, and I have always been ready to assume any risk to achieve this. Risk adds vigor to any organization."[36] As Chung surveyed the new business possibilities under Park Chung Hee in the early 1960s, it was clear that the time had come for greater boldness. Chung set his sights on expanding his construction business beyond Korea's borders. His motivation was simple: "I foresaw that if our construction industry did not make inroads into the foreign market, it would soon reach a dead end."[37] As one senior-ranking Hyundai executive put it, "Chung decided that Korea was not big enough for him."[38]

In late 1964, Chung sent his younger brother, Se Yung, to Thailand to survey business opportunities. Shortly after arriving in Bangkok, Se Yung identified a project that looked interesting: a proposed 58-mile highway through thick jungles linking the cities of Pattani and Narathiwat. This was exactly what Park Chung Hee wanted for Korea and Chung Ju Yung wanted for Hyundai. Se Yung went after the contract. But when he asked if Hyundai could bid on the project, he was told that they would first have to buy $2 million in equipment. No problem, thought Se Yung. Hyundai contacted the Korean government back in Seoul and was immediately granted credit for the entire project. Hyundai then outbid 29 companies from 16 countries with a low bid of $5.2 million. No other government in the world supported its contractors to such an extent. Indeed, during Park's entire administration, Korean companies could count on low-interest, government-backed loans for any reasonable export project.

The departure of Korean workers for an overseas work site in 1965 represented a source of national pride and was front-page news in Seoul. The Korean Broadcasting System (KBS) broadcast the airport departure of Hyundai's work crews live and interviewed an exuberant Chung Ju Yung, who likened the experience to that of a frog who had lived his entire life in a well and had now finally gotten the chance to escape. For his part, President Park saw this new venture as proof of the success of his economic policies, noting that "Korea was making great strides in earning foreign currency."[39]

As Hyundai was about to learn, however, winning the contract was one thing, fulfilling it quite another. The Thai highway project ran into trouble from the outset. First, Hyundai tried to save money by purchasing antiquated equipment, including some Japanese trucks left over from World War II. Then, they decided to save money by paying local workers less than their Korean counterparts. Finally, the company naively assumed that they could continue normal construction efforts in the middle of the monsoon season. Their troubles multiplied. Continual equipment failures finally forced Hyundai to purchase all new machines and vehicles. Thai workers began a series of violent strikes against the company to gain pay equity. And the pavement laid down in the heavy rains soon buckled or was washed out by floods and overflowing rivers. When the highway was finally completed, Hyundai had incurred a net loss of $3 million. Their international debut was not much of a success. Even so, Chung Ju Yung called his experience a "coming-of-age initiation."[40] He concluded that the experience had been a good investment because it taught Hyundai managers how to compete in global markets. It taught them the importance of meeting world standards, a lesson that would be of vital importance to them in the years to come.

After Hyundai's initial international trial-by-fire, the company set its sights on Vietnam. The Vietnam conflict was just heating up in the mid-1960s, and U.S. forces and their allies were again seeking help with numerous construction projects. Brother In Yung rekindled his old contacts with the Americans and moved to Saigon. There he set up offices in the Continental Palace Hotel and remained for the next several years picking up as many construction contracts as he could. For most of its projects, Hyundai served as a subcontractor, most frequently to a U.S. conglomerate called RMK-BRJ. Hyundai built military camps, dredged rivers, and helped build the U.S. naval base at Camranh Bay. During the 1968 Tet offensive, Hyundai workers could be found dodging enemy bullets to finish dredging the Mekong River. They even ran a lucrative laundry and dry cleaning service on the side. Opportunity was everywhere, as was risk. So great was the total Korean civilian involvement in the war—23,000 workers—that it accounted for 10 percent of Korea's foreign exchange earnings in 1966 and nearly 20 percent in 1967. After five years' involvement in Vietnam, over $660 million in foreign exchange earnings had flowed into the Korean economy. President Park was again pleased.

Other major construction projects followed. Building on his relations with the Americans, Chung secured construction contracts for bridges, military bases, and military housing in Guam and Alaska. He secured a major harbor-dredging project in Australia and a hydroelectric plant project in Papua, New Guinea. Hyundai was rapidly establishing itself as a strong contender in the Pacific Rim construction bonanza. Meanwhile, back home, two major projects emerged that would solidify Hyundai's reputation not just as a contractor but as a world-class leader in engineering.

BUILDING A BETTER DAM

Since 1957, the Korean government had wanted to build a dam across the Soyang River (65 miles south of Seoul) as part of its national water resource

Graduation from Songjun Primary School in 1931. (Chung Ju Yung is standing in the fourth row, third from left.)

Chung Ju Yung (center) in a 1932 photograph with his brother In Yung (right) and cousin Won Yung (left).

Chung Ju Yung with the wife of the owner of the Bokheung Rice Store in Seoul, where he worked as a delivery man (1936).

Seoul's Shindangdong in 1938, location of Chung's Kyungil Rice Store.

金剛山探勝紀念
九　龍　淵

Chung (center) hiking with employees on Keumkang Mountain in 1946.

Chung and his wife, Byun Joong Suk, in the early 1950s.

First bridge over the Han River, built by Hyundai Construction in 1958.

hung relaxes with his wife in the front yard of their home in Seoul (1965).

Aerial view of the Kyungbu (Seoul-Pusan) Expressway, completed in 1970.

President Park Chung Hee and his wife at the official opening of the new Kyungbu Expressway in 1970. (Chung is standing at the ribbon to the right of the picture.)

Soyang Dam, completed by Hyundai Construction in 1973.

A Korean 500 won note like the one Chung used to convince the British to help him secure financing for his shipbuilding business.

Official ceremonies marking the launching of Hyundai Heavy Industries' first ship, the *Atlantic Baron,* in 1974.

Jubail Harbor Port, Saudi Arabia, completed in 1979 by Hyundai Construction Company.

Chung laughing with employees during a 1975 beach outing.

Chung engages in traditional Korean wrestling with an employee (early 1980s).

Chung working in his Seoul headquarters office (early 1980s).

Chung standing in front of an exhibit of the Hyundai Pony and a Hyundai-built bulk carrier (1980).

Using a submerged oil tanker to block ocean currents during the construction of a dyke to create Seosan Farm (1984).

Chung helping with rice planting at Seosan Farm (early 1990s).

Chung inspecting Seosan Farm's rice fields from the air (early 1990s).

Chung creating a piece of traditional Korean calligraphy in his home (1981).

Malaysia's Penang Bridge, completed by Hyundai Engineering and Construction Company in 1985, remains one of the longest bridges in the world.

Chung celebrating his 70th birthday with his wife, November 25, 1985.

management plan. The dam was intended to provide hydroelectric power, water, and flood control for the area. But technical problems, inaccessibility, and monumental cost estimates caused repeated delays. A full decade later, the dam was still not under way, and President Park was losing patience. The Ministry of Construction had brought in one of Japan's most prestigious engineering firms, Nihon Kyoei, to design the project. They recommended construction of a conventional concrete gravity dam for the site. A concrete dam would be the strongest type of construction possible and would likely endure for centuries. It also would be the most expensive to construct, and most of the profits would go to Japan, a point not lost on President Park. Even so, it was commonly assumed—even by the Korean government—that Korean firms were incapable of managing a project of this magnitude, especially in such a remote and inhospitable environment.

With little progress to show and huge construction costs looming on the horizon, Park approached Hyundai and asked for engineering advice on Nihon Kyoei's proposal. Chung studied the situation carefully and concluded that a zone-fill dam, made with earth and gravel instead of concrete, would be far cheaper to build and better suited to the topography. He based his conclusion on the experience of a French-designed dam in Thailand with which he was familiar. For dams over 100 meters in height, earthen construction was more cost-effective than concrete and was believed to be equally safe. Chung estimated that building an earthen dam would save 30 percent on construction costs; these funds could then be used for other national development projects. When confronted with Chung's report, the Japanese were outraged. Nihon Kyoei's top negotiator, a graduate of Tokyo Imperial University, reportedly asked: "President Chung, what do you know about dams? Where did you study about dams? Our design team is made up of Tokyo University graduates who have designed dams around the world. Do you mean that a man who completed only elementary school knows more than we do about dam construction?"[41] Chung did not reply.

Ironically, Korean government officials in both the water resources development department and the Ministry of Construction also were outraged at Chung's audacity. They had already approved Nihon Kyoei's designs, and their reputations were at stake. Besides, an earthen dam might collapse, sending a wall of water surging through the valleys toward downtown Seoul, with disastrous results, whereas a concrete dam would be less likely to collapse. What kind of impudence was this—a local construction company challenging the expert opinions of both their own government and one of the world's most respected engineering design firms? In taking on his own government officials, Chung later likened his behavior to "poking at a tiger's nostril and getting oneself killed."[42] The meeting broke up in complete disarray.

When the final proposal was made to President Park, ministry officials recommended the concrete dam and gave only brief mention to Chung's earthen dam proposal, which they dismissed as an unsafe alternative. President Park's response surprised everyone. He asked if anyone had considered the issue of national security in the design. Although it was true that a 100-meter-high earthen dam would cause significant damage if it broke open, wouldn't a 126-meter-high concrete dam cause more? Should the North Koreans bomb the dam—not an unlikely prospect in the volatile 1960s—the concrete dam would inflict significantly more damage than the earthen dam. An air raid on a concrete dam would blow a massive hole in the structure, sending millions of gallons of water rushing toward Seoul. An earth-filled dam, however, was more likely simply to collapse if struck, creating a new barrier and releasing far less water. From a national security standpoint, didn't the earthen dam make more sense?

The experts were stumped. President Park asked Nihon Kyoei and the ministry to study the issue and report back with their findings. Two months later they returned with the conclusion that Chung's proposal had been correct. Not only was an earthen dam equally safe and more cost-efficient than a concrete dam, but in the event of attack a concrete dam across the Soyang River could yield catastrophic results for the people of Seoul. Chung's proposal carried the day, and the new dam was begun in 1967 under a contract with Hyundai Construction. At the age of fifty-two, Chung was taking on one of his biggest challenges.

The Soyang Dam was completed six years later at a cost that was 30 percent below original estimates. Hyundai had completed the largest civil engineering project in Korea to date and had learned skills that they could later apply in even larger and more complex projects. With a touch of irony, Chung later recalled watching the new dam's dedication ceremony on television and seeing ministry officials explain how *they* had rejected the Japanese design and replaced it with a superior one.[43] Even so, the engineering prowess of Chung's company was now firmly established.

KOREA'S AUTOBAHN

About the same time as the Soyang Dam was being constructed, President Park turned his attention to Korea's primitive road system. During a 1964 visit to Germany, he was astonished to see the autobahn system that served as a lifeline to German industry. He determined that Korea would have such a system, beginning with a modern thoroughfare from Seoul to Pusan, a distance of 266 miles. Pusan was Korea's second largest city and its largest port. An expressway would open up large sections of Korea to economic development; it would spread the benefits of industrialization well beyond the city of Seoul.

In April 1967, Park announced the Seoul-Pusan (or Kyungbu) Expressway as part of his second five-year plan. When cost estimates for the project were released, widespread opposition erupted. Korea was a poor country and could not afford such an extravagance, many argued. In an extensive analysis of the proposed project, the World Bank advised the Korean government that the plan was economically and technologically infeasible and would add little to Korea's economic development prospects. The Korean legislature agreed: it would be too expensive.[44] Park saw things differently. To him, an expressway linking the principal population centers of Korea "would be a better investment of our limited funds than railroads and harbors for solving our transportation bottleneck."[45] Besides, building such a project would "give the Korean people a new confidence that they can do whatever they want."[46]

President Park summoned Chung to the Blue House, the presidential residence, to discuss the project. It was Chung's first private face-to-face meeting with the president. Park told Chung that he was familiar with Hyundai's experience in building highways in Thailand and wanted to know what Chung thought of the project. Park then asked him for an estimate of the cost of such a project. Chung spent the next three weeks surveying the proposed route. He studied maps and photographs and flew over the area several times. Chung concluded that the engineers who had initially planned the highway had failed to study the terrain sufficiently and instead had relied too heavily on textbooks and theory. They had proposed that the road be built essentially as almost a straight line from city to city. When Chung returned to President Park, he presented his proposal. Chung proposed digging fewer expensive tunnels through the mountains and, instead, building more of the road surface around the mountains. He further proposed that the inclines of several stretches of the highway could be increased slightly above the normal 6 percent maximum grade. The resulting highway could be built more quickly and with less money.

Park, though impressed with Chung's knowledge of the details of the project, still felt that Chung's cost estimates were unrealistically low. Indeed, Chung estimated the entire project would cost approximately 28 billion Korean won. By contrast, the Korean Ministry of Construction estimated the cost at 65 billion won, whereas the Army Engineering Office estimated 49 billion won and the Ministry of Finance estimated 33 billion won.[47] Hyundai's estimate was substantially below what various "experts" said the highway would cost. Moreover, because of the difficult terrain through which the road had to be built, many experts in both Korea and the United States thought the project was simply technically infeasible. It couldn't be done, some argued.

When Park asked Chung if the project could be accomplished, Chung replied simply, "I can do it."[48] Chung knew that no other Korean company had Hyundai's experience in road building. Here was a chance to put the competitors to shame on the home field.

Although some government officials ridiculed Hyundai's estimate as "uneducated" and "incomplete" and others challenged the project's overall feasibility, President Park nonetheless gave orders for Hyundai to take the lead in organizing a consortium of 17 firms to construct the highway. Hyundai would be assigned 133 miles of the project across some of the most difficult terrain. Groundbreaking ceremonies were held in February 1968.

As Chung set about construction of the highway, Park watched intensely over his shoulder. Park considered himself a nation builder, and the Kyungbu Expressway was much more than a road: it was a symbol of Korea's emerging status as a developed nation. Hyundai and the other companies working on the highway project must do their job correctly. A former engineer who worked closely with the Korean president later observed:

> Mr. Park is not an easy man at the best of times, and he certainly was far from
> that during our project. But after a while, I found myself thinking of him as a
> sort of conductor of an orchestra—with a helicopter as his baton. Up and down
> he would go, this time with a team of geologists to figure out what was wrong
> with some mountainside that had crumbled on our tunnel-makers, the next
> time with a couple of United Nations hydrologists to figure out how our survey-
> ors had got some water table wrong. If he didn't know the answer on Tuesday,
> Mr. Park was back with it on Thursday.[49]

To meet its deadline, Hyundai had to work around the clock and use multiple work crews. Chung personally moved to the construction site to oversee the work and drive his employees, sleeping only periodically in an old jeep used by the company. In the beginning, most workers followed Chung's lead and remained on the site day and night, returning home for only a day or two each month. Constructing the Kyungbu Expressway—accomplishing what Germany had accomplished—became a national cause. Over time, however, construction slowed as the terrain became more difficult. Several workers died in landslides and cave-ins. Accidents were frequent. Thirteen serious cave-ins occurred during the drilling of the Tangjae tunnel alone. Machinery and equipment broke down constantly. Fearful workers began leaving the work site in droves. When some workers complained that evil spirits were living in a particular tree near the construction site, an army officer cut the tree down, only to suffer a serious accident the next morning. More workers left. Chung doubled wages but was still short of workers. To maintain the schedule, Chung had to find ways to enhance the mechanization of the work. In this effort, he spent over $8 million to purchase 1,900 pieces of heavy equipment for the job, a huge amount considering that the entire nation had only 1,400 such pieces at the time.

President Park grew increasingly impatient with Hyundai's slow progress on the project. Chung responded by again giving up any hope of making a profit on the project. Instead, he determined to spend whatever it took to meet his deadline for completion. To Chung, Hyundai's name—and future— was more important than short-term profits. At long last, the Tangjae tunnel, the last and most difficult part of the entire expressway project, was completed in June 1970. When the expressway was officially dedicated in July, President Park was triumphant. "How much energy do our people have? How much technology do we have? We will test our nation's potential with this expressway."[50] The Seoul-Pusan Expressway was a triumph for Hyundai as well as for Korea. Chung's cost estimates for the project, as low as they were, turned out to be correct when adjusted for inflation. In the end, Chung finished his portion of the project—building two-fifths of the entire expressway—with a modest profit. More important, he had won the admiration and trust of Park Chung Hee. He was now 54 years old.

Hyundai thrived under President Park's rigidly controlled regime. To business executives, Park's government was seen as having a clear and realistic plan for economic development. The rules were well known to all, and companies could invest with reasonable confidence. Moreover, despite Park's autocratic style, his government was largely free of graft and corruption. It was clear that Park was committed to enriching Korea, not himself, and the business community trusted him. They also feared him. The only requirement for companies was that they meet their production targets without excuse. Failure to do so removed the company from Park's inner circle and from future government loans and contracts. It was clearly a case of shared destinies, and Korea's best entrepreneurs took up the challenge.

Along the way, Chung also grew to have considerable respect for President Park. Before long, Chung was a frequent visitor at the Blue House, joining Park on Thursday evenings for informal dinners in the private second-floor quarters. The two would sit for hours, dressed in casual clothes, drinking *makkolli*, a traditional fermented rice drink, and discussing Korea's future. Park often referred to Chung as his "minister of construction" in recognition both of Chung's considerable accomplishments in the field and of the respect Park had in his judgment and foresight. A mutual friend observed, "both men believed in the power of human will. They believed that Korean economic development must be built on that work ethos, but both of them also believed in using Western technology."[51] In many ways, President Park became a second father to Chung, and an enduring friendship developed that lasted until Park's assassination in 1979.

By 1972, however, Park became increasingly concerned that his control over Korea's future was waning. He had won the 1972 presidential election by a narrow margin against Kim Dae Jung (whom he later had arrested and jailed for six years), but dissent against his authoritarian regime was increasing. Park's response was to declare marshal law and force through the government-controlled legislature the so-called Yushin Constitution in October 1972. (*Yushin* is Korean for "revitalizing.") This document effectively gave President Park dictatorial powers to censor anyone who disagreed with or criticized his programs. Labor leaders, journalists, and political opponents were routinely jailed if they spoke out against Park's policies. The widely feared Korean Central Intelligence Agency (KCIA) soon became an instrument of the government's autocratic policies. This political crackdown, supported by the repressive Emergency Decree on National Security, lasted well into the early 1980s and made Korea one of the most repressive of the newly industrializing nations of Asia.

The Yushin period has been described by historians as one of Korea's darkest hours in terms of political freedom, but Park and his colleagues believed they were purifying Korea from the effects of partisan politics. "Before Yushin," observed one of Park's assistants, "I think the economic mechanism ran less smoothly because of political input. Park used to refer to that period and speak contemptuously of how businessmen used to lobby through political party bosses to affect government policy. After Yushin there was a belief on the inside [of the Blue House] that we had succeeded in freeing economic policy making from the pressures of politics and business."[52] Park used the Yushin Constitution to take a firmer grasp of economic development. In Park's view, Yushin removed many dysfunctional political influences from Korean's economic development efforts. There would be time for democracy later; for now, Korea had to grow. As one of Park's aides later observed in defense of Park's takeover, "If you agree on high growth, industrialization, expansion of trade, then this [Yushin] gives you a set of parameters. The less you are subject to pressures to swerve away from those objectives the better it is. This is the assumption you inculcate yourself with. Park was confident, sure of his performance, sure of the direction. He had no doubts."[53]

Chung Ju Yung had learned a great deal from his construction projects over the past decade. From the jungles of Thailand and Vietnam to the mountains and valleys of Korea, Hyundai had repeatedly proved that it was capable of the toughest jobs. Moreover, these experiences had created for a Hyundai a cadre of experienced managers and technicians who were capable of tackling almost any project in any kind of environment. Chung had also learned how to work effectively with the autocratic President Park. However repressive the government was, Chung understood and supported its goals—a stronger, more prosperous Korea. To accomplish this, both Park and Chung knew that Korea needed more foreign exchange; it needed more exports. To Chung, this meant finding new areas of endeavor. He set his sights on two new arenas about which he knew practically nothing: automobile manufacturing and shipbuilding. He would learn on the job. And Park Chung Hee would be standing right behind him.

C H A P T E R   5

DRIVING IS BELIEVING

"That man [Chung Ju Yung] is so bright, it's unbelievable. He's practical to the point where it hurts. He must have taught himself finance, and he's a great motivator. He put the fear of God into people."

—GEORGE TURNBULL, FORMER VICE PRESIDENT,
HYUNDAI MOTOR COMPANY[1]

With the completion of the Soyang Dam and the Kyungbu Expressway, Hyundai's construction credentials were firmly established. It was now the preeminent construction firm in Korea and had more business than it could handle. Chairman Chung was now in his early fifties, a time when many entrepreneurs begin solidifying their accomplishments instead of seeking new adventures. But for Chung, the hunt was just beginning. Hyundai was clearly off to a solid start, but Chung had dreams of becoming one of Korea's leading conglomerates, not just a construction firm. He wanted new challenges that would not only enhance his company but also improve the standard of living for his fellow Koreans.

To Chung, the strategy was obvious. Korea had an ample supply of educated and dedicated people who had no jobs. At the same time, Korea had to buy most of its industrial products from abroad because of the weakness of its own manufacturing infrastructure. If Korean firms could secure the necessary technological support, why not use local talent to build the industries that would build Korea's future? Again, President Park and Chairman Chung were on the same track. Korea needed to build its heavy industries, and Hyundai intended to take the lead.

There is a popular myth that when Hyundai was busily working to complete the Seoul-Pusan Expressway, President Park Chung Hee asked Chairman Chung if he knew anything about cars. Chung reportedly replied that he had run an automobile repair shop during and after World War II. Park thought for a minute and then said: "You're building the road. Now we need cars." There is little truth to this myth; Hyundai had already entered the automobile business before it began constructing the expressway. But the story symbolizes Park Chung Hee's strategic way of thinking, as well as the confidence he had in Chung Ju Yung.

Although Chung had been forced to sell his Hyundai Motor Service Company shortly after the Korean War to pay off some of his debts, he never forgot his dream that someday Hyundai would actually build cars for Korea's roads and highways. To Chung, it was a matter of national pride that Korea should build its own cars. Automobile manufacturing was widely considered a key economic indicator of industrialized nations; it was a symbol that a nation had arrived. Chung was determined that Korea be counted among this group. In addition, he realized early on that a domestic automobile industry meant greater employment and economic prosperity and less dependence on foreign suppliers. Korea's fledgling economy could not fully develop without a solid—and independent—transportation industry. Chung's dream of an empire based on heavy industries mandated that he try to take the lead in this endeavor.

However, two recent failures by Korean companies attempting to assemble cars had convinced most other industrialists that such a bold move was premature. The wise money went into making auto parts, not cars. When Chung announced that he would build cars, the reaction in the business community was shock. Although Chung had run a car repair service, he had no experience making car parts, let alone entire cars. Korea was simply not ready to tackle this industry. But Chung was undeterred: Hyundai would build cars.

Once again, Chung and the Korean government were heading in the same direction. In 1967, Park's government announced its second five-year plan (1967–1971). The plan included a call for increased industrialization, including the production of automobiles (see Table 5-1). The plan offered tax incentives for plant construction and car assembly, removed tariffs on imported automobile components and assembly equipment, and increased tariffs on fully assembled imported cars. Two other manufacturers also took up the challenge: Shinjin teamed up with Toyota to assemble Coronas, and Kia, a bicycle maker, teamed up with Honda to assemble Civics. Both cars would be made from kits imported from Japan and then assembled on Korean assembly lines.

But while Kia and Shinjin inched into the market, Hyundai jumped in with both feet. In 1967, Chung established an automobile office within Hyundai Construction and used a government-secured loan to purchase

TABLE 5-1

KOREA'S SECOND FIVE-YEAR PLAN: 1967–1971

STRATEGIES	OBJECTIVES	LONG-RANGE GOAL
Attain self-sufficiency in food; develop fisheries and forestry.		
Lay the foundation for industrialization, including automobile assembly and other heavy industries.	Modernize industrial structure.	
Improve the balance of payments.		Improve industrial performance, farm output, and living standards.
Institute employment creation, family planning, and population control.	Promote self-sustaining economic development.	
Raise farm household income. Improve technological acquisition and industrial productivity.		

82 acres on the Taehwa River in Ulsan for an assembly site. Ulsan was perfect for his long-term plans. A port city with a deep-water harbor, Ulsan would soon be connected to all major Korean cities by highways and was also suitable for the construction of a jetty from which Hyundai could import equipment and assembly parts and eventually export its cars abroad. In December 1967, Chung formed Hyundai Motor Company (HMC) as a separate company from Hyundai Construction (see the timeline in Table 5-2). He appointed his younger brother, Chung Se Yung, as president. Se Yung would remain as head of HMC until shortly before his retirement in 1996, when he appointed his son to replace him. At the same time, brother Chung In Yung, who had been indispensable in securing construction contracts in Southeast Asia, was appointed president of Hyundai Construction Company. Chung Ju Yung would officially become group chairman of the entire enterprise.

TABLE 5-2

TIMELINE: HYUNDAI MOTOR COMPANY

DATE	EVENT
1967	Hyundai Motor Company founded.
1968	HMC begins assembly of Ford Cortinas for Korean market.
1973	HMC signs technical assistance agreements with ItalDesign and Mitsubishi for help designing its own car.
1974	Hyundai Motor Service established to distribute cars.
1976	Hyundai Pony rolls off the assembly line.
	HMC experiments with car exports to various overseas markets.
1982	Hyundai Pony II launched.
1983	Hyundai Pony II cars exported to Canada.
1985	Hyundai Motor America established in California.
1986	First Hyundai Excels shipped to United States.
1987	Hyundai Excel rated #1 import car of the year in the United States.
	Korea Electronic Fuel Injection Corporation (KEFICO) founded.
1988	Hyundai Sonata introduced in U.S. market.
1989	Hyundai Excel reaches 1 million in worldwide sales, while HMC total cumulative sales reach 3 million.
	HMC's North American assembly plant opens in Bromont, Quebec.
1990	Hyundai Elantra launched.
1991	HMC builds its first independently designed Alpha engine.
	HMC builds its first electric car.
1992	HMC reaches 5 million cars in cumulative sales.
1994	Hyundai Accent launched.
	HMC builds its first solar-powered car.
	Bromont, Canada, plant closed.

DATE	EVENT
1995	Hyundai Avante launched.
1996	Cumulative HMC sales reach 10 million units, 4 million in exports.
	Hyundai Tiburon and Sonata III launched.
	HMC builds its first hybrid car.
1997	Hyundai launches 800cc Atos mini car.
1998	HMC initiates a major campaign to gain market share in North America through the introduction of several newly redesigned car models.

APPRENTICESHIP WITH FORD

In February 1968, Chung Se Yung reached an agreement with Ford Motor Company for Hyundai to become an assembler of complete knockdown sets of Ford Cortinas that would be manufactured by Ford and then shipped to Ulsan for final assembly.[2] Ford also agreed to provide all the necessary equipment for assembly. Hyundai rejected an early offer from Ford for management participation (or part ownership in the enterprise). In a later agreement, Ford further agreed to allow Hyundai to use Korean parts and materials where possible and to provide technical assistance to the Korean auto parts industry. Hyundai was eager to get started. Indeed, in constructing its initial assembly factory, Hyundai set a record for the quickest time between ground-breaking and full-scale operations for any Ford assembly plant around the world—just under six months.[3]

As originally planned, Hyundai would assemble 3,000 vehicles per year. Eighty percent of the parts would come from the United States and 20 percent would be locally sourced. Within two years, production was increased to 5,000 cars. Soon, diesel trucks and buses were added to the product mix, with 80 percent of the required parts coming from Ford-Europe and 20 percent being locally made. Ford engineers taught Hyundai the business from start to finish, including planning, scheduling, product assembly, inspection, and quality control.

After the initial two years, Hyundai and Ford began discussions about future cooperative ventures. These negotiations were spurred on by the Korean government's insistence that local-content requirements (the percent of locally made parts) be raised from 20 to 60 percent. Chung proposed that Ford and Hyundai establish a second company on a fifty-fifty basis to build engines for the assembly line. In November 1970, Ford agreed. Soon, however, the joint venture was in trouble as each side fought for management control. Increasingly, Chung took the position that building a Korean car was required for the nation, and that the Americans were interfering with Korea's drive for self-sufficiency and economic well-being. Although Park's second five-year plan envisioned Korea assembling cars, it assumed that the actual design and manufacture of a uniquely Korean car was too ambitious—even for President Park. Chung, however, soon concluded otherwise. He felt that simply assembling cars designed by others, such as Ford, would neither be profitable in the long run nor help significantly in the development of Korea's infrastructure.

At the same time, Ford increasingly began to question its return on investment in Korea. Ford had established a complete factory and taught the Koreans how to build cars. In return, they expected some degree of allegiance, as they had received from Ford-Europe and other Ford operations. Instead, they came to feel that Hyundai, supported by the Korean government, was simply milking them for technology and engineering expertise. Both sides resisted honoring their financial commitments for the new joint venture.

Finally, Hyundai made a proposal that Ford thought was outrageous: they proposed that Hyundai-made Fords be sold throughout Ford's global distribution system. This offer was consistent with President Park's grand plans to increase both exports and foreign reserves, but Ford rejected it and noted that the Ford distribution network was for Ford cars exclusively. Hyundai did business with Ford, but they were not considered part of the family. Ford did not control them. Besides, Ford argued, no one but Koreans would willingly purchase Korean-made cars.

Then Ford made an equally outrageous counterproposal. Why not make Hyundai part of its emerging "world car" effort? Hyundai could build Ford-designed engines that would be put on chassis made in Australia with transmissions made in Japan. To Chung, this represented a national insult. How could Hyundai and Korea gain international stature as an auto maker by participating anonymously in a grab-bag assembly scheme? Ford was being imperialistic in pursuit of its own global objectives, as Chung saw it. In January 1973, Park's government withdrew its support for the joint venture, and Hyundai followed suit two months later. Although Hyundai continued to assemble Ford Cortinas for several more years, trust in the partnership had evaporated.

Chung immediately set about finding alternative paths to his dream of becoming a global car maker. To learn more about how the entire industry worked, Chung sent experts to Australia to study production technologies, to Japan to study after-sales service, and to the United States to study marketing and distribution systems. He wanted to learn the entire business from the ground up.

BUILDING A NATIONAL CAR

With the breakup of the Ford-Hyundai partnership, Hyundai needed another source for supplies and technical assistance. They still required foreign support. Chung Se Yung searched the world for suitable partners. After talking with General Motors, he concluded that "we wanted to run the company our way, but GM wanted to run the company their way. That was the point of disagreement."[4] (GM went on to form an unsuccessful alliance with Shinjin, known as Saehan, that later formed the basis for the creation of Daewoo Motors.) Hyundai then approached Volkswagen and Alpha Romeo, but fared no better. No one offered the independence that Hyundai wanted, and probably for good reason: Hyundai could shortly become a competitor in their own markets.

Finally, HMC turned to the Japanese, their one-time oppressors, for help. Chung Se Yung noted: "We were very happy to go with Mitsubishi because we could run the company our way. They didn't touch our management. This way, we could do better business than arguing with the partner all the time."[5] At the time, Mitsubishi Motor Company was desperately trying to expand its markets and compete with the larger Japanese auto firms of Toyota and Nissan. Mitsubishi offered Hyundai a technical licensing agreement, which meant that Hyundai could build its own nameplate cars using technical designs from Japan for everything from engines to transmissions. No financial partnership was required, only licensing fees, although Mitsubishi would later buy 10 percent of HMC stock to help finance expansion and technological development.[6] Moreover, Mitsubishi agreed to buy up to 30,000 of the cars to sell in Japan under the Precis nameplate. The agreement was signed in 1973. It was a dream come true for Hyundai and Korea.

As fast as Hyundai moved, it sometimes seemed that the Korean government moved faster. Within months of the signing of the Mitsubishi agreement, President Park issued a directive governing the development of the automobile industry. This was quickly followed by several more directives, including one that specified that Korean car makers must build a "citizens' car" to be made almost entirely with Korean parts. These cars would in reality be runabouts, with engines of less than 1,500 cubic centimeters. Hyundai, along with Shinjin and Kia, were designated as prime contractors. Se Yung immediately set out for Europe in search of design assistance. First, he met with Giorgetto Giugiaro of ItalDesign, the car stylist for Alpha Romeo and Fiat. Next, he met with George Turnbull, who had recently resigned as president of British Leland over a policy dispute with the company's chairman. Turnbull was invited to Korea for an inspection tour of the Hyundai facilities and was immediately impressed with both of the Chung brothers. In recalling his first impressions of Chung Ju Yung, Turnbull noted that he was a man of vision who had boundless energy: "That man is so bright, it's unbelievable. He's practical to the point where it hurts. He must have taught himself finance, and he's a great motivator. He put the fear of God into people."[7]

George Turnbull was hired in February 1974 as an HMC vice president reporting directly to Chung Se Yung to help make Chung's dream a reality. Turnbull immediately hired six European chief engineers to assist him, including a body designer, two chassis designers (for cars and trucks), two production engineers, and a test engineer. All were given three-year contracts. The new team returned to Italy to consult again with Giugiaro. The design they selected was simple but not elegant; Hyundai still lacked the sophistication for complex designs.

Upon his arrival in Ulsan, Turnbull set about building an engineering center and a new assembly plant. Normally, it took four years to put a car into production, but HMC required only two. Turnbull was amazed at Chung's resolve. When engineers tried to tell him that he had selected a swamp for the plant site, Chung resolutely stood by his initial decision. They drained the swamp. Turnbull concluded that Chung thought he could accomplish anything if he just put his mind to it. Building in a swamp was bad enough, but it was winter and the concrete pilings for the factory walls repeatedly cracked in the extreme temperature. Chung was again unmoved. This was where he wanted his factory. Some of the equipment was installed before all of the factory walls were even in place. It made little sense to the conservative British executive. Nor did he understand Hyundai's approach to building a test track. Most U.S. and European test tracks at the time cost over $1 million to build, but HMC spent only a fraction of this. It was rough, to be sure, but it worked all the same.

Throughout construction, Chung made frequent inspection visits to the plant site. To do so, he would leave his home in Seoul at 4:00 A.M. with one or two assistants for the long drive to Ulsan. For Chung, however, the drive was an enjoyable experience because it was on the new Kyungbu Expressway. As he would often say, he was driving on *his* road, and he was happy.

Turnbull's expertise proved to be invaluable to Hyundai throughout the start-up phase. On one occasion, Mitsubishi attempted to supply HMC with an underpowered engine for their new cars; they wanted to keep their superior engines for their own Japanese models. Turnbull would have none of this and sent HMC executives to Tokyo to insist on the better engine. HMC also insisted that Mitsubishi provide sufficient spare parts for the engine. Slowly, the Japanese were learning that the Koreans could stand on their own two feet. After working with the Koreans for several years, one Mitsubishi executive concluded, "Hyundai Motor's ability to put everything into practice is really amazing."[8]

While Turnbull built the factory, Chung set about securing financing for the new venture. With government backing and loan guarantees, he secured a $100 million loan on favorable terms from a consortium of Japanese, British, French, and Korean banks. Hyundai managed to get the loans for 1½ percent below prevailing market rates, with up to ten years to repay. This was the first time that European banks had made a significant loan to any Korean company and was all the more impressive because HMC's entire paid-in capital at the time was a mere $5 million.[9] The banks would take the risks; Hyundai would take the profits.

By 1976, the new plant was completed and the first cars began rolling off the assembly line. Chung named the new model the Pony, a familiar name to many Koreans who were brought up on American Western movies. The Pony was a 1.2 liter rear-wheel-drive subcompact of modest quality. No market research had been done. Chung and his company had simply designed and built the car they thought the Korean people should have. President Park guaranteed the financing; Hyundai built it. It was Korea's first national car.

WORKING ON THE LINE

Working for Hyundai Motor Company during these early days was no easy job. The normal work shift lasted from 8:00 A.M. to 8:00 P.M., six days a week. With mandatory overtime, the average assembly line worker was often in the plant from 8:00 A.M. to 10:00 P.M., six days per week, and sometimes on Sunday depending on production demands.[10] Workers received time off for lunch, dinner, and two breaks at the work site. This meant that workers were frequently in the factory 14 hours a day, or 84 hours each week.[11] Women typically worked about nine hours per day, arriving each morning at 8:00 and usually leaving around 6:00 P.M. to return home to help the family with dinner.

A good example of how difficult the job could be is found in a 1979 account of assembly workers at Hyundai Motor Company by award-winning journalist David Halberstam. Halberstam tells the story of Park Chin Keun, an HMC foreman.[12] Like many Koreans, Park had left a farming village to enter the industrial world because he felt it had greater promise for the future. He moved to Ulsan in 1974 and applied along with four hundred others for the fifty blue-collar jobs that were open. He was very nervous during the selection interview and gave what he thought were wrong answers to several questions (e.g., "If something bad happens inside the company, would you tell anyone from the outside?"). But he got the job.

In the early days the work was very hard. The Pony assembly line was not automated, and the workers were inexperienced. The parts made by suppliers were of poor quality, and the men had little idea of what they were doing. Park remembers that the assembly line usually worked only about 20 to 30 percent of the time and that a shift could only produce about twenty cars per day. Park knew that the cars were not very good but, like the other workers, he was told by his supervisor that things would improve and that it was his obligation to persevere. He did, and slowly the situation got better. Gradually, the workers at Hyundai came to understand what was expected of them. Their technical knowledge improved, as did the quality of parts from suppliers, and productivity began to climb.

The critical year was 1979. Before this, the company had achieved a level of production of one car every four minutes and thirty-eight seconds. As the technical assistance began to come together and a new semiautomated assembly line was put into place, production surged to one car every two minutes. The work pace was exhausting, but Park never complained. He worked twelve hours a day, six days a week. He had no effective union representation. He lived with his wife and two children in a small, company-owned high-rise apartment near the factory. Throughout, however, he was convinced that his new life in the industrial world was far better than that of his parents on the farm.

EXPLORING OVERSEAS MARKETS

Within weeks of the opening of the new Pony assembly line in Ulsan, Chung announced that he would export five thousand of the cars overseas. Turnbull was shocked. Koreans might buy a car of dubious quality because they had no alternative, but foreign buyers usually had many more options. If they rejected the Pony in favor of cars of higher quality, it would injure Hyundai's future reputation and sales. Chung was undeterred: he would export. He had promised President Park he would do so. But instead of exporting all of the cars to a single test market, he would spread them out across several countries in different parts of the world, including Nigeria, Taiwan, Peru, Ecuador, and Saudi Arabia. In this way, he could test his vehicle's performance and stamina in different markets, climates, and road conditions. He would do his test market *after* the cars were built and, in the process, would learn how to improve future versions. He also would learn something about selling cars around the world.

Chon Sung Won, a young HMC manager at the time, was sent to visit thirty countries—including some that had no diplomatic relations with South Korea—in search of markets. Looking back on his adventure, Chon admitted: "We didn't have any basic knowledge of exports. We just thought that someday we should export. That was the natural thinking in South Korea at that time."[13] Where possible, they relied on what they had learned overseas in the construction industry, but Hyundai had little real experience in dealing with foreigners. In the end, although customers frequently spurned the car, Hyundai learned a great deal about how to sell overseas. They also learned how different physical environments affected their automobiles. In hot tropical climates like Nigeria, the vinyl roofs peeled off like banana skins. In Saudi Arabia, the excessive sun caused the paint to fade. And in several locations, Ponys experienced numerous mechanical problems, especially with steering and brakes, as the cars were driven across miles of primitive roads. As a result, HMC was forced to upgrade the quality of its cars significantly, probably sooner than it would have had it remained exclusively in the protected Korean market.

In these early days, quality control was always problematic. Hyundai was still learning how to make good cars and lacked many of the more sophisticated quality control methods used by the leading producers in Japan and the West. Instead, they had to improvise. As HMC Chairman Chung Se Yung noted in a 1997 interview, one crude but reasonably effective method that was used to determine the relative quality of Hyundai cars was to drive along the highways and count the number of disabled cars on the sides of the road. Chung knew that his company had 60 percent of the Korean market, but routinely counted only about 50 percent Hyundai cars among those stopped along the roadside. He concluded that, compared to the competition, Hyundai must be doing O.K.[14]

In 1977, after their three-year contracts expired, Turnbull and his associates returned home to Europe, leaving behind a motor company that felt it was ready to take on the world. HMC still had much to learn, but it had come a long way from its humble beginnings. It was no longer just an assembler of foreign cars but a full-fledged Korean automobile manufacturer, managing everything from design to manufacture to marketing and distribution. Significant progress had been made. Even so, profits were tardy in arriving. As one Hyundai executive observed, "Between 1972 and 1978 Hyundai Motor was essentially a bankrupt company supported by other Hyundai companies."[15]

The audacity of Chung Ju Yung and his brother Se Yung during this period can be seen in their decision to build a new automobile factory with a production capability well beyond any reasonable market forecast. In the mid-

1970s, the total car market in Korea hovered around 30,000 units per year. With the recent success of the Pony, Chung announced plans to construct a major new manufacturing plant. At the time, General Motors was launching a new "world car" assembled from parts manufactured in different countries that could be sold around the world. To accomplish its plan, GM targeted worldwide sales of 300,000 and began constructing a new $3 billion factory. Chung studied GM's plans and strategies and came to two conclusions. First, Hyundai would also build a new factory capable of manufacturing 300,000 cars per year—almost ten times Korea's current total market. Second, he would do so for about one-tenth the cost; Hyundai would build its factory for only $300 million.

Both of these goals seemed unrealistic to Chung's colleagues. Who would buy 300,000 cars? And how could Hyundai, even with its lower labor costs, construct such a large factory for so little investment? Chung explained that Korea's car market would grow significantly as its people emerged from poverty as a result of the country's new industrialization. In addition, Hyundai would build an entirely new car designed principally for export. If General Motors could do this, so could Hyundai. To keep construction costs of the new facility down, Chung personally reviewed all aspects of the plant design with his engineers. The bricks used to construct the factory walls were reduced in width. Window sills, which had to be made from expensive imported wood, also were reduced in width. The windows themselves were made from glass that was slightly thinner than the norm. Costs were shaved in any way possible. The resulting factory, opened in 1980, was functional if not attractive. It would produce the targeted number of cars and cost just what Chung had estimated. Hyundai was now prepared to take on the world in cars.[16]

Soon, with their new capacity, HMC's exports began to climb, as did local sales. Hyundai had long ago surpassed the other Korean manufacturers to become to dominant industry leader, both locally and internationally (see Table 5-3). But HMC was just beginning. In 1982, an improved version of the Pony—dubbed the Pony II—was launched that incorporated what HMC had learned about car manufacturing. The new car was exported as far away as Africa, Latin America, and Canada and was well received as a modestly priced compact car. By 1986, HMC's sales had risen to more than 400,000 vehicles, and profits began to stream in. As if to show the Japanese that the Koreans were indeed capable of succeeding in this highly competitive industry, Chung published a book in Japanese in 1987 entitled *Pony Ga Hashiru— The Pony Runs*. HMC would be a global player in the automobile industry.

TABLE 5-3

EARLY GROWTH OF KOREA'S AUTOMOBILE INDUSTRY: 1970–1990

Annual Production (# Units)	1970	1975	1980	1985	1990
Hyundai	4,300	7,100	61,800	240,700	676,000
Kia	5,700	20,000	34,100	87,200	337,300
Daewoo[a]	16,600	9,300	25,700	45,000	201,200
Others	1,700	400	2,800	7,500	48,000
Total	28,400	36,800	124,400	380,400	1,302,500
Annual Exports (# Units)					
Hyundai	—	—	16,200	120,000	225,400
Kia	—	—	4,700	1,400	85,800
Daewoo	—	—	4,200	5,600	34,200
Others	—	—	100	900	1,700
Total	—	—	25,200	127,900	347,100

[a]Includes knock-down kits assembled by Shinjin before Daewoo Motors was formed in 1980.

Source: Based on data provided by the Korea Automobile Industry Council; Linsu Kim, *Imitation to Innovation: The Dynamics of Korea's Technological Learning* (Boston: Harvard Business School Press, 1997), Chapter 5; "Automobile Exports Increase 8.2% in 1997," *Korea Herald*, January 13, 1998, p. 1.

EAST TO AMERICA

By the early 1980s, the Hyundai Business Group had grown into a major international corporation. It had been listed as an International Fortune 500 company since 1975 and had proved its capabilities in a wide array of industries. Now Hyundai felt it was ready for the world's largest and toughest automobile market: North America. If Hyundai could succeed there, it could easily become one of the truly major international players and a force to be reckoned with in the emerging global economy. As Hyundai saw it, they had reasonably high quality entry-level products, a well-trained and inexpensive labor force, and the financial backing of their government. What they lacked was North American marketing know-how. This they would buy.

In 1985, Hyundai began a serious study of the North American automobile market. HMC Chairman Chung Se Yung thought that he had found just the right niche in this competitive market. With the Japanese car companies scrambling for the compact market and the U.S. companies still focused primarily on the mid- and large-sized market, HMC would go after the subcompact market. By undercutting Toyota Corollas, Nissan Sentras, and Mazda 323s, as well as Ford Escorts, Hyundai would aim to capture the market then held by the notoriously unreliable Yugo. With a starting price of $4,995, the new Hyundai Excel, recently designed with the export market in mind, would be priced well below the $6,000-plus compacts. Industry analysts agreed: Hyundai would become the next Toyota.

HMC set out in earnest to establish an American-style car company capable of successfully entering the U.S. market. Based on two years' experience selling cars in Canada with modest success, it formally established Hyundai Motor America (HMA) in late 1985. Headquarters were opened in Garden Grove, forty miles south of Los Angeles in car-crazy southern California. The new HMA hired several senior U.S. executives away from their Japanese competitors to help run it. For the Americans who joined HMA, it was a chance to get in on the ground floor on what would undoubtedly be a major adventure. For Hyundai, it was a chance to use American know-how to leapfrog over their Japanese rivals. Park Sung Hak was sent to California from Hyundai's Canadian operations to become HMA's first president. From the beginning, Hyundai established a two-tiered company consisting of Korean executives transferred in from other Hyundai companies and Americans hired in from the outside. This class system would later return to haunt the fledgling company.

HMA engaged Backer, Spielvogel, & Bates, a leading American advertising firm, to develop a marketing campaign with the theme "Cars That Make Sense." Hyundai would focus its efforts on lower income used-car buyers. Now, instead of buying a used car, these drivers could buy a simple but attractive new car for the same money. For a little extra, they could even have an automatic transmission and air conditioning. No one claimed they were selling premium cars. The fit and finish were not perfect; indeed, no one could remember a car with a worse paint job. Reliability and performance could have been better. Nonetheless, in the you-get-what-you-pay-for car market, the Excel was instantly recognized as a good compromise for low-end buyers. Besides, it came with a five-year limited warranty.

By any measure, Hyundai's initial entry into the U.S. market was an unqualified success. On December 23, 1985, *Business Week* graced its cover with a picture of the Hyundai Excel to accompany an article on Korea's new export drive to North America. Hyundai—and Korea—had arrived on the U.S. scene as a major player in a wide range of labor-intensive industries, ranging from automobiles to home electronics. While Hyundai was selling cars, other Korean giants like Daewoo, Samsung, and Lucky-Goldstar (later LG) were beginning to flood the U.S. market with inexpensive televisions, VCRs, and microwave ovens, usually with someone else's brand name printed on them, like Kenmore or J.C. Penney. Daewoo would shortly sign a joint venture agreement with General Motors to assemble Pontiac LeMans cars in Korea for export to the United States. But Hyundai wanted no part of such OEM (original equipment manufacturer) operations; it wanted to use its own brand name. It wanted people to know who Hyundai was.

With little idea about potential market size—or, for that matter, the number of cars they might be able to receive from the Ulsan assembly plant—Hyundai Motor America initially took a conservative approach to establishing dealerships. Since the Excels would be shipped through just three U.S. ports (Los Angeles, California; Portland, Oregon; and Jacksonville, Florida), it was important that the initial dealers be located near these ports. Moreover, dealers would need to have sufficient funds to staff and equip a full-service dealership adequately. Dealers also would need to guarantee that they would sell no other brands; a Hyundai dealership would not simultaneously carry Volvos or Chevrolets. Hyundai would look carefully at applicants' sales history, customer satisfaction index, and reputation in the industry. It would not be easy to become a Hyundai dealer. Even so, over 4,000 applicants eagerly fought for the first 75 dealerships. By 1988, the number of dealerships would rise to 300, still a small number in comparison to their Japanese or U.S. competitors, but sufficient for Hyundai's initial needs.

The first cars arrived in the showrooms in February 1986. The success of the Hyundai Excel was swift and sure. Sales for 1986 surpassed the initial 100,000 projections and reached 168,000. In 1987, sales reached 264,000. The Excel was rated the number one imported car for both years in sales. No other car company in history had achieved such initial success. With its new styling, front-wheel drive, and inexpensive price, the Excel was off to a good start in an unbelievably competitive industry. To keep things moving, HMC built a massive automobile storage facility and a four-ship dock adjacent to its assembly facilities back in Ulsan to handle the huge car-transport ships destined for the U.S. market. HMA dealers were invited to Ulsan on a regular basis to inspect the cars and advise the Koreans on how to improve them.

In an interview at the time, HMC Chairman Chung Se Yung, reflecting on HMA's early success, noted that, like Americans, Koreans were highly individualistic people: "The key to our success is good planning and good leadership."[17] These qualities, Chung observed, would allow Koreans to catch up to Japan in the near future. What about the Americans? Chung thought for a moment and then replied, "When [Americans] get rich, they work less." The United States, he believed, has a "structural problem" that, if unchecked, would likely inhibit future entrepreneurial endeavors. They needed to get back to work.

In support of its entry into the American car market, Hyundai purchased a 420-acre site in Bromont, Quebec, 50 miles east of Montreal, to build a North American assembly plant. Here they would assemble both Excels and the larger Sonata, which they hoped to sell eventually in the United States. At $300 million, the Bromont plant was the largest factory ever built by a Korean firm outside of Korea. It promised to provide Hyundai with the ability to rapidly assemble and deliver more cars built to exacting North American standards than would be possible from its Ulsan factory. Initially, 120 Koreans were brought in to complete the factory and train the work force. Soon, this number would fall below 40 as 1,200 Canadian employees reported for work. The plant opened its operations in December 1988 with a capacity of 100,000 cars per year.

Despite its initial success, however, and unbeknownst to many HMA managers at the time, the fledgling U.S. car company was headed for serious trouble. The first sign came in April 1987, when HMA's affable and well-respected president was recalled to Seoul. Although it is unclear why he left, many American managers on the scene at the time felt that he had allowed them too much independence in decision making. Others believed that Hyundai had concluded that it had learned everything it could from the locals and now intended to assume more direct control over operations. Whatever the reason, 1987 signaled a turning point in U.S.-Korean relations within the firm. Henceforth, American executives saw their roles eclipsed by a steady stream of Korean managers sent from the home office. All major financial and marketing decisions would henceforth be made in Seoul.

Inexperience and nationalism were apparently holding back Hyundai's charge into the global marketplace. In an effort to incorporate more Korean-made parts into the U.S. vehicles, HMC began dropping its European and Japanese suppliers in favor of less experienced Korean ones. As a result, the quality of the Excels, never outstanding, began to deteriorate. Everything from electrical motors to steering units to brakes became a problem. A good example of this can be seen in the inferior paint jobs used on the Excels. HMC turned to a paint company owned by one of Chung's brothers. The company, Korea Chemical, had little experience making high-quality automotive paint and initially produced paint of very poor quality. Because the company was owned by a family member, however, it retained the contract. It took several years and foreign assistance before Korea Chemical could approach world standards for the product. When the American managers complained about such issues, their concerns were brushed aside. HMC knew what it was doing. But the marketplace was telling a different story. New Japanese and U.S. entries into the subcompact market—including a new Ford Festiva assembled by Hyundai's rival, Kia—raised the stakes for quality and value. Hyundai sales remained static in 1988 at 263,000 units, well below the targeted 300,000.

Then, the new Sonata, Hyundai's answer to the Toyota Camry and the Honda Accord, was introduced in the U.S. marketplace in December 1988. Problems began almost immediately. First, Ulsan was late in shipping parts to Canada, where the new car was to be assembled. This was caused by repeated labor strikes that had erupted throughout Korea during this period (see Chapter 9). Potential customers visited empty showrooms and went away angry. When the parts finally arrived and the cars were assembled and shipped, they were not supported by a serious advertising campaign. Customers began looking elsewhere, and sales plummeted. Then the United States was hit by a severe economic recession, and overall car sales began to decline. Despite the reasonably high quality ratings the car received, sales were sluggish in a crowded market.

By 1989, total Hyundai sales in the United States had dropped to 188,000 vehicles. HMA responded by terminating several U.S. executives, notably those who had disagreed with Seoul on matters of policy and strategy. By 1991, total sales had dropped to 120,000 vehicles. By 1992, this figure had dropped again, to 77,000, with an operating loss of $140 million. HMA was now in serious trouble. Consumers began to complain more vociferously about poor quality and poor resale value.[18] When the remaining American managers proposed investing additional funds in rebates and advertising to reinvigorate sales, they were overruled by their Korean bosses, who looked instead for new ways to reduce costs. To many American managers, it appeared that orders were coming directly from Seoul to cut their losses.

In 1992, only 14,220 Sonatas were assembled at the new Bromont plant, less than 15 percent of total plant capacity. Excels were never manufactured there, as originally planned. In October 1994, the Bromont plant was closed.[19] Hyundai called this a temporary measure, but no one expected the plant would ever reopen. Hyundai's rush into the marketplace—perhaps before they were ready—cost them dearly in terms of brand image and corporate reputation. Poor-quality products, combined with poor marketing and after-sales service, tarnished the company's reputation in the U.S. marketplace for years to come.[20] It would be a bitter lesson.

At least part of this conflict came about because the Americans failed to understand Korean culture. Had they done so, they might have pursued different strategies that could have met with greater success. Instead, they saw this as an American problem and tried to solve it using direct American means. It did not work. As the British journalist Simon Winchester concluded after trekking across Korea from the southern tip of the peninsula to Panmunjom, the last thing a manager should do in dealing with Koreans is to say or do something that causes someone else to lose face. This especially applies to one's boss. As Winchester counsels: "If you see a Korean on a golf course, do not approach him, no matter how dreadful his play might be, and advise him on how he might improve matters; he would be deeply offended, and you would be deeply wrong. 'To lose face is bad,' Confucius is supposed to have said. 'To make someone else lose face is unforgivable.'" Since the Koreans didn't seem to understand the problem and the Americans didn't seem to understand the solution, no serious timely remedy was in sight.

The problems at HMA can be viewed in terms of cross-cultural communication and conflict, but they also can be viewed as a failure of management. Indeed, a major factor that seems to have influenced the conflict and resulting loss of market stems from the fact that some of Chung's own managers forgot his admonition to be creative in all things. Available evidence suggests that several Hyundai managers sought to apply traditional textbook solutions to problems that required innovative interventions. Had they remembered Chung's advice as envisioned in the Hyundai spirit—creative wisdom, unyielding will, indomitable driving force—perhaps they would have tried harder to understand the issues surrounding the crisis and moved earlier to find a suitable remedy. As it was, they failed to do so, with distressing results.

GLOBAL AMBITIONS

Learning from its mistakes, Hyundai Motor Company has recently begun to accelerate its rate of product development. Indeed, the company has come a long way from its earliest days learning the car business. Today, HMC continues to build global market share with newer, more stylish—and higher quality—cars. Quality control is now recognized as a vital aspect of the production process. Parts are made to higher specifications; even the paint is vastly improved over the old Excel days. New or updated models, like the Elantra, Accent, Avante, Tiburon, and Sonata, were all launched to highly successful reviews. In 1997, HMC launched the Atos, an 800 cc. mini car designed to meet Korea's tough new pollution control standards. The Atos set a record at Hyundai for having the shortest development time: only 23 months from initial designs to mass production. It cost $155 million to design and build. Hyundai-manufactured cars began winning sports rallies and design awards around the world in places as diverse as China, Chile, Zambia, Thailand, Greece, Switzerland, Canada, and the United States.

In 1991, HMC celebrated the launch of its first engine that was developed completely by Hyundai with no foreign technical assistance.[21] Called the alpha, this engine exceeded the performance specifications of the previous Mitsubishi-designed engines HMC had been using. Developed at a cost of $140 million, the alpha engine again signaled Hyundai's principal of developing its own technology whenever possible. Also in 1991, HMC developed its first electric car. Then, in 1994, HMC developed its first solar-powered car. In 1996, it developed a hybrid car, featuring an electric engine supplemented with a small internal combustion engine for additional power when needed. This system overcomes many of the shortcomings of pure electric cars, including limited driving distance, while simultaneously minimizing auto emissions.

Car sales continue to increase annually. In 1997, Hyundai sold 645,600 cars in Korea and exported another 565,300 cars worldwide. In the Korean market, Hyundai captured the top two slots in sales performance with the Sonata (158,400 units) and the Avante (130,900 units). Cumulative HMC sales since their founding surpassed 10 million cars as of 1997, including 4 million exports. These two records were achieved in 28 and 20 years, respectively. This compares favorably to Toyota and Nissan, which required 36 and 37 years, respectively, to reach the 10 million vehicle mark. Cumulative exports by geographic region currently stand at 2.1 million cars for North America, 830,000 for Europe, 350,000 for Asia and the Pacific, 330,000 for the Middle East, and 310,000 for South America, and 90,000 for Africa.[22] HMC has indeed become a global marketer for cars. And as Hyundai grew, so too did Korea, becoming one of the world's top five automobile manufacturers by 1995 (see Table 5-4).

In Korea, HMC now has an annual production capacity of 1.33 million vehicles at its Ulsan plant, the single largest automotive production site in the world.[23] Hyundai also boasts the largest commercial vehicle production site in Cholla Province, opened in 1997. This facility can produce 18,000 buses and 82,000 trucks and specialty vehicles annually. These trucks and buses are exported throughout the world.[24] In 1995, HMC began producing cars on a limited scale in Indonesia, Egypt, Malaysia, and the Philippines.[25] In 1997, HMC built an assembly plant in Botswana in southern Africa to cater to the growing African car market. Plant capacity there is 40,000 units, and HMC plans to have 30 percent of its cars made from locally produced components.[26] HMC also established a new $1.1 billion automobile assembly plant in India in 1997, with an annual capacity of 200,000 cars, and a smaller plant in Turkey, with an annual production capacity of 120,000 cars.[27] Localized pro-

TABLE 5-4

RANKINGS OF TOP TEN AUTOMOBILE PRODUCING COUNTRIES: 1970–1995

(In Thousands of Units)

1970		1980		1990		1995	
U.S.A.	8,300	Japan	11,000	Japan	13,000	U.S.A.	12,000
Japan	5,300	U.S.A.	8,000	U.S.A.	9,800	Japan	11,000
Germany	3,800	Germany	3,900	Germany	5,200	Germany	4,500
France	2,600	France	3,400	France	3,800	France	4,000
U.K.	2,100	USSR	2,200	USSR	2,100	**Korea**	2,400
Italy	1,800	Italy	1,600	Italy	2,100	Canada	2,400
Canada	1,100	Canada	1,300	Spain	2,000	Spain	2,100
USSR	900	U.K.	1,300	Canada	1,900	U.K.	1,700
Spain	500	Spain	1,200	U.K.	1,600	Brazil	1,600
Australia	500	Brazil	1,200	**Korea**	1,300	Italy	1,500
[Korea	**28]**	**[Korea**	**123]**				

Source: Based on data reported by the Hyundai Business Group; *Automotive News*, 1995; and Linsu Kim, *Imitation to Innovation: The Dynamics of Korea's Technological Learning* (Boston: Harvard Business School Press, 1997), Chapter 5.

duction is seen as imperative by Hyundai as it tries to get closer to its new markets while also avoiding increasingly high labor costs at home. Korea's financial crash in late 1997 slowed several of these expansion efforts, but the company remains committed to the long-term success of its global automobile enterprise.

Research and development has always played a prominent role in the success of HMC. As shown in Table 5-5, investment in R&D in terms of both money and human resources has more than kept pace with the growth of the company. In 1997, HMC spent $42 million to construct one of the world's most advanced automotive technical centers and proving grounds, called the Namyang Technology Research Center.[28] The proving grounds at Namyang can simulate driving conditions in virtually any part of the world. HMC is committed to becoming one of the world's ten largest automobile manufacturers.

TABLE 5-5

R&D INVESTMENTS AT HYUNDAI MOTOR COMPANY: 1975–1994

YEAR	CAR SALES (IN DOLLARS)	R&D EXPENSES (IN DOLLARS)	R&D AS % OF SALES	NUMBER OF RESEARCHERS
1975	$3,000,000	$110,000	3.5	197
1978	21,600,000	540,000	2.5	381
1982	43,000,000	790,000	1.8	725
1984	66,900,000	2,270,00	3.4	1,298
1986	190,600,000	7,950,000	4.2	2,247
1988	341,100,000	11,600,000	3.4	2,459
1990	465,600,000	19,000,000	4.1	3,418
1992	607,900,000	24,880,000	4.1	3,192
1994	905,200,000	40,000,000	4.4	3,890

Source: Adapted from Linsu Kim, *Imitation to Innovation: The Dynamics of Korea's Technological Learning* (Boston: Harvard Business School Press, 1997), Chapter 5.

To accomplish this, current HMC chairman Chung Mong Kyu (son of Chung Se Yung) notes that the company will need to make significant strides in technology development and in labor-management relations, two historic trouble spots for the company.[29]

Underlying this drive to succeed in the world automotive market is a fundamental motivation to meet and beat the Japanese. As Chung Se Yung notes: "We have a competitive mind like the Japanese. But, in some ways, we think we are more clever than they are. We think we have better brains. That's why so many Koreans excel when they attend American universities."[30] Japanese car makers are seen as the real competition in the quest for market supremacy. To those who question Hyundai's ability to compete head-on with the Japanese in this arena, Chung observes that the same thing used to be said about shipbuilding, where Korea now has a commanding lead (see Chapter 7). If Korea can win in shipbuilding, why not cars? What holds Korean back in this endeavor? According to Chung, it may be Korea's traditional lack of cooperation as a people. "They say one Korean can beat two Japanese, but three Koreans can beat five Koreans," Chung notes. "That's very bad."[31] Korea as a nation must learn to work together to solidify its gains in the industrial world.

Meanwhile, back in the United States, Hyundai Motor America has been busy reestablishing itself in the marketplace. Under the leadership of President Juhn Myung Hun, who has worked with HMC since 1977, HMA has begun an aggressive campaign to rebuild both its 500 dealerships and its customer support base for the new cars Hyundai is now building. Juhn, who worked for HMA in California between 1989 and 1992, is familiar with the company's previous personnel problems, in which some American managers felt excluded from executive decision making. He is convinced that the situation has changed considerably in recent years. "When sales were good between 1986 and 1989, everybody was a hero. But when sales began to fall, everyone looked for someone else to blame," Juhn said in a recent interview.[32]

Today, Juhn pays considerable attention to ensuring cultural harmony between Korean and American managers who must work together for the success of the enterprise. "My job as president is to make sure that everyone is a member of the same team. We have a new work atmosphere here now."[33] To maintain this culture, the president meets once a week with his Korean staff to emphasize the importance of building one multicultural team. "I tell my Korean staff not to separate themselves from the Americans. We must all be team members. Don't stand against each other," Juhn observes.[34] And he tells the Americans the same thing. But something else is different with the new HMA. Today, all but two of the top management team are, in fact, Americans—one more indication of Hyundai's commitment to globalization.

HMA's current plans call for laying a solid foundation on which to rebuild sales over the coming years. It is a long-term developmental strategy, in contrast to their initial hasty market entry. Current sales stand at a modest 110,000, close to two percent of the U.S. market. To increase this, HMA plans to invest heavily in the coming years in building brand image and customer service. This, combined with several new models arriving in the showrooms shortly, will, they hope, convince a skeptical marketplace that Hyundai is a solid, reliable, value-for-money car. The company's new theme—"Driving is believing"—is designed to lure customers back into the showrooms for a closer look. "Frankly speaking, in the past, the durability of our product was not what our customers had expected. We learned from that experience. Now we are busy trying to show Americans that our products have improved considerably. It will take time to accomplish this, but I believe we are off to a good start," the president concluded.[35]

VICTORY AT SEA

"A ship order placed at Hyundai took half the time it would in a European yard—and at a price a good 10 percent lower than the nearest-priced competition."

—SIMON WINCHESTER, JOURNALIST[1]

B y the early 1970s, Hyundai was firmly established in two major industries: construction and cars. The company also was beginning to grow in other new directions by entering industries that supported its two principal businesses. When it needed building materials for its massive construction projects, it formed Hyundai Cement. When it needed engineering services, also for construction, it formed Hyundai Engineering. When it needed miles of pipe for various projects, it built Hyundai Pipe. When it needed hotel space for visitors to its Ulsan industrial site, it created Keumkang Development Company and built the Diamond Hotel. And when it needed a distribution system for its cars, it formed Hyundai Motor Service. All were formed as spin-offs of Hyundai Construction Company and, in fact, reported to the construction firm. Indeed, by the early 1970s, Hyundai had grown to eight companies in highly diversified business fields. Now, Chung needed a new adventure. For this, he would look to the open seas.

Chung envisioned a global conglomerate that would not only bring him wealth but also bring economic prosperity and national pride to his fellow Koreans. To accomplish this, he needed to enter new business arenas. His company was already one of Korea's most successful firms, but it was small compared to the major Japanese and U.S. conglomerates of the time. Hyundai had yet to become a major player in the global economy. In 1970, Chung vowed to change this situation by entering the shipbuilding business.

As noted in Chapter 1, Chung and his company had no previous experience in this industry. They had never built a boat or ship of any size. They didn't even own a shipyard. But Chung was undeterred: he would enter the shipbuilding business. It fit Chung's long-term strategy for developing both his company and his country. Korea would gain valuable technological expertise and tens of thousands of new jobs, and Hyundai would continue to grow and prosper. With his success in securing a major loan from Barclays Bank in London and with orders in hand for two VLCCs (very large crude carriers) from Greek shipping tycoon George Livanos, Chung knew he could succeed here.

LAUNCHING THE *ATLANTIC BARON*

When Chung returned to Korea from London in 1971 with his shipbuilding contract in hand, many of his executives were uneasy about the commitment he had made on behalf of the company. Failure in this venture would likely bankrupt the entire firm. It would also incur the wrath of President Park. Chung was undeterred. "What's the big deal?" he asked. "A ship has an engine inside and an exterior made of steel. . . . Ships resemble power plants, which Hyundai has built many times."[2] After a lavish groundbreaking ceremony for the new venture in March 1972, construction began on both the shipyard and the two ships *simultaneously*. Hyundai Heavy Industries (HHI) was officially established several months later, in 1973.

Throughout the project, Chung squeezed as much performance out of his workers at all levels as he could. The Hyundai spirit of hard work and ingenuity had to prevail. Whereas the typical Japanese shipbuilding firm had 20 percent of its work force engaged in engineering and technical support, HHI had only 11 percent. And whereas Japanese firms had an average of 14 percent of their work force in supervisory positions, HHI had only 7 percent. As a result, more direct labor (82 percent vs. 66 percent) was available for the actual work of constructing the vessels.[3]

At times, as company executives readily admit, they really didn't know what they were doing. In one case, the conditions laid down by the European bankers required that much of the money be spent purchasing equipment from the countries making the loans. To meet this requirement, Hyundai decided to purchase a Goliath crane from a prominent German manufacturer, even though they were not quite sure what such a crane looked like. They just knew they needed one. Later on, when it was time to install the wiring in their first ship, they realized that they had no wiring diagrams, and the engineer assigned to the task had never worked on a ship before. They decided to improvise.[4] On several occasions, entire parts of the ship were assembled incorrectly and had to be dismantled and then reassembled. But construction continued.

There were also times when the construction of the ships outpaced that of the shipyard. At one point, the forward section of one of the tankers was completed before the German-made Goliath crane required to move it had arrived on site. Chung was again undeterred. He simply ordered the massive section put on a trailer and rolled into place, with a bulldozer pulling in the opposite direction to maintain sufficient tension on the trailer to keep it under control. Amazingly, the technique worked. On another occasion, in November 1973, Chung himself almost drowned when he swerved to avoid some boulders while driving through an early morning rainstorm and crashed his Jeep into the bay. He struggled to get out of the car, yelled for help, and clung to a stone retaining wall until a guard finally arrived to rescue him.[5]

While the first two ships were still under construction, more business began to arrive. HHI received contracts to construct four more supertankers for Japanese and Hong Kong businesses. HHI, which had ruthlessly underbid its competitors by 15 percent to win new contracts, now had to fulfill its obligations. As a result of his success, Chung was now pressed to launch his first two ships to make room for the next four. Before its first launch, HHI had acquired a backlog.

Finally, in June 1974, two years after construction had begun, President and Mrs. Park were invited to the christening of the two ships and the official opening of the shipyard that produced them. It would be one of Mrs. Park's last public appearances.[6] Two months later, on August 15, as Park was officiating at a Liberation Day celebration at the National Theater in Seoul, a North Korean sympathizer who had entered South Korea through Japan suddenly jumped up from the audience and fired several shots at the president on stage. His wife, seated directly behind him, was fatally struck by a stray bullet. President Park dropped to the floor when the firing began, but after police had removed the assassin, Park stood up again and calmly finished his speech. He then picked up his wife's handbag and shoes from the stage floor and left.

On the day of the christening, however, this tragedy lay in the future, and happiness and national pride prevailed. The first ship launched was the 260,000 DWT VLCC *Atlantic Baron* (see the timeline in Table 6-1). President Park's confidence in Chung Ju Yung had been vindicated, and Hyundai—and Korea—were now in the shipbuilding business. It was a glorious beginning. Once again, Hyundai was out in front, ahead of its rivals. Chung was very pleased.

TABLE 6-1

TIMELINE: HYUNDAI HEAVY INDUSTRIES AND SEOSAN FARM

DATE	EVENT
1971	Chung signs agreement to construct two VLCC (very large crude carrier) ships.
1972	Hyundai breaks ground on new shipyard in Ulsan; begins construction of VLCCs.
1973	Hyundai Heavy Industries established.
1974	HHI successfully launches first two ships, *Atlantic Baron* and *Atlantic Baroness*.
1975	Hyundai Mipo Dockyards established to refit and refurbish ships.
	Hyundai Pipe established.
	HHI begins building platforms and jackets for offshore drilling.
1976	Hyundai Merchant Marine established.
1977	Hyundai Precision & Industry established.
1978	Hyundai assumes control of Inchon Iron & Steel.
1979	Chung purchases land surrounding Seosan Bay.
1982	Seosan land reclamation project begun.
1983	First Seosan dyke completed using "net method."
1984	Second Seosan dyke completed using "oil tanker method."
1989	Exxon Harmony and Exxon Heritage launched.
1992	HHI becomes first company to receive ISO 9001 Quality Assurance certificate in shipbuilding and offshore construction.
1993	HHI launches its first Moss-type LNG carrier.
1997	HHI completes 700 vessels since its founding; marks delivery of 50 million DWT of ships.
	Seosan farm produces 1.6 million bushels of rice annually, making Chung Ju Yung Korea's biggest farmer.
1998	HHI sets three new records for the largest number of new ship orders, annual construction, and orders-on-hand. HHI remains the world's largest shipbuilding company.

CAPITALIZING ON ADVERSITY

Now a new challenge emerged on the horizon that would severely test Hyundai's entrepreneurial talents. Just as HHI's first ships were reaching completion, skyrocketing oil prices following the Arab-Israeli War caused a significant world economic downturn. The market for VLCCs collapsed. Livanos abruptly canceled his contract for Hyundai's second ship and forfeited his $2 million down payment. The Japanese and Hong Kong orders were canceled as well. Hyundai had learned to build ships no one could afford to buy in the new market realities.

Faced with this new disaster, Chung moved swiftly. With his new fleet of VLCCs, he created Hyundai Merchant Marine Company in early 1976 to carry crude oil across the Pacific. Hyundai's entry into the oil transport business was backed by President Park, who quickly introduced new regulations requiring all crude oil transported to Korean refineries to be carried on Korean ships. Hyundai was now in the transport business, with monopolistic control over Korean oil supplies. Soon, Hyundai Merchant Marine ranked as one of the world's largest shipping firms. Necessity was indeed the mother of invention.

When the market for large ships returned, Hyundai was well positioned to exploit it. The firm had acquired shipbuilding technology and had a skilled and inexpensive labor force that global competitors found difficult to match. A phalanx of British technicians and advisors—many formerly employed by Britain's stagnating shipbuilding industry—moved to Ulsan as contract workers in support the new venture. Soon, Chung added the Mipo Dockyards near HHI to his gallery of businesses. With the technical assistance of Kawasaki Heavy Industries, Mipo Dockyards quickly grew into a world-class ship repair facility, doing everything from routine cleaning and servicing to major ship redesign and refitting. If a customer's ship requirements changed, Mipo would redesign the vessel to suit its new needs.

By the early 1980s, the Korean government was routinely purchasing a quarter of all the ships built by Hyundai. When foreign competitors cried foul, HHI President Chung Mong Joon (one of the chairman's sons) pointed out that it was not uncommon for the Japanese government to purchase between 60 and 90 percent of the ships built there. And the U.S. government had long provided healthy subsidies for its own merchant marine.[7]

Throughout its growth and development, a hallmark of HHI has always been its emphasis on frugality. Following Chung's fundamental dictate, money—"my money," as he would say—was to be conserved at all costs. At several locations throughout the HHI shipyard, visitors can see large billboards on which are mounted samples of key supplies used by the workers.

These included work gloves, small tubes or cans of adhesives and lubricants, sandpaper, and nuts and bolts. Beside each sample is its cost, usually just a few cents or dollars. The billboards plainly show workers and managers how such small costs can add up. Everyone is encouraged to make supplies go as far as possible, and nothing is to be wasted.

From the HHI guest house on a nearby hill overlooking the shipyard comes another example of the chairman's obsession with frugality. When Chung visited HHI, he usually stayed in a private room at the guest house, originally built to house short-term visitors to the company. Once, during his absence, a maid noticed that the slippers in his room were literally falling apart. No chairman of a great company like Hyundai should be seen in such slippers, she thought, so she discarded them and replaced them with a new pair. When Chung returned to Ulsan several weeks later, he was reportedly furious to learn that his slippers were gone. They could have been used for several more years, he yelled. As in everything else, Chung set the example.[8]

Part of Korea's competitive edge against foreign companies comes from the drive and diligence of its work force. As one U.S. supplier to HHI observed, "The Koreans are competent, they work hard."[9] When asked what differences he saw between Korean workers and their American counter-parts, he responded, "I work with [Korean] welders. They will work ten hours a day. The arc time—the time a welder is actually applying heat to metal—is about eight hours. The American welder works about eight hours, but it's really seven and a half hours, and their arc time is only two hours. I like the Korean attitude. The American welders don't work."[10]

Trying to understand what made Hyundai—and Korea—so successful in ventures such as shipbuilding, British journalist Simon Winchester visited HHI's Ulsan facility in 1985. Winchester could not help but compare HHI's success with the demise of his own country's shipbuilding industry. Whereas Britain's shipyards were nearly empty, HHI routinely had thirty to forty vessels in various stages of assembly. What impressed Winchester most was the speed with which HHI completed their work. "From the moment the immense plates of steel were cut in the foundry shops until the dry-dock sluices were opened and the sea waters were allowed to float a new behemoth away, it took the Korean workers only nine months. With a further nine months spent in the fitting-out yard, this meant that any new Hyundai vessel took just a year and a half to make. A ship order placed at Hyundai took half the time it would in a European yard—and at a price a good 10 percent lower than that of the nearest-priced competition."[11]

What Winchester failed to notice in his assessment of HHI, however, were the benefits it received from belonging to the Hyundai chaebol. Membership definitely had its privileges in the case of Hyundai. This can be seen in a number of ways. First, as a member of the larger Hyundai network, HHI had ample access to skilled engineers and technicians from other Hyundai companies. In the beginning, HHI had no ship construction experience, so Hyundai Construction sent in construction engineers to transfer their knowledge. Indeed, the first president of HHI came from Hyundai Construction. Hyundai Construction engineers also taught HHI how to schedule work. Hyundai Motor Company engineers taught HHI how to reduce throughput time, as well as how to establish and balance an assembly line. HMC also provided help in developing training programs for workers. HHI control systems were established with the assistance of Hyundai Cement personnel. As MIT economist Alice Amsden observes, "the possibility of mobilizing such personnel enabled HHI to act quickly and to avoid the delays of recruiting fresh talent from the market."[12]

A second advantage of chaebol membership accrued when HHI needed to hire talent from the outside. The Hyundai group could bring substantial resources together to hire the very best talent available. Indeed, Korea Shipbuilding and Engineering Company (KSEC), a major competitor, claims to have lost one-third of its best engineers to HHI. HHI simply outbid KSEC in both wages and career opportunities.[13]

Third, membership in the Hyundai network also allowed HHI to integrate vertically at a rapid pace. One example of this has been noted: the move from shipbuilding to shipping. Another example can be seen in Hyundai's move into ship engines. When HHI needed high-quality ship engines, it initially had to buy from Japanese suppliers, which routinely charged foreign customers more than their Japanese customers. Wanting to remain competitive and reduce the overall price of each ship, HHI formed Hyundai Engine Manufacturing Company (HEMCO) in 1978 and began building engines under license from several European engine manufacturers, including MAN of Germany and B&W of Denmark. As a result, HHI was more easily able to access high-quality engines on site. This operation also allowed HHI and HEMCO to gain access to state-of-the-art technology that would prove useful as they progressed further in the industry.

Fourth, the Hyundai network allowed HHI to take a long-term approach to profit maximization. When the market for ships decreased, the markets for automobiles typically increased. As a result, Hyundai made large profits from cars and transferred some of these profits to HHI to help it retain its stability in the marketplace. Competitor KSEC, for one, unable to do this because it was a specialty company, soon went bankrupt.

Finally, HHI, like its mother company, firmly believed in research and development and was provided with sufficient funds to invest in the future. At HHI, two innovative R&D facilities were established: the Welding Research Institute, which focused on improving welding techniques and quality-control methods, and the Maritime Research Center, which focused on improving ship design. Together, these two institutes provided invaluable service to HHI at a time when it sought to become the preeminent fully integrated shipbuilding company in the world.

Another thing that Simon Winchester overlooked was the military-style discipline that characterized the Hyundai shipyard. In contrast to European and U.S. shipyards, which labor under inefficient and noncompetitive work rules and union contract provisions, Hyundai Heavy Industries is organized and operated on principles not unlike those used in the Desert Storm invasion of Kuwait. As Jack Kamont, a West Point graduate and long-time consultant to HHI, noted in the early 1990s: "Everything at Hyundai is run on a fairly military basis.…A director is a director everywhere in terms of social position and rank. If a vice president from another Hyundai company goes to see the shipyard, he won't be ignored. They know where they are, who they are. They even dress in uniform," referring to the company jackets worn by everyone from the president to manual laborers.[14] Kamont observed military reservists lined up in the yard for training exercises. "They're organized to defend the yard. You probably have enough for a light division.…They have an armory in the yard. The guys who are educated all know what to do if a war breaks out," Kamont concluded.[15]

David Gregg, a British engineer associated with HHI agrees. "It's a very military-oriented society. In the morning you can go there, and you will have a line of people. They'll all be standing at attention to get a work assignment." Typically, once a week, the director of the division will address the workers using a loudspeaker to psych them up: "We expect the best. We are Koreans. Show the world we are Koreans," Gregg recalled hearing.[16] Tony Robinson, another British engineer, comments on Hyundai's can-do approach to manufacturing. "You couldn't believe what they do. They break all the rules. Their equipment is old. They make their own tools. Nobody else would use them," Robinson observes.[17] Even so, the results speak for themselves: "They deliver what we ask for, on time. I don't understand it but whatever they do, it works," he concludes.[18] With organization, discipline, and persistence like this, it is no wonder that both the West and Japan have lost so much of the business to Hyundai and Korea.

DIVERSIFYING OFFSHORE

Because of the cyclical nature of the shipbuilding industry, HHI never could count on keeping its expensive plant and equipment operating at full capacity. As a hedge against industry downturns, they began producing platforms and jackets (or frameworks) for offshore oil rigs in the mid-1970s. Hyundai initially learned the technology through joint ventures in Japan and India. Soon, however, HHI was on its own producing the equipment necessary for offshore oil exploration and production. To provide it with a stable source of raw materials and a more vertically integrated manufacturing process, Hyundai established Hyundai Pipe adjacent to HHI in Ulsan in 1975 and later acquired Inchon Iron and Steel in 1978. Henceforth, supplies would be more readily available.

HHI's venture into platforms and jackets for offshore rigs brought it into contact—and conflict—with the Americans. Exxon contracted with HHI to fabricate two of the largest jackets ever manufactured. These giant structures were named the *Exxon Harmony,* measuring 375 meters long and weighing 45,000 tons, and the slightly smaller *Exxon Heritage.* They were launched in Ulsan in August 1989 and were to be towed across the Pacific for service in the oil fields off Santa Barbara, California. At the ribbon cutting celebrating the completion of the jackets, Exxon officials spoke with praise of their partnership with Hyundai and noted that there had been only 28 injuries throughout the 2.5 million man-hours required to build the two structures. The Americans publicly applauded the ability of both sides to work through cultural conflicts and disagreements to achieve two state-of-the-art jackets containing 36,000 tons of steel and 8,000 parts.

HHI officials told a quite different story. As Hyundai saw it, Exxon had repeatedly delayed the project because of an environmental controversy in Santa Barbara over the installation of such rigs, and these delays had cost HHI over $130 million. The only good news for Hyundai was that they charged Exxon $30,000 per day storage fees while the Santa Barbara controversy raged on, thereby canceling out their loss and breaking even on the entire project. Throughout the four-year project, both sides argued incessantly over costs and fees. In fact, over 4,500 letters and faxes were exchanged on this single topic. Exxon wanted Hyundai to slow down so they could manage the environmental crisis in California; Hyundai wanted to hasten construction to keep its costs down. At the same time, however, labor strikes at Hyundai served to disrupt the production schedule, frustrating HHI's own plans.

In the end, the Americans came away from the venture convinced that HHI had a lot to learn about doing business in the Western world. The Koreans seemed too much like bulldozers to the Americans; they were not as globally sophisticated as their Japanese rivals. For its part, Hyundai came away from the experience believing that the Americans were very arrogant and shortsighted. They lacked respect for the Koreans' know-how and accomplishments. Ultimately, perhaps both sides learned from each other. Indeed, when a senior Exxon executive was asked if Exxon would do business with Hyundai again, his reply was immediate: Definitely!

CULTIVATING NEW FRONTIERS

An ocean adventure of a different sort occurred when Chung Ju Yung decided to reclaim a huge tract of land from the ocean and put it into productive farming. Chung always reminded people that he was a simple farmer at heart. He was proud of his peasant background and frequently scoffed at the middle class backgrounds of some of his chief rivals. He was close to his roots. Amid all of his travails at home and abroad, Chung decided he needed a challenge of a very different sort. For many years, he had been concerned about the inefficiencies of family farming in Korea, where a typical family barely had enough land to support itself and sell a bit of rice on the side. Although Chung believed in supporting rural communities, he felt that at least some farmers should become sufficiently large and productive to be able to export rice. If Korea could export industrial goods, why couldn't it export agricultural products as well? But to accomplish this, they—and Korea—would need more land. In typical Chung style, he set about showing firsthand what could be accomplished.

In 1979, at the age of 64, Chung purchased the land surrounding much of Seosan Bay, near the southwest corner of Korea. Here he was determined to reclaim 38 square miles of land from the Yellow Sea and convert it into Korea's largest mechanized rice farm. Chung traveled to California's Sacramento valley to observe how huge mechanized farms could efficiently produce food. His dream consisted of two parts. First, he wanted to demonstrate that Hyundai could succeed in reclaiming a vast piece of land from the ocean. Second, he wanted to demonstrate that Korea could become a major exporter of rice. The two goals complemented each other nicely, and Chung set about his land reclamation project with enthusiasm. After he had received government approval and the requisite land reclamation permits, actual construction began in April 1982.

The Seosan land reclamation project required that two large dikes be constructed to close out the seawater. To construct the dikes, workers would use a textbook operation of building two narrow peninsulas out from each shoreline toward one another. Eventually, the two peninsulas would meet in the middle of the bay, thereby closing off the sea. The reclaimed area could then be drained, and new soil could be brought in to create the rice fields. The first and smaller of the two dikes proved difficult because of the turbulent waters.

As rocks were poured into the sea to form a barrier, rushing waters would repeatedly wash them away. To overcome this, Chung invented a method—widely used today—of wrapping several rocks and boulders in a wire net and lowering the net into place. The combined weight of the encased rocks was sufficiently heavy to remain in place. Using this method, the new dike was successfully completed in late 1982.

Chung then began constructing the second dike in July 1983. This four-mile-long dike proved to be far more difficult. As the two sides of the dike grew closer together, the space through which the turbulent ocean current flowed grew smaller, increasing both the speed and strength of the current. As a result, with the two ends of the dike still far apart, the strength of the current repeatedly washed out the rocks and dirt intended to close off the sea. Time after time, armies of dump trucks dropped rocks and dirt into the chasm to close out the sea, but each attempt ended in failure. Even the "net method" that had proved so effective on the first dike failed to hold against the rushing waters.

Chung consulted with engineers and engineering professors, to no avail. No one seemed to have a solution other than to keep pouring rocks and dirt into the bay. Chung realized that such action would only serve to pollute the area further and destroy fragile fishing grounds near the edge of the bay. There must be a better way. Finally, Chung had an idea. In March 1984, he called HHI and ordered them to sail a large tanker that was destined for the scrap yard to Seosan Bay. The ship he selected was 1,050 feet long and weighed 226,000 DWT. Chung had the old tanker pulled into place across the 886-foot opening in the dike, then scuttled in 65 feet of water. This effectively blocked the tide from entering the bay while workers completed filling in the dike. As usual, many experts thought he was crazy but—also as usual—his scheme succeeded. With the dike filled in, the ship was refloated and led away. To this day, many engineering textbooks refer to the "oil tanker method" or the "Chung Ju Yung method" of completing dikes in treacherous waters. Referring to his academic critics who told him his idea would fail, Chung wryly commented, "These professors don't know everything."

A short time later, Chung had a sign placed in the elevator at Hyundai's corporate headquarters back in Seoul that read, "Experience without knowledge is better than knowledge without experience." This reflected Chung's most basic belief, that practical experience and the will to succeed, not abstract theories, are the keys to success.

With the two dikes completed, Chung set about building his farm. He repeatedly told visitors that he would eventually retire to Seosan to become a farmer again, as in his youth. New soil was brought in, and the vast area was divided into numerous, precisely measured plots for rice planting. Several crop-duster airplanes were purchased and painted bright yellow. Jokingly referred to as the "Hyundai Air Force," the planes were, in actuality, Korea's first effort to seed rice fields by air. A cattle-raising business was also established at one end of the farm. Korea's largest grain silo and a processing plant were constructed on site to store, process, and package the grain. All told, Chung spent $760 million on the Seosan project. Everything was ready.

Unfortunately, the soil did not cooperate. It remained too salty for quality rice production. It took Chung years to improve the soil enough to grow sufficient rice to make it commercially viable. To this day, there remain major patches of salt-ridden soil at Seosan, which inhibit full-scale operation. Even so, Hyundai had accomplished what it set out to do. It completed one of the world's largest land reclamation projects, creating new productive agricultural lands while protecting the ecology of the bay. The project created thousands of new jobs during construction and hundreds of permanent jobs after completion. Currently, the Seosan farm has a capacity of producing 1.6 million bushels, or 54,000 metric tons, of rice annually.[19]

Fifty years after escaping from what he described as the worst job in the world, Chairman Chung was once again a farmer. When asked if he still detested farming, Chung responded: "I didn't like it in the past because at that time it was done on a small scale. Now that I can do it on a large scale, it's fun." This was vintage Chung. Asked if he was now Korea's largest farmer, he smiled and replied, "Yes."[20]

SETTING NEW RECORDS

In 1994, Hyundai Heavy Industries reached another significant milestone, which turned out to be a mixed blessing. It produced 26 ships, 40 percent of Korea's total output. Total company sales reached $3.1 billion, with net profits of $360 million—four times larger than those of Daewoo Shipbuilding and eight times larger than those of Samsung Shipbuilding. As a result, HHI earned the dubious distinction of becoming Korea's highest taxpayer, with a corporate tax bill of just under $70 million.

Much of HHI's more recent profitability has resulted from its entry into the most sophisticated shipbuilding arena: liquefied petroleum gas (LPG) and liquified natural gas (LNG) carriers. Since launching its first such vessel in 1986, HHI has manufactured two dozen LPG and LNG carriers, with capacities of up to a million tons. In recent years, HHI has significantly expanded its research efforts in order to remain ahead of the competition. Each year, it invests up to $40 million on R&D activities in various enterprises, ranging from specialized ships like the LPG and LNG carriers, offshore structures, enhanced welding technology, and shore-based industrial plants and bridges. HHI plans to remain a leader in heavy industries for decades to come.

HHI retains the record as the world's largest shipbuilding company, with 27,000 workers and over $6 billion in annual sales. Its Ulsan shipyard, substantially larger than any competitor, covers 7 million square meters of land and contains nine dry-docks.[21] HHI operates the world's largest dock, with a capacity to build ships of up to one million tons. Six medium- or large-sized ships can be built at this dock simultaneously.[22] Each year, it delivers about thirty of the most technologically advanced ships afloat, including bulk carriers, tankers, VLCCs, container ships, LNG and LPG carriers, naval frigates, and corvettes. It also has constructed hovercrafts, hydrofoils, diving support vessels, passenger ships, and patrol vessels. All told, HHI has produced over 700 vessels with a total weight of over 50 million DWT since it opened in 1973.

HHI also operates the world's largest ship repair and conversion facility, the Mipo Dockyard. Hyundai ships also receive high marks for quality and dependability. In fact, in 1992, HHI became the first company in the world to receive the ISO 9001 Quality Assurance certificates in shipbuilding and in offshore construction.[23]

In addition to shipbuilding, HHI is actively engaged in manufacturing industrial and marine engines, robots, steel transmission towers for microwave and power transmission, offshore drilling rigs, wastewater treatment plants, industrial power systems, hydromechanical equipment, material handling systems, and construction equipment. HHI manufactures industrial plants for a wide range of purposes, including power and co-power generation, nuclear power, desalination, environmental engineering, and iron and steel mills.

Throughout its twenty-five-year history, Hyundai Heavy Industries has grown from obscurity into a world leader in shipbuilding and associated industries. It has achieved a well-deserved reputation around the world for quality and dependability. Although some economists have argued that the time has come for the Hyundai Group to shift its attention away from such traditional "old" industries and concentrate more on the high-tech arena, logic suggests that HHI will remain a cornerstone of the group. HHI is one of Chung Ju Yung's prized accomplishments, and to the extent possible the company will likely honor his wishes to retain the business. Beyond such sentiment, however, the hard fact is that the world will always require ships and, for now, HHI can produce these ships better and cheaper than anyone else. HHI invests considerable sums to remain ahead of the technological curve in this business. Finally, if Korea is to enhance its position as a global economic power, it must advance into new business arenas, such as advanced electronics, telecommunications, and aerospace, while simultaneously maintaining its competitive edge in some of its traditional industries. Ceding the shipbuilding industry to China or Vietnam, as some have suggested, is not only bad policy for Hyundai, it is also bad policy for Korea. Korea requires a solid, broad-based industrial infrastructure to remain competitive with Asia's new emerging tigers. For these reasons, HHI's future should remain bright for decades to come.

CHAPTER 7

CONTRACTOR TO THE WORLD

"The conditions here are impossible, but we are surviving. I know we can make it here."

—HYUNDAI PROJECT MANAGER IN THE DESERT OF IRAN, 1975[1]

P ark Chung Hee's economic development efforts depended on massive imports of petroleum to keep Korea's factories and transportation systems running. As oil prices began to rise sharply in the early 1970s (from $1.75 per barrel in 1973 to more than $10 per barrel just two years later), the Korean economy was being hammered in ways that threatened its long-term stability. The government responded by encouraging Korean firms to seek new business in the increasingly prosperous Middle East. Since its founding, Hyundai had grown from a local construction company into a major conglomerate making cars, ships, aluminum, pipe, and cement. With this knowledge, and with increasing pressure from the government, Hyundai Construction set its sights on the emerging construction opportunities in the Middle East. The company was convinced it could succeed on the basis of its previous experience in Southeast Asia with such projects as Thailand's Patanni-Narathiwat Highway in 1965. But Hyundai did not just want to be a player in this arena; it wanted to be the biggest player. It set its sights on becoming the contractor to the world.

In 1972, Chung Ju Yung's brother, In Yung, was named president of international operations for Hyundai and sent to the Middle East in search of business. As Chung noted later: "I could not miss this once-in-a-lifetime opportunity. I knew we lacked the experience to work in the unforgiving desert environment but, as we did in the shipbuilding business, I believed in the power of imagination and a willing heart. I felt that my motto never to quit would see me through the difficulties and obstacles."[2] In early 1975, when Chung was nearing sixty years of age, Hyundai landed its first Middle Eastern construction project (see the timeline in Table 7-1). The $10 million project from the shah of Iran involved building a Mobilization and Training Shipyard for the Iranian navy near Bandar Abbas. This was a major opportunity for Hyundai, if they could succeed. A spirit of optimism spread through company headquarters in anticipation of the construction gold mine they had discovered in the Middle East. In preparation for the venture, Hyundai even offered classes in Arabic for interested employees slated for the overseas service.

However, once the project was under way, initial reports from the field were not encouraging. Iran knew what they wanted in a shipyard, but they had little knowledge of how to construct it, so they asked Hyundai to construct the facility as a turnkey project. But Hyundai engineers had no experience designing or constructing the launching mechanisms Iran wanted. The navy wanted rail equipment that jutted into the sea, lifted ships out of the water, and then transported them to a dry work area for repairs. The same equipment would then be used to return the ships to the sea. Hyundai had experience building dry-docks, but this was something new to them. They had to travel to Europe and the United States to learn the technology involved. Korean managers and workers also complained of the unbelievable heat and humidity. The construction site was desolate, and Koreans were not made welcome by the mostly Muslim inhabitants. Well into the project, one Hyundai crew leader reported back that "the conditions here are impossible, but we are surviving. I know we can make it here."[3] Hyundai's can-do spirit was alive and well in the deserts of Iran.

In the end, Hyundai successfully completed the project, and Chung was eager for more business in the Middle East. Brother In Yung, however, was not so confident. He worried that even Hyundai was not up to the challenge of constructing major projects in the region on a sustained basis. Prevailing temperatures were unbearable, much worse than the Koreans had experienced in Southeast Asia. Design and construction specifications were much more rigid than those common throughout much of Asia at the time. And Koreans often felt that their wealthy Middle Eastern customers looked down on them and could not be trusted. In Yung was not convinced Hyundai could succeed here.

On several occasions, In Yung tried to block the signing of major contracts that he felt were beyond the company's expertise, despite Ju Yung's encouragement from Seoul. When a major contract for a dry-dock and repair facility in Bahrain became available in late 1975, Chung Ju Yung instructed his people to go after it. But younger brother In Yung disagreed, and Hyundai executives were caught in the middle. Whom should they obey, Chung Ju

TABLE 7-1

TIMELINE: HYUNDAI'S MAJOR ACCOMPLISHMENTS IN OVERSEAS CONSTRUCTION

DATE	EVENT
1965	Pattani-Narathiwat Highway begun in Thailand by Hyundai Construction.
	Hyundai initiates major construction projects in Vietnam, Guam, Papua New Guinea, Alaska, and Australia.
1975	Hyundai Construction signs its first Middle Eastern construction contract for the Mobilization and Training Shipyard in Iran.
	Hyundai contracts to build a dry-dock and ship repair facility in Bahrain.
1976	Hyundai begins Jubail Harbor oil terminal port facility in Saudi Arabia, the world's most expensive construction project to date.
1979	Jubail oil terminal project completed.
	Hyundai initiates major construction projects in Iran, Iraq, Abu Dhabi, the United Arab Emirates, and Kuwait.
1985	Penang Bridge completed in Malaysia, the longest bridge in Asia and third longest in the world.
1989	Hyundai Construction Equipment Service Company established.
	Hyundai Construction records $20 billion in overseas construction work.
1997	Hyundai Construction reaches $6 billion in total annual sales.
	Hyundai awarded contracts for 35 major new overseas construction projects totaling $4 billion, an all-time overseas sales record for the company. Projects include orders from Singapore, Indonesia, Malaysia, Hong Kong, Tunisia, Tatarstan, Saudi Arabia, and Yemen. These contracts represent 28 percent of the total overseas contracts for all Korean construction firms.
1998	Hyundai wins best project engineering award from the Construction Industry Development Board for its $635 million Suntec City project in Singapore.

Yung back in Seoul or Chung In Yung sitting next to them in Bahrain? The conflict burst into the open when the Koreans were called to a meeting in London to meet with their proposed British partners for the venture. (Even Chung Ju Yung recognized the need for British technical assistance to compete for the $30 million dry-dock project.) During the meeting, Ju Yung's young protégés led the fight to sign the contract over their boss's objections. The young Turks reasoned that Hyundai's can-do spirit would guarantee success against all odds; they could not fail. In Yung was compelled to yield, even though he disagreed. Following the contract signing, In Yung flew back to Seoul and resigned from the Hyundai Group. No longer would he follow his brother's bold adventures. No longer would he accept the increasing risk that accompanied every new venture. Instead, he would form his own company, the Halla Group, to pursue his own endeavors. Chairman Chung assumed personal control over the new enterprise.

JUBAIL HARBOR AND THE SPIRIT OF ADVENTURE

Shortly after the contract-signing ceremony, Chung met with his senior executives in early 1976 for the traditional New Year's celebration. "We have suffered the pain of deciding on stability or adventure," Chung observed in his opening comments. "We have concluded that we will accept the challenge of a major adventure called the Middle East." Was Hyundai up to the challenge? Of course, Chung reasoned. Hyundai would find "the spiritual strength that exists within people, companies, and nations," he told the gathering. "If an enterprise does not have within itself an ability to adapt to change, it is obvious in a capitalist society that the enterprise will fail." Hyundai needed to be challenged; it needed to find its own way. But, most important of all, according to Chung, "we have the burden of carrying the fate of life and death of our people [on our shoulders]....We cannot fail."[4]

The Iran and Bahrain projects had lured Hyundai to the Middle East. Once there, however, Hyundai decided to stay. Its next major project would again put the company on the map for demonstrating superhuman efforts to accomplish what other companies were convinced was impossible. Hyundai was invited to bid on a project to build a new open-sea tanker terminal and harbor facility in the port city of Jubail in Saudi Arabia. The scale of the project was monumental, as was the risk. Building a terminal facility in open seas was never easy, but to build one of this magnitude had many experts in the construction industry referring to it as one of the construction "wonders of the world." In addition, Hyundai had no experience in designing or building such complex facilities. Chung was betting the company on his ability to secure foreign technical assistance to support the project. The stakes were exceedingly high. Should Hyundai secure the contract but then fail to build the facility properly, it would likely be banned from further business in the entire region.

Even so, the project had the firm backing of President Park, who, according to one observer, "ordered Chung to secure the project."[5] Park needed foreign projects not just to reaffirm Korean national pride, but also to help stabilize its currency. Korea in 1975–1976 desperately needed foreign exchange; indeed, its minister of finance was then traveling the world in search of additional foreign aid. Middle Eastern construction projects by several Korean companies, including Hyundai, were just the ticket to salvage Korea's sagging economy.

Chung personally took control of the bidding process for the Jubail harbor project. Estimating the cost of a project of this magnitude was no easy task. No one at Hyundai had any real idea how much it would cost to build the open-sea tanker terminal. When Chung first estimated how much Hyundai should bid on the project, Chun Kap Won, a subordinate, insisted that the bid was too low to cover costs, especially in a region of the world where the company had little experience. Chung should raise his bid by $100 million, his subordinate argued. Chung rejected the aide's proposal, saying simply, "No, we have to secure this project. Otherwise, I cannot face President Park."[6] Finally, Chung determined he would bid $870 million, less than half the amount bid by several of his competitors, as it later turned out.

The final bidding in Riyadh was tense. Chun Kap Won was sent to carry Hyundai's offer to the bidding ceremony. Remaining convinced that the company's bid was too low and that his boss had made a costly error, Chun made the unparalleled decision to raise Hyundai's bid to $931 million—a full $60 million over what he had been ordered to bid—without consulting the chairman. He reasoned that, according to his calculations, his bid was more realistic. Besides, Chun was convinced that Hyundai's bid would still be well below those of the competition. After what seemed like an eternity, the Saudi minister of communications announced that Brown and Root had bid $903 million on the project. Chun was horrified; he had miscalculated. To make matters worse, Chairman Chung walked over and congratulated him; Chung still assumed that his lower bid had been submitted. When Chun told the chairman what he had done, Chung grew furious and walked away. Chun knew his career was over and seriously considered committing suicide by drowning himself in the Gulf. Almost miraculously, however, the Saudi minister then announced that the Brown and Root bid covered only the marine side of the project, whereas Hyundai's bid covered the entire project. Hyundai had won, and Chun's status in the company changed instantly from an insubordinate saboteur to a corporate hero. He had taken a Chung-like gamble and won. The contract was officially granted to Hyundai. Chung later commented with a bit of a smile, "I was glad that Chun did not have to kill himself and that our country earned an additional $60 million."[7] At $931 million, Hyundai's Jubail project was equivalent to half of the Korean government's entire annual budget for 1976.

A final footnote to this story provides additional insight into the inner workings of the chairman. After winning the contract, Chung was approached by a Saudi official, who told Chung that it was customary to pay a 5 percent commission, or agent's fee, on all such contracts. Chung resisted, arguing that such a fee was not customary in the business. The official grew angry and told Chung that he had the power to rescind the contract if the fee was not paid. Reluctantly, Chung offered to pay a 2 percent fee but adamantly rejected 5 percent as excessive. The Saudi official, who had never before witnessed such audacity in dealings with his government, finally agreed to accept the lower fee. Chung had saved another $3 million.

Winning the Jubail Harbor contract was one thing; actually building it was something else. Hyundai would need to marshal an army of 3,000 construction workers to apply technical expertise beyond their capabilities to complete the project in record time. To Hyundai management, it was the perfect challenge with which to demonstrate their can-do spirit. Like other Korean companies working in the Gulf region, Hyundai had a competitive trump card in its labor force. Highly trained and motivated, virtually all of Hyundai's workers had completed two or three years of mandatory military service back in Korea. They were used to military-style discipline. And former junior military officers made ideal unit supervisors. Added to this was a significant infusion of technical expertise that was provided by losing bidder Brown and Root, which agreed to serve as a Hyundai subcontractor on the theory that having some of the business was preferable to having none.

The size and scope of the Jubail Harbor project was immense. Hyundai's task was to construct a terminal that could berth four oil supertankers simultaneously in the middle of the sea, seven miles from the coastline. Worse still, all of the materials would need to be manufactured in Ulsan by HHI to save money and time, and therefore would have to be transported more than 7,000 miles across typhoon-ridden seas to reach the Gulf. The terminal design consisted mainly of steel jackets that were driven into the seabed at 70-foot intervals and then connected to form the foundation of a long pier. Each jacket was over ten stories high and weighed over 500 tons. The project required 89 such jackets, plus thousands of tons of steel pipe piles and concrete slabs, all to be made in Korea. To get the materials to Jubail, Chung ordered that each of his ships be loaded with 120,000 tons of materials and then towed across the open seas to the construction site by 10,000 horsepower tugboats. In all, nineteen shipments would be required. Chung even hired computer programmers to plot the safest route from Korea to Saudi Arabia so the threat of typhoons could be minimized.

To add to the risk, however, none of the cargoes was ever insured, because Chung thought it would be too expensive. His subordinates considered this sheer lunacy. If a ship or its contents was lost, they argued, Hyundai would suffer a massive financial loss. Chung reasoned differently. To him, if a ship was wrecked and its contents lost at sea, an insurance company—despite collecting huge premiums in advance—would likely require extensive, time-consuming investigations before any possible reimbursement. By that time, Hyundai would be in breach of contract with the Saudi government and would lose anyway. To Chung, the materials simply couldn't be lost at sea. Instead, he designed a way to seal the ends of the jackets and pipes, thereby creating huge air pockets that would make them float in case of a shipwreck. If some of the jackets or pipes went overboard, they could be retrieved from the ocean surface by a second ship. On average, Chung sent one ship each month on the thirty-five-day voyage to Jubail. In all, only two minor mishaps occurred throughout the entire operation. The project went as planned, and the Jubail Harbor project was completed within budget and on time. The Saudi government was pleased.

WORKING IN DESERT SANDS

Working conditions at Jubail and elsewhere in the Gulf region were relentlessly austere. To complete projects on schedule, Hyundai decided that its crews would work around the clock in shifts. This was unheard of in Western companies; many considered it inhumane. Huge lighting systems were erected so workers could see what they were doing throughout the night. Moreover, again in contrast to Western competitors, workers' families were required to remain behind in Korea. Workers could visit home for brief holidays once a year on average. A case in point is Park Il Kwon, a career Hyundai manager. Park had joined Hyundai in 1977 after graduating from college and almost immediately volunteered to go to Saudi Arabia. "I wanted to go for several reasons," noted Park. "Yes, it was a good opportunity to make money, but it was much more than that. To me, it was an opportunity to serve my country. I wanted to help build Korea so my children would have a better life."[8] Park and others typically worked ten hours a day, seven days a week. His first visit home came after one year on the job; his second visit came eight months later. Like many employees, Park would spend three years working in Saudi Arabia.

Hyundai employees were known for their tenacity and hard work. One

Brown and Root engineer working with Hyundai crews even wrote a poem about their dedication. In the spirit of Rudyard Kipling, the engineer wrote:

> *When we're hungry, they smile,*
> *When we're tired, they get up,*
> *When we're sleeping, they hustle,*
> *It's the epitaph for a Brown and Rooter.*
> *This man lying here is the most foolish one.*
> *He ruined himself working like a Hyundai man*
> *Whom he couldn't catch up with.*
> *It's not good for Brown Rooter's health*
> *To bustle with Hyundai style.*[9]

In its own way, Hyundai went to great lengths to keep its workers happy and productive. For starters, employees earned two-and-one-half times their regular salaries for going to the Middle East. Beyond this, Hyundai flew in Korean cooks to make traditional foods, including *kimchi*, the spicy-hot pickled cabbage that is a dietary staple and is served at most meals. When not on the job, workers could go to the company canteen for snacks and soft drinks (liquor was forbidden by Saudi authorities) and listen to music or play games in the company recreational facility. Park used his leisure time—what there was of it—to improve his golf game by practicing in the desert sands. "Not the easiest course I've ever played," Park commented wryly, "but most instructive."[10]

Frequently, Chairman Chung would make unannounced visits to the work site. These visits always instilled considerable fear in the site managers. Chung would inspect everything and usually had some suggestions for improvement. His eyes continually scanned the work site. One Hyundai manager noted that Chung was particularly interested in the location of storage facilities. "It doesn't matter how creatively you arrange things; he will find a better way."[11] Chung also was always looking for ways to save money. On one occasion, he discovered that project accounts were being kept in expensive ledger books and immediately ordered them replaced with cheaper ones. Such actions continually set an example of frugality for others to follow.

During these inspection trips, after reviewing construction plans and progress reports, Chung would always insist on spending time with his workers, regardless of their rank or status in the company. Such a sight is rare indeed among Western, or for that matter other Korean, CEOs. Chung was particularly fond of playing sports or wrestling with workers, and he usually won. (As in the West, beating the boss in athletic competition was probably

not considered conducive to a good career.) What was important for workers—
and, indeed, demanded by the chairman—was showing a team spirit and personal resolve. The can-do spirit meant that workers could rely on and support
one another. Workers were not allowed even to consider giving up on a task,
regardless of its difficulty or risk. Above all, honesty was required in all
things. Hyundai managers at all levels repeatedly tell visitors that the quickest way to get fired by the chairman was to intentionally give him false or
misleading information. This he would not tolerate, and stories abound in
Hyundai's culture of Chung personally firing even good friends because they
lied to him.[12]

On one occasion, a group of Hyundai dump truck drivers learned that a
rival construction company at an adjacent work site had raised the wages for
their drivers. Specifically, the rival firm had begun paying drivers on a per-
load basis instead of by the hour. Hyundai drivers asked for the same compensation plan. Supervisors initially rejected this method of payment because
they felt it would cause workers to drive too fast, thereby risking increased
accidents. When the Hyundai drivers complained, several overly zealous
supervisors refused to listen and instead criticized the drivers for not working
hard enough. A wildcat strike erupted, involving several hundred workers.
Saudi troops were called in to surround the work site in case the strike got out
of hand. Hyundai's future prospects in the Gulf lay in the balance. Chung personally intervened in the ensuing negotiations and instructed both sides to
calm down. He lectured both sides that such turmoil would only give their
competitors an unfair advantage in future project bidding, to the detriment of
everyone. The overzealous supervisors were removed, and the company offered
pay raises and a forty-eight-hour work week to help quell the dispute. Chung
also ordered changes in company personnel practices, requiring supervisors
to pay more attention to workers' attitudes, opinions, and grievances. At last,
peace was restored, and Hyundai went back to work on the project.

In February 1979, Jubail Harbor was officially opened, and Hyundai was
firmly established as a major player in the global construction industry.
Indeed, Hyundai earned $2 billion in gross income from foreign construction
projects for the year, making it the fourth largest construction company in the
world. Company revenues had expanded over a hundredfold in just five
years. The Korean economy benefited considerably from Hyundai's efforts,
as well as the efforts of other firms. As one senior Hyundai executive noted,
"It was the first time in our five thousand year history that Korea was making
big money."[13] Looking at the Jubail project and roughly fifty other successful
projects in the region, another senior Hyundai executive summed up his feelings of pride, saying: "The Japanese couldn't put up an operation in the Middle East like we did. Not many Japanese wanted to go there."[14]

Working in Saudi Arabia was good for both Hyundai and Korea. The Jubail project alone was equivalent to 50 percent of Korea's annual budget for 1976. It was the largest single construction contract ever awarded to any company to that time. Other Korean companies also found fortune in the desert sands. All told, from 1977 through 1979, nearly 300,000 Korean workers from two dozen companies were sent to the Middle East. But Hyundai far surpassed every other company in both the size of its projects and its profits. For Hyundai, Saudi Arabia and the Middle East would prove to be a bonanza. For the decade ending in 1979, the Hyundai group would accumulate an incredible *annual* growth rate of 38 percent.[15]

Hyundai's efforts in the Middle East were not without their problems, however. On one occasion, at a construction site in Iran in 1979, Islamic revolutionary soldiers forced 450 Hyundai workers to flee for their lives from attacks on all "foreign devils." In the rush to escape, five workers were killed and twenty others wounded in a traffic accident. Survivors were eventually flown out of the country by a Korean Air pilot sent in for the rescue.

Meanwhile, Chung began looking elsewhere in the region for more opportunities. Projects soon followed in Kuwait, Abu Dhabi, and the United Arab Emirates. The company also followed many Western firms into Iraq. Despite its conflict with Iran, Iraq had vast sums of money to invest in infrastructure development, and Hyundai would soon be its largest contractor. During the 1980s, Hyundai constructed highways, apartment buildings, supermarkets, power plants, sewage treatment plants, and a medical city. All told, the company received over $5 billion in contracts from Iraq, although Iraq would later become delinquent on many of its loans.

At the same time, Hyundai Construction continued to work in Southeast Asia. One notable success here was the Penang Bridge, begun in 1981 at the request of the Malaysian government to connect the Malaysian mainland with Penang Island. The bridge cost $235 million to build and ranked as the longest bridge in Asia and the third longest bridge in the world when it was opened in February 1985. Hyundai would go on to secure more construction work in Southeast Asia as the market in the Middle East declined. Indeed, today most of the company's emerging overseas business opportunities are in this growing region.

CHANGING POLITICAL FORTUNES

Although Park's government has been widely criticized for its authoritarian style, per capita income in Korea during his regime rose from $94 in 1960 to $1,589 in 1980. Exports grew from $33 million to $17 billion during the same period.[16] Life expectancy increased by ten years, while infant mortality was cut in half. Clearly, the Koreans had begun the long march toward economic prosperity.

While Hyundai and other Korean companies were succeeding in the desert sands and elsewhere abroad, a major political battle was looming on the horizon back in Seoul. President Park had always been a strong supporter of the Korean conglomerates, especially Hyundai. Although he was strong-willed and dictatorial in manner, most corporate leaders believed that he had a clear vision for expanding Korea's economy, and they understood their role in that vision. They were to grow, with government support and encouragement. Indeed, to most business leaders—especially Chung Ju Yung—Park Chung Hee was a hero, a national leader worthy of respect. All this changed on October 26, 1979, when Park was assassinated at a private dinner party in Seoul by the director of Korea's Central Intelligence Agency. It was reported that the assassin was distressed over Park's increasing control over every segment of Korean economic and political life and felt that democratic reforms would never be possible under his regime.

Following the arrest of the assassin, Major General Chun Doo Hwan, Korea's defense security commander, was put in charge of the investigation. In December, in a lethal confrontation at the home of his superior, Chun arrested more than thirty military leaders—including his boss—on trumped-up charges of complicity in the assassination. Chun was assisted by his military academy classmate, Major General Roh Tae Woo. By May of the following year, student riots erupted in both Seoul and Kwangju. Students were demanding an end to military rule and a return to democracy. Seeing a threat to his authority, Chun brought in troops loyal to him to suppress what he called the Communist-inspired riots. They killed hundreds of students and innocent bystanders. In August 1980, Chun formally overthrew Park's constitutional successor, the civilian prime minister, and had himself appointed president by his military supporters. Chun claimed that he was forced to accept the position in order to help rid Korea of rampant corruption, but many political observers felt that what he really wanted was a larger share of the payoffs.

Hyundai's troubles were just beginning. Chung Ju Yung had always felt that President Park suited the times of Korea. He was a brilliant economic strategist at a time when Korea was impoverished and in need of direction. In his dealings with Hyundai, Chung felt that Park consistently demonstrated high personal integrity. And although he was an unforgiving taskmaster—like Chung—he always acted in the best interests of Korea. With Chun Doo Hwan, all that changed. Although Chung understood that he needed to work with President Chun, he lacked confidence in Chun's insight and vision and distrusted his motives. Close business-government relations would continue, but on a very different course.

Even before Chun was appointed president, he and his fellow generals had decided that the chaebols were too powerful, both politically and economically. He wanted them constrained or, better yet, broken up. Moreover, Chun disapproved of Korean companies competing against each other in such industries as steel and automobiles. Korea needed a new industrial policy, as Chun saw it.

In the summer of 1980, a government minister summoned leaders of both Hyundai and Saehan Motors (jointly owned at the time by General Motors and Daewoo) and told them that he saw no reason for both companies to manufacture cars. He proposed that one company choose cars and the other choose power generators. Each company would then be given exclusive rights to their respective product line by the government. Having produced cars for twelve years and having just acquired a power generator manufacturing facility in 1979, Chung saw little reason to drop either line. At stake were assets worth well over $1 billion. To Chung, the policy was crazy.

Even so, both Hyundai and Daewoo agreed to the government's proposal for Hyundai to specialize in cars and Daewoo to specialize in power generators. Based upon this agreement, Chung opened negotiations with General Motors to establish a new joint venture to manage Saehan Motors. But he soon concluded that GM was not seriously interested in an equal partnership, and negotiations broke down. As a result, Daewoo retained control of Saehan and continued its partnership with GM. Soon, Saehan became Daewoo Motors and began assembling the GM-designed Pontiac LeMans for both the domestic and foreign markets. Other car models would follow, using Japanese designs. Hyundai now had another major competitor in the car business. At the same time, Daewoo was allowed to assume control over Hyundai's power generator business. However, after only three months of operation, Daewoo announced that it was unable to make the power generator venture work and gave it back to the government. The government then proceeded to operate the business for several years as a money-losing venture under the name Korea Heavy Industries. But despite their losses, government officials refused to let Hyundai reenter the power generator industry. Hyundai had lost a profitable business and gained nothing in return. Chung would later remember this moment as one of the most bitter experiences in his life. He felt that he had been double-crossed.

President Chun continued his attacks on Hyundai, as well as other firms. In the late 1970s, Hyundai had invested heavily to acquire liquefied natural gas (LNG) terminal technology. They used this knowledge to win a government contract in 1981 to construct a LNG terminal. However, Chun soon told Hyundai to give up the contract in favor of rival Hanyang Group. Chun claimed that he was concerned about Hyundai's dominance in the field but he failed to mention that his brother, Chun Ki Hwan, was the agent for Hanyang. Then Chun asked Hyundai to take over several smaller construction firms that had gone bankrupt through headlong expansion into the Middle East. Chung refused on principle. As a rule, Hyundai would always insist on building its own companies, not taking over bankrupt ones. Chun was not happy to be rebuffed. (By contrast, rival Daewoo grew largely through government-brokered takeovers of bankrupt firms, which were then reorganized to make them more efficient. The two companies, Hyundai and Daewoo, in fact have diametrically opposed growth strategies, both of which seemed to have been successful in the Korean business climate.)

Under former President Park, the government set goals but left it up to the companies to determine how best to achieve them. Chun's government, however, wanted to micromanage the companies themselves. Increasingly, Chun's government advisors began dictating which businesses to enter or how and where companies could expand. This ran contrary to everything Chung believed in. Moreover, President Chun's personal style began to offend many business leaders, including Chung. A prominent business leader of the time compared Chun and Park Chung Hee as follows: "If Park held a meeting with business leaders for three hours, he talked fifteen minutes and listened the rest of the time.... He knew how to use us. But he still listened. In a three-hour dinner with businessmen during the Chun years, Chun may have spoken two hours and fifty minutes on business matters.... If someone else had an idea in his presence, Chun didn't like that."[17] The highly successful business-government partnership that had created the engine of growth for Korea was rapidly unraveling.

Another Chun project in the early 1980s was the so-called Peace Dam. The National Security Planning Agency believed that a dam North Korea was building near the DMZ above Seoul might be used to unleash a torrential flood that could inundate South Korea's capital city. This was referred to as the North Korean "water bomb." Although several experts pointed out the impossibility of the plan, the Korean government took it seriously and mounted a mass mobilization effort. Chun sought "donations" from companies and individuals to pay for the construction of a defensive counter dam to collect the flood waters should they be unleashed. Chung had grown up near the site of the North Korean dam, and he knew that President Chun's expressed concerns were unfounded. On one occasion, Chung visited the Blue House to try to persuade the president to drop the plan. A friend of Chung observes: "He [Chung] knew the terrain, he knew how the water flowed. He knew that the dam could not be 180 meters high, because of gaps in the mountains, and he knew that it would take much longer to fill than the government was saying. He went very quietly to President Chun and told him this. His advice was rejected. He felt angry and humiliated."[18] In all, $70 million in "donations" were raised for the project, but the dam was never built. It remained in the "planning phase" for several years, until President Roh Tae Woo declared the dam unnecessary in 1988. When it was all over, the money raised for its construction had conveniently disappeared.

President Chun and his advisors correctly assumed that Chung would consistently resist government intervention in private industry. One of Chung's power bases for doing so was his chairmanship of the powerful Federation of Korean Industries (FKI). FKI was made up of chaebol owners, and when they spoke with one voice it was exceedingly difficult for Chun's government to overrule them. Chung was first elected to a two-year term as FKI chairman in 1977 and, despite strong government opposition, was reelected to four additional two-year terms before he finally stepped down in 1987. During this time, he successfully used his position to rally other chaebol leaders to resist the increasingly arbitrary policies of a corrupt Chun government. Over the years, Chun tried repeatedly, but without success, to have him removed.

On the other hand, Chung continually sought ways to placate the president and his government when he could in the interest of good business. In 1983, his opportunity came, or so he thought. In October of that year, President Chun led a group of senior-ranking government officials and business leaders to a summit in Rangoon, Burma. Chung Ju Yung was invited to join the delegation. Shortly before a major ceremony at Rangoon's Martyr's Mausoleum, a bomb set by three North Korean terrorists who had infiltrated the country exploded, killing seventeen high-ranking Korean officials and four Burmese dignitaries. Included among the dead were the best and the brightest of Chun's cabinet. President Chun was not injured in the explosion. En route back to Seoul following the tragedy, President Chun approached several business leaders and suggested they help establish a foundation to care for the surviving relatives of the victims. It was suggested that each major corporation contribute $15 million. Chung immediately agreed. The charity would be called the Ilhae Foundation, a name derived from Chun's pen name.

Soon, however, the Ilhae Foundation began asking companies for further donations. It became increasingly apparent that the contributions were going to support Chun and his cronies, not the victims' families. Companies that refused soon found that their government credit lines had dried up. Some, like the unfortunate Kukje Group, Korea's seventh largest chaebol with 38,000 employees, were forced into bankruptcy within a matter of weeks.[19] Ultimately, over $90 million in "donations" were given to Ilhae.[20]

Finally, public pressure forced the scandal into the open. During a 1988 legislative investigation and a 1989 criminal investigation into the scandal, accusations were made that Chung and other business leaders had willingly paid the huge bribes to the Ilhae Foundation to keep Chun's government happy. A more accurate description was that many business leaders knowingly paid the bribes because they understood that, under Korea's prevailing system of government, failure to comply meant the likely termination of one's enterprise. Chung himself noted at the time: "First, I was eager to pay [because it went for a good cause]. Then, I paid voluntarily. Finally, [after I realized that I was trapped], I paid because I thought it would be a lot more convenient."[21] The lesson of Kukje was not lost on the business leaders.

As chairman of FKI, Chung came under particular scrutiny during the investigation for supposedly leading the fundraising campaign for the foundation. Chung acknowledged raising the funds, but only under Ilhae directives. He was nevertheless criticized for his participation. In the end, President Chun left office in disgrace but was protected from prosecution for a time by the newly elected President Roh Tae Woo, his old comrade. However, several of his Chun's associates were sent to jail for corruption.

As for Chairman Chung, his directness and candor in describing the inner workings of Korean business-government relationships during the televised investigations catapulted him into something of a media star. His pictures were frequently seen in newspapers and magazines, and he was widely sought for interviews on subjects ranging from the economy to North-South Korean relations. People wanted to learn more about this plain-talking business tycoon who had amassed such wealth and power and who had stood up to his accusers and won. Chung was described by one newspaper as Korea's "economic president,"[22] and another called him "the great tree of the business world."[23] Chung was now looked upon by many Koreans as "clearly different [from the other business leaders], distinguished among others....He exercises his influence and power without regret."[24] At the age of 73, Chung had become a national icon, not unlike H. Ross Perot or John Wayne in the United States.

JOINING THE HIGH-TECH RACE

"We did not avoid competition; competition only made us stronger."

—CHUNG JU YUNG[1]

By the late 1970s, Chung Ju Yung had become increasingly concerned about the future of heavy industries and construction, the backbone of his conglomerate. Both markets were soft, and Chung felt he needed a hedge against economic downturns. Looking for more balance in his company, he became interested in developing a new product line that he could export. In 1978, Chung created the Hyundai Heavy Electrical Company to explore the feasibility of manufacturing home appliances for both the domestic and international markets, but he soon concluded that this industry offered insufficient prospects to justify the investment. His attention then turned from electrical products to electronics. In 1982, at the age of sixty-six, he formed KDK Electronics, a joint venture designed to secure advanced electronics technology. His strategy was simple. He would combine American technology and engineering expertise with Korean production capabilities to manufacture and sell state-of-the-art electronic products at bargain-basement prices. The products would be designed in the United States, manufactured in Korea, and then sold in the United States and anywhere else he could find a market.

Hyundai's initial move into the field of electronics complemented Chung's continual drive for vertical integration at the group level. Hyundai was now emerging as a major global automobile company. As Chung saw it, cars were increasingly becoming high-tech vehicles. In addition to the obligatory radio, many younger customers were demanding tape players and multiple speakers. Soon, CD players and integrated sound systems would be added to the list of customer demands. New cars also required other sophisticated electronics, including fuel injection systems, climate control systems, and anti-lock braking. At the same time, HHI's ships were also becoming electronic fortresses on the high seas, with sophisticated navigational, communications, and radar systems. Even Hyundai's elevator business was becoming increasingly high tech, requiring integrated electronic control systems. If Hyundai could succeed in securing a solid foothold in the electronics industry, it could remain ahead of the competition in several of its key markets.

Chung concluded that the future of Hyundai depended on capturing a major share of the market for electronics equipment. As he noted at the time, "Without a presence in electronics we cannot survive in the future."[2] He was determined to have a piece of this action. But whereas other Korean firms relied principally on Japanese technology and product designs, Chung would again attempt to leapfrog over the competition by doing his own design work as well as manufacturing. And this time he would begin his venture in the heart of California's Silicon Valley, not in Korea.

CALIFORNIA DREAMING

To get his fledgling American-based electronics venture off the ground, Chung hired Bae Myung Seung away from Xerox Corporation in late 1982 and made him executive vice president of the new American venture. It was called Hyundai Electronics America (HEA), and it was officially opened in 1983 (see the timeline in Table 8-1). Property was leased in San Jose, California, for company facilities. Bae set about drafting a comprehensive plan of operation to build a first-rate electronics company in the heart of Silicon Valley. When it was finally submitted to Chairman Chung, Bae's plan called for an $83 million initial investment. HEA would first learn the business and then prepare for head-to-head competition with its U.S. and Japanese rivals. But when Chung read the plan he immediately dismissed it as being too timid. Instead, he drafted a new plan calling for an initial $300 million investment. HEA was born, and Hyundai officially entered the high-tech race.

From the beginning, however, Hyundai acted more like a naïve trailblazer than a significant foreign threat to the U.S. high-tech industry. Early in 1983, several senior Hyundai executives were sent to California from the newly formed Hyundai Electronics Industries (HEI) back in Korea to serve as Chung's eyes and ears for the project. HEI would be the principal owner of HEA and would manage every detail of its operation. From the outset, the Koreans insisted that things be done on a grand scale. Their plans frequently came into conflict with the thinking of the more experienced Bae, who had worked in the industry for thirty years in the United States. Bae was con-

TABLE 8-1

TIMELINE: HYUNDAI ELECTRONICS INDUSTRIES

DATE	EVENT
1978	Hyundai Heavy Electrical Company established.
1982	KDK Electronics formed as a joint venture.
1983	Hyundai Electronics Industries and Hyundai Electronics America established.
	Hyundai enters the DRAM market.
1985	HEI's Inchon Semiconductor facility opened.
	HEA stops development of work stations after producing Smart Alec.
1988	HEI records first profitable year, five years after entry into field and a record in electronics industry.
1989	HEI builds 1M DRAM.
	HEA introduces Korean-made Blue Chip PCs to U.S. market; discontinued in 1992.
1991	HEI builds 4M DRAM.
1992	HEI builds 64M DRAM.
	Hyundai begins PC production in the United States; discontinued in 1994.
1993	HEI builds Korea's first HDTV prototype.
	Hyundai Information Technology Company established.
1994	Hyundai becomes tenth largest producer of DRAMs in the world.
	HEI joins GlobalStar satellite consortium.
	HEA acquires Maxtor.
1995	HEI opens semiconductor plant in Shanghai, China.
	HEA selects Eugene, Oregon, as the site for its future U.S.-based semiconductor manufacturing facility, called Hyundai Semiconductor America.
	HEA purchases Symbios Logic.
1996	Hyundai becomes seventh largest producer of DRAMs in the world.
	HEI develops world's first 256M DRAM.

DATE	EVENT
1997	HEI develops world's first 1-gigabyte DRAM.
	Hyundai Semiconductor America opens in Eugene, Oregon.
1998	HEI completes Korea's first complete HDTV broadcasting transmitter/receiver system.

cerned that Hyundai was too inexperienced in the field to prosper in the short run. Instead, they should start slowly and learn the business, perhaps beginning with automotive electronics and other industrial materials, as Chairman Chung had originally envisioned. But the expatriates wanted the sizable profits that could only come from semiconductors and personal computers. They instructed that 80 percent of HEA's investment be put there. They also wanted HEA to design and make work stations. One year into the venture, Bae had over two hundred people on the payroll and the plant was in full operation in both R&D and manufacturing, just as he had ordered.

Unfortunately, what HEA lacked was a well-reasoned corporate strategy or even a coherent business plan in one of the United States' most competitive industries. At one point, HEA's stated plan was to conduct R&D on semiconductors in Silicon Valley, send the plans back to Korea for manufacture, and then return the finished chips to the United States for sales and distribution. Later, however, the plan changed and HEA determined that it should research, design, *and* manufacture products for sale in the United States. Above all, HEA was to make money. With a conflict over mission, as well as a conflict of wills between senior executives, disaster loomed. Right or wrong, Bae increasingly saw himself as an outsider who had lived far from the inner circles of power at Hyundai's headquarters. He knew he did not have the ear of top Hyundai officials. It was clear to Bae who would win in any major policy conflict.

Indeed, many executives—both Koreans and Americans—would come and go in short order at HEA. Some were fired because they challenged the prevailing order; others quit when they concluded that all major decisions were being made in absentia back in Seoul. One Korean-American engineer who passed through HEA, John Nam, felt that Hyundai experienced so many troubles in HEA because it was essentially a heavy industry firm that always tried to muscle its way through problems. Electronics, on the other hand, required considerable expertise in both technology and marketing; it required a patient and delicate approach to business. This was not Hyundai's strong suit, according to Nam. In particular, he thought that HEA made two serious errors in its operations. First, it hired exclusively technicians and engineers; no professional managers were brought on board. Second, it failed to understand the gap between culture and business. Nam explained: "The way Silicon Valley works, you have to have imagination in products and technology. You develop a product. If it works, you produce and sell it. Hyundai did it the other way around. They built a huge manufacturing facility in Inchon, Korea, and hired 3,000 people right away. R&D and marketing in Silicon Valley couldn't follow the speed with which they were building in Korea."[3] Although it would likely take three to five years for HEA to develop a suitable product for market, Hyundai built its factory in Korea in six months and then demanded that HEA send it something to make. Hyundai's top executives in Seoul, all schooled in the construction industry, failed to understand the electronics business. They had made their mark, like other Korean firms, by getting a quick turnaround on its invested capital. The idea of long-term investments—*very* long-term investments—had never occurred to them. Nor had it occurred to the Korean government that was backing Hyundai's efforts.

One of HEA's initial plans to design and make personal computers was soon scrapped. Concluding that they were too late to capture a significant share of this market, they decided instead to try and design low-cost engineering and scientific workstations. Workstations, referred to in the industry as "PCs on steroids," represented a smaller but more sophisticated segment of the computer market. In pursuing workstations, HEA hoped to build upon Hyundai's noted technical expertise in engineering. But corporate Hyundai again intervened, demanding a finished product from HEA before one could realistically be developed. "We have a huge factory; you have to fill it," Nam recounted Hyundai executives saying.[4] The pressure was on in typical Hyundai fashion; results were needed now, not later.

As it turned out, design efforts on the workstations progressed slowly due to the difficulty of hiring the best available engineers. Not only did HEA face a tight labor market for engineers, but they were unable to make competitive offers to recruit and retain the Valley's best minds. The best American engineers expected to be offered either high managerial positions or equity shares in the company. Moreover, they tended to see their employment as a partnership among equals and resented the authoritarian climate of the firm. At HEA, most of the highest positions were held by Koreans sent from Seoul, and the Chung family was not about to give equity shares in one of its companies. As a result, many of the best U.S. engineers stayed away from the new venture. "We ended up hiring left-over guys," Nam observed. "But if you want to develop, you have to be a little better than someone else."[5] This only exacerbated the cultural conflict by convincing many Korean managers that the Americans were simply not up to their standards and were therefore probably not worthy of their trust.

Despite these problems, by October 1983 HEA had completed prototypes of four different workstations, including one for color graphics. They called the product line Smart Alec. A major ribbon-cutting ceremony was held at the upscale Lotte Hotel in downtown Seoul. Headlines and photographs in the Korean newspapers celebrated Hyundai's entry into the field of high technology. In many ways, however, the celebration was misleading. Although the workstations functioned reasonably well, Hyundai proved incapable of converting the prototypes into production models. Hyundai had never taken the time to develop the manufacturing know-how or technical expertise to become a high-tech producer. In all, just eight workstations were produced before Chung finally called a halt to the entire project in early 1985. Korean engineers were transferred back to Seoul, while the Americans were given four weeks' severance pay and terminated. The newly constructed HEA facility was closed. Hyundai's first venture into the world of high technology had been a complete failure, with a loss of $50 million.

But it also had been a significant learning experience for the company. Hyundai would be back, and next time it intended to do better. We obviously had not heard the last of HEA. Meanwhile, Hyundai would convert its Inchon factory to the manufacture of DRAM chips. DRAMs required sophisticated technology, originally secured from the Americans and Japanese, and were very profitable, especially with cheap labor. Hyundai Electronics had found its niche. By 1986, the Inchon facility would become one of the world's largest fabrication facilities for DRAMs, with 12,000 assembly employees and well over $1 billion in investment.

Learning from the HEA debacle, Hyundai Electronics Industries soon established a major R&D facility at Inchon that was staffed with the best engineers Hyundai could find. These included many Korean-Americans who were enticed into returning to their homeland by generous salaries and appeals to nationalism. Hyundai—and Korea—were beginning to learn the value of research and development. While their first ventures into R&D were relatively small—spending far less on average than their Japanese and U.S. competitors—with time and experience Hyundai would begin making the kinds of investments required to become a global player in the electronics industry.[6]

Perhaps more than any other Hyundai company, the road traveled by HEI and its U.S. subsidiary, HEA, has been a bumpy one. In the late 1980s, HEA reopened its doors and formed an alliance with a small U.S. distributor to manufacture and sell Korean-made personal computers in the U.S. market under the Blue Chip brand name. It was one of the few times that Hyundai executives decided against using their own "Hyundai" name for the product, and it proved to be another costly mistake. A lack of brand identity and disagreements between the parties over cost and revenue distributions caused an early split in the partnership. Blue Chip computers came and went before most customers even noticed them.

In 1992, Hyundai decided to shift production of its PCs for the U.S. market to HEA in San Jose, California, and relaunch its business once again. They would try again in the U.S. market. HEI also continued its Inchon production facilities for PCs destined for the Asian market. In the United States, Hyundai targeted the low-end market, where they hoped they could carve out a sizable niche among cost-conscious buyers. This time they insisted on using their own name. If Hyundai was going to make a mark in the U.S. electronics market, they wanted it to be on their own terms; they wanted nothing more to do with OEM manufacturing. Indeed, 95 percent of its PCs sold in the 1990s were marketed under the Hyundai brand name, compared to only 20 percent for rival Samsung.[7] Hyundai had its work cut out for itself, however, in large measure because of its poor showing in the 1980s. As *Electronics Business Asia* observed at the time: "Company sources admit they've been saddled with resentful customers, a bloodied dealer network, and low name recognition among potential PC buyers, few of whom know that in 1991 Hyundai sold more PCs in North America than CompuAdd and pulled in more revenue than Acer or Zeos....Hyundai will need much more than clever marketing and aggressive pricing to restore the fractured relationships among its dealers and customers."[8] At issue was whether Hyundai had the ability—or even the inclination—to develop smooth, mutually beneficial relationships with its U.S. partners for the long term.

Once again, Hyundai soon found the U.S. market for PCs to be too competitive. PC prices dropped an average of 30 percent each year, leaving little if any profit for manufacturers. Despite its conservative goal of capturing only 5 percent of the U.S. market, it had difficulty maintaining a mere 2 percent. Although Hyundai PCs were inexpensive, many customers complained about poor service from the resellers (the companies that actually sell the PCs to the public), which, in turn, felt they had insufficient incentives to push the Hyundai line over competitors. Samsung and Goldstar had similar troubles in the market. In 1994, citing lagging sales, Hyundai discontinued its U.S. PC production—for the second time in less than a decade. Indeed, in 1993, its last full year of operation, HEA earned a paltry $34 million on PC sales, hardly sufficient to justify its continued massive investment. Hyundai was not giving up, however, and made it known that they would return. "We never give up," stated Lee Sung Hee, a Hyundai executive. "It's not the Hyundai way."[9]

Even so, it is reasonable to ask why Hyundai so missed the mark in its repeated ventures into the U.S. electronics market. Was it Hyundai's traditional impetuousness that caused them to jump before they completely understood the market? Was it inexperience with the prevailing practices, conventions, and norms of the electronics industry? Or was it their heavy industry mentality that assumed that brute strength could overcome all barriers? Perhaps they sent the wrong people to lead the effort. Perhaps they lacked adequate technologies to attempt a successful market entry. Or perhaps they knew less than they originally thought about globalizing their business efforts and working with people from other cultures. Maybe all of these reasons combined to lead to repeated failures. Whatever the reason, Hyundai proved to be a slow learner in this important industry and lost valuable time in gaining a foothold. If, as Chung had noted, Hyundai required a presence in the field of electronics to survive in the long run, they would have to do better in the future.

THE BATTLE FOR SEMICONDUCTORS

The major battles over semiconductors had long been fought principally between Japan and the United States. The Europeans had largely ceded the market in the early 1980s, after struggling unsuccessfully to develop their own indigenous industry. At the time, few industry experts considered Korea a possible contender in this industry. Korea had no comparative advantage in semiconductors: capital was scarce, semiconductor design capabilities were nonexistent, and the major markets were overseas. It was widely assumed that the Koreans were highly ambitious but woefully unprepared for the challenge. In fact, many Japanese executives felt that the Koreans "could not master the complexities of semiconductor manufacturing," echoing a similar sentiment made by the Americans about the Japanese just two decades earlier.[10] To the surprise of many observers, however, Korea would emerge as a major player in the industry in the late 1980s and today enjoys a tremendous competitive edge in memory devices.

As early as 1976, the Korean government made a decision to promote semiconductors as a strategic industry. Within a year, the government had created an electronics research institute, an industrial estate for semiconductor manufacture, and its own semiconductor manufacturing facility. In Korea's fourth five-year plan (1977–1981), semiconductors became a specific target for development with formal, quantified industrial objectives. In 1982, the government's Semiconductor Promotional Plan led to supportive measures to enhance semiconductor capability, including subsidized capital and tax benefits for semiconductor investments, increased funding for government research, and continued import protection for domestic producers.

Convinced that the only way to crack the world semiconductor market was through massive developmental projects, the government launched the VLSI Project. This research and development venture aimed to create a 4M DRAM chip by 1984. The VLSI Project had an initial budget of $199 million shared by the government and participating firms. The industry portion was subsidized by government-guaranteed, low-interest loans. The visibility of the project was so pronounced that Korean industry officials called it the Blue House Project, in reference to the official residence of Korea's president. Within just four years, in 1989, Korea's presence was felt when the country's rapidly increasing production and aggressive export methods drove down DRAM prices worldwide. Korea's continued progress in penetrating the semiconductor market is shown in Table 8-2.

In 1990, three of Korea's largest industrial groupings—Samsung, Goldstar, and Hyundai—all declared semiconductors as one of their top industrial priorities. Initially, these firms tried to develop semiconductor technology through foreign licensing agreements, cooperative research efforts, and government-assisted reverse engineering methods. Later, they realized that success was only possible if they became more independent of Japanese and U.S. technology. When Korean firms entered full-scale production of 64K

TABLE 8-2

KOREA'S PRODUCTION AND EXPORTS OF SEMICONDUCTORS: 1966–1995

(In Millions of Dollars)

	1966	1970	1975	1980	1985	1990	1995
Production	0.002	32	231	424	1,200	5,100	17,500
Exports	0.002	32	178	415	1,100	4,500	13,500
Stage of Development	Multinationals enter assembly operations in Korea (1965).		First Korean firm begins to fabricate wafers and produce LSIs (1975).		Korean firms enter VLSI production under foreign licenses (1984).		Korea becomes independent in DRAM design and production (1988).

Source: Adapted from Linsu Kim, *Imitation to Innovation: The Dynamics of Korea's Technological Learning* (Boston: Harvard Business School Press, 1997), Chapter 7.

DRAMs in late 1984, attempting to be cost leaders, they quickly discovered that they could not compete with the Japanese on the basis of price alone.[11] Even so, the Koreans proved to be quick learners as they finally dislodged the Japanese in the DRAM market by copying their marketing and pricing strategies.

During their initial take-off stage, Samsung acquired most of its technology from U.S. corporations. Design specifications for the 64K and 256K DRAM came from Micron in 1983. And leading-edge MICOM and EPROM technologies came from Intel in 1985 and 1986. Once Samsung became the leading company in DRAM production, it progressed by cross-licensing advanced technologies with global competitors. Specifically, they exchanged some 64K DRAM technology they independently developed with Intel's MPU technology and NCR's ASIC and chip-set technology. Samsung also jointly developed the RISC CPU with Hewlett Packard and cross-licensed related semiconductor patents with IBM. In 1993, Samsung initiated a large-scale joint production with Texas Instruments in Portugal to produce and market Samsung's 1M, 4M, and 16M DRAMs and Texas Instruments' high-quality logic DRAMs throughout Europe. Samsung and Texas Instruments have also expanded the cooperative relationship further for joint development of new products.

Also in 1993, Samsung participated in a Korea-based joint venture with Dai Nippon Screen of Japan to build a next-generation production facility for 64M DRAMs. In the same year, it concluded a joint-venture contract with Towa of Japan and Hanyang Precision of Korea to produce auto molding systems, an important part of semiconductor manufacturing facilities. Shortly thereafter, Samsung announced plans to forge a technical partnership with NEC to develop next-generation 256M DRAM chips. In 1993, Samsung overtook Toshiba as the world's largest supplier of metal-oxide semiconductors, forcing Toshiba to forge an alliance with eighth-ranked IBM and Siemens to develop 256M DRAMs. Then, second-ranked Hitachi teamed up with the seventh-ranked Texas Instruments. The alliance between Samsung (number one) and NEC (number three) was described by their executives as a reaction to the collaborative networks formed among their major rivals.[12] Currently, Samsung is investing over $8 billion to enter the logic chip market, where it believes it can gain significant profits and diversify itself away from the memory chip market.[13]

Meanwhile, rival LG has relied heavily on technological alliances to catch up with Samsung. Since the late 1980s, Hitachi of Japan has contributed most to LG's growth. LG began its semiconductor business through a joint venture with AT&T, which was consolidated into Goldstar Electron in 1989 to utilize the 1M DRAM technology Hitachi offered.[14] Hitachi willingly provided the

1M DRAM technology to LG because it wanted to focus on 4M DRAM technology and catch up with its main rival, Toshiba. The LG-Hitachi alliance also cooperated in developing 4M and 16M DRAMs. Recently, as LG has become more technologically competent while Hitachi has lost some competitiveness due to the continual appreciation of the yen, the role has been reversed, and Hitachi has been more anxious to open additional alliances with LG. The LG-Hitachi alliance has been a good marriage for both partners. LG has been able to narrow the technology gap with Samsung and Hyundai in a short period of time on the basis of Hitachi's DRAM technology, and Hitachi secured a cheap supply of 1M DRAMs and was able to reinvest profits from 1M DRAM business in the development of 4M DRAMs. LG also cooperated with Hyundai and Samsung to develop 16M and 64M DRAMs. Recently, LG formed a new alliance with IBM to use its technologies to manufacture computer notebooks, PC servers, and computer peripherals.[15]

For its part, Hyundai approached the memory chip business with the same drive and determination that it had with ships and automobiles—a brash, aggressive, straight-on approach. Since Hyundai entered the standard memory market in 1983, it has joined a series of technological alliances, mostly with U.S. and Japanese corporations (see Table 8-3). In the 1980s, Hyundai operated under various vertically related OEM contracts with Texas Instruments, General Instruments, and Intel. Since the early 1990s, however, Hyundai and Fujitsu have become inseparable business partners. In 1993, Hyundai and Fujitsu reached an agreement to start full-scale cooperation in development, manufacturing, and marketing semiconductors. The two corporations exchange various DRAM technologies. Also, Hyundai is now able to use Fujitsu's manufacturing plants in the United States to produce 4M DRAMs and other products and to sell them in local markets. This helps protect the company from antidumping lawsuits. The Hyundai-Fujitsu alliance was expanded further for cooperation on 64M DRAMs, ASIC microcontrollers, and specialized chip technologies. The alliance helped Hyundai in the ASIC business and Fujitsu in the DRAM business, where it has been traditionally weak.

In 1988, Hyundai Electronics Industries reached an important milestone. It experienced its first profitable year after being in business for only five years—a record for firms in this industry. Its recent success in semiconductors has propelled it to a par with its competitors. In 1989, it was selling the 1M DRAM. By 1991, it was selling 4M DRAMs and, more significantly, the actual chips were designed by Hyundai, not by Japanese or American engineers. This represents a significant accomplishment for any Korean latecomer into the industry.[16]

By 1992, semiconductors ranked as Korea's single largest export, grossing

TABLE 8-3

HYUNDAI'S EARLY TECHNOLOGICAL ALLIANCES IN SEMICONDUCTORS

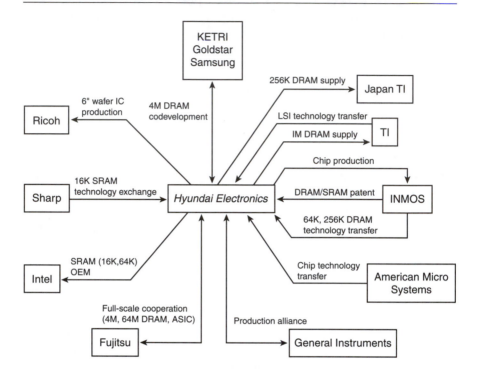

Source: Reprinted with permission from Gerardo R. Ungson, Richard M. Steers, and Seung-ho Park, *Korean Enterprise: The Quest for Globalization* (Boston: Harvard Business School Press, 1997), p. 145. Copyright 1997 by the President and Fellows of Harvard College. All rights reserved.

$6.8 billion in foreign sales, including $3.9 billion in sales of chips actually fabricated in Korea and another $2.9 billion from those assembled and packaged in Korea for foreign makers and reexported.[17] By 1994, Samsung had overtaken the Japanese to become the top-ranked DRAM manufacturer in the world, and Hyundai was ranked tenth in the world in DRAMs. By 1996, Hyundai had risen to seventh in the world in sales of DRAMs, with total sales of $2.3 billion. Hyundai accounted for 17 percent of Korean exports of semiconductors but was well behind Samsung, with $6.7 billion in sales.[18] Beating Samsung at its own game had become Hyundai's new ambition.

As part of its globalization strategy, Hyundai is determined to expand its presence overseas. In addition to its new semiconductor production facility in Shanghai, China, Hyundai has also targeted both the United States and the

European Union. After a lengthy search for a U.S. location for the manufacture of DRAMs, the company announced in May 1995 that it would build a $1.4 billion semiconductor plant in Eugene, Oregon. The facility, named Hyundai Semiconductor America (HSA), would initially employ up to 1,000 people and produce 64M DRAMs, with a monthly capacity of 30,000 8-inch wafers.[19] It would be one of the ten largest fabrication plants in the world. HSA was officially opened in December 1997, after several delays caused by construction problems and protests by local environmentalists who opposed city growth. Indeed, HSA's arrival in Oregon served as a lightning rod for several antibusiness groups opposed to economic development. Local groups tried to have HSA property rezoned to create environmental wetlands for habitat, to cancel previous city and county commitments for temporary tax abatements, and to prohibit the transportation and use of chemicals used in the manufacture of chips.[20] In the end, these efforts served to slow but not derail Hyundai's progress in gaining a foothold in the U.S. semiconductor market. At the same time, a similar plant was announced for Dunfermline, Scotland.[21] With the December 1997 Korean economic crash, however, completion of the Scottish plant was delayed as investment capital dried up and Hyundai put a hold on several overseas projects.

JOINING THE TECHNOLOGY CLUB

Today, HEI and its U.S. subsidiary, Hyundai Electronics America, have reached levels of technological sophistication widely considered impossible only a few years back. In the field of electronics, HEI has complemented its extensive DRAM semiconductor business with a wide array of memory applications that include video RAM, mask ROM, flash memories, and various IC cards. It also has strengthened its base in nonmemory semiconductors, including systems ICs, various ASIC products, and other compound semiconductors. Recently, it added LCDs (liquid-crystal displays) to its product mix through a technical alliance with Image Quest Technologies.[22]

Currently, HEI—not unlike the competition—invests 10 percent of annual sales in R&D efforts. This investment has led to over 20,000 patents in recent years. As a result of these targeted efforts, HEI now has a string of recent successes that hold the potential to catapult the company into one of the world's truly significant high-tech companies. Witness just a few of HEI's recent achievements:

▶ Developed the first Korean-made car navigation system (1993).

▶ Developed the first Korean-made high-definition television (HDTV) system (1993).

▶ Joined a consortium of companies to develop the GlobalStar communication satellite system that will connect the world through a network of 56 satellites (1994).

▶ Developed the world's first MPEG II decoder chip (1995).

▶ Developed the world's first commercial CDMA system (1995).

▶ Developed the world's first 256M Synchronous DRAM (1996).

▶ Completed a $200 million state-of-the-art direct broadcasting system for China (1996).

▶ Developed the world's first 1 gigabyte synchronous DRAM (1997).

▶ Developed the first silicon-on-insulator DRAM chip (1997).

▶ Developed Korea's first composite EDL (embedded DRAM in logic) chip by embedding a memory chip on a nonmemory logic chip to improve date handling and system performance (1997).

▶ Developed a new 14-inch LCD that is the thinnest and lightest of its kind in the world (1998).

▶ Developed Korea's first complete HDTV broadcasting transmitter/receiver system (1998).

Indeed, HEI has come a long way in the electronics business. What is crucial to its future, however, is its ability to begin creating more of its own advanced technologies to compete head on with the Americans and the Japanese. Korean firms began as imitators and progressed to partners through a series of strategic alliances and joint ventures. Now, Hyundai and other Korean firms must move ahead of their rivals and establish themselves as significant technological leaders. Above all, as Korea University professor Kim Linsu notes in his recent book, *Imitation to Innovation: The Dynamics of Korea's Technological Learning*, Korean firms must become true innovators.[23]

Just such a move can be seen in the recent developments at Hyundai. In their Inchon research facilities, Hyundai Electronics Industries is gearing up to develop the next generation of electronic products. Over the next five years, it plans to significantly expand its production facilities, research and development laboratories, and marketing efforts, with the aim of becoming a major contender in this highly competitive industry. As ambitious as this may appear, industry experts are confident the company can achieve its goals.

Meanwhile, back in California, Hyundai Electronics America now seems to have a clear game plan for the future. Under the initial leadership of former President Kim Young Hwan (who was subsequently promoted to president of

HEI in Seoul) and current President Park Chong Sup, HEA has developed a two-pronged strategy to gain a major foothold in the U.S. electronics market. First, HEA serves as the North American marketing and sales arm for Hyundai's electronic products, including DRAM chips, monitors, flash memories, and LCDs. These products come from both Korea and the United States Second, HEA has emerged as a major holding company for several leading-edge high-tech firms that have prospered under the wing of the Hyundai group.

Learning from past mistakes, HEA now goes to great lengths to ensure harmony between Koreans and Americans. Indeed, most of the executive team at HEA are now Americans, as are all of the CEOs of HEA's subsidiary firms. HEA also goes to great lengths to provide local autonomy for each company. HEI President Kim notes: "*Globalization* has become a catch word for many corporations, but there is a distinct difference in HEI's strategy. We are providing support for our overseas subsidiaries by endowing them with independent decision-making rights and responsibilities, so they can build a global outsourcing structure and concentrate their efforts on developing their core businesses."[24] President Kim continues: "Decentralization is our best course of action. As long as our subsidiaries are profitable, we will leave them alone. In fact, the reason we bought these companies in the first place is because of their expertise. Why should we stifle this enterprise?"[25]

This policy was quick to produce positive results among its American employees in terms of corporate culture. One U.S. engineer recently noted, "I expected a lot of changes, such as management turnover, when Hyundai came in and took over, but they have pretty much left us alone. They have had a positive influence, increasing our business focus and making us pay more attention to profitability, strategic direction, and new production."[26]

At the same time, HEA's new policy has led to positive financial results. Whereas subsidiaries like Maxtor and Symbios Logic were both money-losing ventures when they were first acquired by HEA, they are now highly profitable companies. The same cannot be said for the U.S. subsidiaries of Hyundai's Korean rivals, which continue to lose money. At Maxtor, HEA offered low-cost manufacturing facilities in Asia to keep its products competitive. Maxtor is now a $2 billion company. "We build partnerships," explained HEA President Park Chong Sup. "That is the key to our recent success."[27] When Symbios Logic was owned first by NCR and later by AT&T, the company was not allowed to make capital investments. When HEA acquired the firm in 1995 for $340 million, it was given considerable discretion over such investments. In 1997, the company made a profit of $68 million on sales of $614 million. By the time that Symbios Logic was sold to LSI Logic in 1998, HEA had more than doubled its three-year investment and sold the firm for $760 million.

Throughout these efforts, Hyundai seeks a balance between the goals of business and the larger goals of society. As Chung Mong Hun, current HEI chairman and son of the founder, notes: "Though making profits through the development of technology is important, the responsibility of preserving the earth's environment and developing a moral culture is also a major responsibility of HEI. We believe that genuine progress is achieved not only through technical development, but also through valuing human well-being."[28] In the fifteen years since their founding, HEI and HEA have come full circle from naïve trailblazers to full-fledged corporate members of the world's exclusive technology club.

BUMPY ROAD TO LABOR PEACE

"Strikers have to realize that if they go to the extremes of selfishness, they will damage not only their firms but also the national economy, eventually doing harm to their own interests."

—KOREAN PRESIDENT KIM YOUNG SAM, 1993[1]

The plight of Korea's working class has always been problematic. Confucian traditions require hard work and long hours and offer few rewards in exchange. The poverty that pervaded Korea throughout most of the twentieth century only added to their misery and frustration. After the Korean War, as the country's infrastructure began taking shape and its economy began to develop, hundreds of thousands of workers at last found steady employment in the burgeoning factories rising on the banks of the Han River. Companies with names like Samsung, Daewoo, Lucky-Goldstar, Sunkyong, Ssangyong, Kumho—and Hyundai—were building a "New Korea" and, in the process, were creating opportunities for people of all economic and educational backgrounds.

As Korea evolved from an agrarian society toward an industrialized state in the late 1960s and early 1970s, young men and women began migrating in ever-increasing numbers from their small villages and farms to the new factories being built in Seoul, Pusan, Taegu, and Ulsan. Most sought a better life and a higher standard of living, the same motivation that prompted Chung Ju Yung to leave Asan village for Seoul in the 1930s. Farm life was both dreary and hard, and little money was to be made. By contrast, the new factories offered young people an opportunity to learn new skills and make considerably more money. To many, it represented the future and a better way of life.

FROM FARMS TO FACTORIES

During the industrial heyday of the 1970s, when the demand for blue-collar workers increased continually throughout Korea, joining Hyundai or other Korean companies was relatively easy. All you needed was a friend or relative who worked for the company. In the 1970s, roughly two-thirds of the industrial workers employed by Hyundai applied because of a friend or relative who already worked there.[2] In Korea, this is called "back-door recruitment"; in the West, it is called employee referral.[3] Many Korean firms believed that this technique led to hiring good employees, because the company already had someone on the payroll who would vouch for the candidate's sincerity and dedication. The remainder of the openings were filled through "open recruitment," where prospective job candidates heard about jobs through public announcements or direct inquiries.

Later, however, as the manufacturing technology became more advanced, Hyundai became more sophisticated in its hiring procedures and sought industrial workers with more preemployment training. More than two-thirds of the workers hired by the company in the 1980s were graduates of the Hyundai Vocational Training Institute. The Institute provided free training—and even paid a small monthly stipend—to well-qualified students interested in technical careers.[4] Why work for Hyundai? One 14-year veteran of Hyundai Motor Company recalled in an interview: "My father is a farmer, and I graduated from agricultural high school. I thought Hyundai Motor was the best. It enjoyed a good reputation among seniors. Hyundai takes care of diligent workers. The Hyundai spirit is the backbone of this company."[5]

Like most Korean companies, Hyundai considered its employees, once hired, to be the central building block of long-term corporate success. Considerable effort went into the development of employees at all levels. With the increasing competitiveness of the 1980s, the company began establishing a more sophisticated human resource management system to oversee both employee recruitment and development. Most training for blue-collar workers involved on-the-job training aimed at improving job-related skills and "correct" attitudes toward the company. As employees gained more experience, the focus of training tended to shift to the development of future first-line supervisors for the company. This approach to training mirrored the situation in many industrialized countries of the world, including Japan and the United States.

Throughout, emphasis was also placed on developing an all-around "Hyundai man." (At the time, all industrial workers were male, and unmarried women were hired into clerical positions.) One worker interviewed said that his co-workers were all proud to be Hyundai workers. "We sing the company song when we have athletic meetings or special events, at least two or three times a month."[6] Besides, he noted, Hyundai's pay was "as high as anybody's." Fellowship among the workers is important. Another worker observed: "We sometimes have 'survival drives' to test how to survive in bad conditions. We climb mountains or go on overnight trips [usually about eight times each year in groups of between 30 to 40 workers] to test our group spirit. We never refuse to go. We have the team spirit, the feeling that we are in the same boat. Sometimes we keep walking for two or three hours, drink some beer or *soju*, sing the company songs, popular songs, American cowboy songs."[7] While the workers are away, their wives dutifully join teams of women for treks to the beach or religious shrines.

As a result of a Confucian commitment to hard work, combined with company efforts for continual on-the-job training, Korea's workers rapidly earned a well-deserved reputation as being the hardest workers in the world. Labor statistics bear out this accolade. In 1986, the average South Korean male industrial worker worked an average of 54 hours per week, reportedly the longest in the world (see Table 9-1).[8] In many Korean factories, mandatory overtime frequently brought this figure to over 70 or more hours per week. It is estimated that during this time the average Korean male worked at least

TABLE 9-1

AVERAGE HOURS OF WORK FOR MALE INDUSTRIAL WORKERS (1986)

COUNTRY	AVERAGE WORK WEEK (IN HOURS)	COUNTRY	AVERAGE WORK WEEK (IN HOURS)
South Korea	54	Germany	41
Malaysia	48	United States	40
South Africa	47	France	40
Hong Kong	47	Israel	39
Mexico	46	Norway	38
Japan	46	Sweden	38
Argentina	45	Puerto Rico	38
United Kingdom	42	Belgium	34

Source: International Labour Office, *Yearbook of Labour Statistics* (Geneva: ILO, 1986).

2,833 hours per year, compared to 2,168 hours in Japan, 1,898 in the United States, and 1,652 in Germany. Similarly, though entitled to more, the average Korean actually took only 4.5 days vacation *per year*, compared to 9.6 in Japan, 19.5 in the United States, and 30.2 in West Germany.[9] Indeed, many Korean workers referred to their Japanese counterparts as "those lazy Asians."

Eventually, all of this hard work paid off. When President Park Chung Hee assumed control of Korea's fate in 1961, per capita annual income was just $100. By the mid-1980s, it had risen to $2,300. However, as personal income rose, Korea's gross domestic product rose even more, increasing an astonishing 8.7 percent per year on average from 1960 to 1988.[10] Korea had become the world's seventeenth largest economy and the twelfth largest trading nation. In 1970, only 2 percent of Korean households had refrigerators, only 4 percent had telephones, and only 6 percent had televisions. By 1985, just fifteen years later, these percentages had increased to 71 percent, 50 percent, and 98 percent, respectively.[11] Koreans were moving up the economic ladder, in large part as a result of the country's industrialization efforts.

RISING EXPECTATIONS

Although workers were far better off than they had been in the past, they were now determined to get a larger share of Korea's new-found prosperity. If Korea was becoming a newly industrialized country (a so-called NIC), as everyone was claiming, it was time to spread the wealth. To accomplish this, workers would need some form of collective representation; they would need real unions. But in Korea, unions had long been controlled or outlawed as being against national interests. Korean workers would not find it easy to accomplish their goals.

During the Japanese occupation, from the turn of the century through World War II, the Korea economy was dominated by Japanese firms.[12] Korean language, culture, and customs were suppressed by the Japanese rulers. As a result, the early vestiges of labor unions in Korea emerged as part of the resistance campaign against Japanese colonialism. In fact, labor clashes often were seen as patriotic and received widespread support from the Korean people.[13] By the end of World War II, however, with the emerging schism between North and South, South Korean labor leaders were divided into two philosophical camps: those who supported capitalism and those who supported communism. For a time, both communist-oriented and capitalist-oriented unions existed in the south. In 1949, South Korean President Rhee Syngman's government threw its support behind the Federation of Korean Trade Unions, or FKTU (similar to the AFL-CIO in the United States) and helped it defeat the pro-Communist unions.[14] This was the beginning of strong government involvement in union activity in South Korea.

After the Korean War, the Trade Union Act was passed. This act, similar to the National Labor Relations Act of the United States, gave workers the right to organize, bargain collectively, and engage in collective action. One important difference from the U.S. legislation, however, was the absence of an enforcement agency, comparable to the National Labor Relations Board, to protect the rights of the newly created unions and their members. This lack of any enforcement mechanism made the rights of labor difficult to achieve. Almost from its inception, the Korean government controlled the FKTU, and the enforcement of labor laws during the 1950s was minimal. Antigovernment sentiments among unionists increased and, in 1960, labor activists joined student demonstrations aimed at overthrowing the government of President Rhee. The government's response to this threat was to use its security forces to curb labor's new assertiveness. In fact, in some cases, government agents were more aggressively antiunion than many companies.[15] Suppressing labor activity in the 1960s and 1970s represented a principal government strategy to control labor costs, a key ingredient of Korea's economic development plan.[16] The position of the government was that strong labor unions were "conflictful, unproductive, and disruptive in the context of economic growth."[17]

Government pressure on Korea's labor unions intensified during the 1970s and early 1980s under the successive governments of Park Chung Hee and Chun Doo Hwan. In 1971, the Korean government issued the Special Act on National Security, which required government approval to hold any labor negotiations. In 1980, the government banned industrywide national unions altogether and replaced them with enterprise, or company, unions following the Japanese model. Enterprise unions were largely run by labor-management "works councils." Korean labor laws, especially the Labor-Management Council Act as revised in 1988, mandated that every company with over fifty employees create a works council (*nosa hyeobeuihoe* in Korean) designed along the lines of those found in Western Europe. These councils were seen by the government as a substitute for labor unions in handling labor-management relations.

In theory, these works councils provided for equal labor and management representation, and such bodies were meant to serve as a means of democratizing the workplace and providing for labor-management cooperation and productivity enhancement. In actual practice, however, management typically controlled the works councils, which thereby lost their potential as an agent for substantive change in the workplace. The selection of the labor representatives was often influenced by management and acted on its behalf. Moreover, the councils were inexperienced in negotiating, in part as a result of the Special Act on National Security. Thus, during serious disputes, government officials were called in by management to settle differences. The government policy of "growth first, distribution later" typically led to pro-management contract settlements.[18]

An example of how these works councils functioned during the 1980s can be seen in the case of Hyundai Motor Company.[19] At HMC, the council consisted of twelve management representatives (including the factory's chief executive officer, the personnel director, and ten members selected by the CEO) and twelve members elected annually by the workers. The council was required to meet at least once every three months but could meet more often if it wished. Agenda items that could be discussed at the council include productivity enhancement and work efficiency, education and training of workers, prevention of labor-management disputes, workers' grievances, promotion of workers' interests, safety and improvement of the work environment, and mechanisms to enhance labor-management cooperation.

Regulations governing the council at Hyundai also stipulated that the purpose of the council was to foster labor-management cooperation and industrial peace; that members of the council should not engage in any behavior that might encourage a labor-management dispute or break the industrial peace; and that the council could not be used for collective bargaining. In practice, however, many workers felt that these regulations put them in an impossible situation. The law governing works councils required that all worker demands had to be channeled through the works councils, yet real collective bargaining was proscribed. Hence, workers at Hyundai (and elsewhere) could only express their grievances to management but had no mechanism to require management to negotiate on their demands. Even so, this system continued to function throughout most of the 1980s.

RENEGOTIATING THE SOCIAL CONTRACT

Between 1980 and 1987, the number of Korean manufacturing workers increased from 3 million to 4.4 million. During this same short period, the national economy nearly doubled in size.[20] The country had more industrial employees, more middle-class salarymen, and fewer farmers. At the same time, many industrial workers felt that the economic revolution was passing them by. Although they had seen significant wage increases over the past decade, they did not feel they were getting their share of the increasingly prosperous "New Korea." In addition to salary concerns, many workers felt that they had few rights as employees of the major conglomerates. They wanted a stronger voice in how they were treated on the factory floor. In the early 1980s, union membership across Korea hovered around 800,000. The revocation of the Special Act on National Security in 1981 revived the rights of organized labor and increased labor organizing activities. Union membership began to increase sharply in 1985 and grew to over 1,600,000 union members by 1989.[21]

The rapid rise of unionism was aided significantly by the Korean government's Declaration of Democratization on June 29, 1987.[22] This declaration reduced government intervention in labor-management relations and served to revitalize union rights. Under the reform, union shops were now allowed if more than two-thirds of the employees in an establishment were union members. National unions were once again permitted. For the first time, new amendments to the Trade Union Act identified unfair labor practices by management. These included dismissal of or discrimination against workers who joined a union, rejection of a collective bargaining agreement, and interference with workers in the formation and operation of a trade union.[23]

Workers, with their new-found rights but without bargaining experience, took their grievances to the public for support. As Korean companies and the country as a whole became more prosperous, workers and their unions began a concerted drive to improve both wages and working conditions. Nationwide, the number of strikes rose from 300 in 1986 to almost 4,000 in 1987 and continued to increase in 1988 and 1989. Behind these strikes was a widespread feeling by workers that the Korean economic miracle was not being shared equally throughout the country. Many felt that the miracle itself had occurred only as a result of the sacrifice of the Korean work force and that the time had come for a return on that investment. In fact, real wages in Korea had fallen substantially behind both the nation's gross domestic product and industrywide productivity gains.[24] Workers decided it was finally time for a change.

When major labor conflicts arose, Hyundai and other companies primarily involved in heavy industries bore the brunt of union wrath. With more blue-collar workers in one place than any other company, Hyundai's Ulsan operations were especially hard hit. (It is interesting to note that those Hyundai companies that were not engaged in heavy industries—like Hyundai Electronics Industries in Inchon—were largely unaffected by the strife.) Known to many as "Hyundai City," Ulsan at the time had a population of 600,000. Of these, over 80,000 people worked for one of several Hyundai companies, including Hyundai Heavy Industries, Hyundai Motor Company, Hyundai Electrical Engineering, Hyundai Precision, and Hyundai Pipe. Most Hyundai employees and their families lived in a sprawling high-rise housing development known as the "Ten Thousand Apartments."

The new radical labor leaders attacked the existing company-sponsored unions as "company stooges" and demanded that new independent labor unions replace them. Because Korean law outlawed more than one union per company, a choice would have to be made. The radical labor leaders staged sit-ins and protests in support of their new unions, first at Hyundai Electrical Engineering, then at Hyundai Heavy Industries, then at Hyundai Motor, and so forth. Signs were posted saying, "Down with the company labor union; choose the democratic union." Several protests turned violent. When HMC managers met with workers on the assembly line to discuss grievances, several workers began breaking the windows of the cars on the line. When Hyundai Precision managers were late arriving for a negotiating session, angry labor leaders blocked the streets. National police had to be called in to quell the riot, and three labor leaders were arrested.

Initially, these conflicts caught Hyundai executives off guard. Korean tradition demanded absolute loyalty to the company, and many managers were surprised and offended at the strident behavior of the labor leaders. Many executives believed the strife had been instigated by communist agitators or sympathizers.[25] Rumors spread of communist training camps being held in the countryside around Ulsan. At times, management tried to compromise with the radicals; at other times, they resisted firmly.

Chung Ju Yung was personally concerned about attempts by a small group of radical labor leaders to hijack the democratic efforts of rank-and-file union members. He estimated the number of radicals at about thirty, with perhaps two thousand followers, equivalent to about 10 percent of the work force. In a newspaper interview at the time, he confirmed that Hyundai wanted to work with the unions to improve the economic welfare of workers, but he pointed out that for the workers to succeed, the company also had to succeed. If the company failed to make money, there would be nothing with which to pay the workers. Above all, Chung wanted to ensure that a reasonable long-term solution was found to the conflict. "The workers have a right to have a labor union that can guarantee their interests in a logical manner," he argued. "But the government, political parties, and social groups shouldn't stir things up by making unrealistic and provocative claims."[26] By the end of the end of the summer of 1987, Hyundai executives concluded that the time had come to recognize the unions and give workers a greater voice in workplace affairs. New labor agreements were initialed, giving workers paid vacation time, abolishing mandatory overtime, standardizing the speed of the assembly lines, and even ending the requirement that workers wear their hair in short, military-style haircuts.

But more trouble was ahead. The newly formed radical unions next organized a federation of unions in an attempt to bolster their bargaining power against the huge conglomerates. At first, Hyundai refused to recognize the federation, prompting more strikes and closing many of the Ulsan factories. Again, Chung was concerned that a small number of radicals were controlling these efforts. Korea's new labor laws supported Hyundai's position, but, after mounting political pressure, the government ignored its own laws and began pressuring Hyundai and other companies to settle with the unions.[27] Union rallies were held to protest the plant closures and to demand recognition of the federation. At one point, over twenty thousand Hyundai workers rioted and went on a rampage through the streets of Ulsan. They threw rocks and fire bombs and broke several hundred windows, injuring sixty people. Finally, two thousand riot police were called in to help quell the demonstration.[28] Again, Hyundai sought compromise, but to no avail.

Finally, on August 19, 1987, Chairman Chung personally recognized the federation. But this conciliatory action again backfired, encouraging the federation and its unions to make even more demands. One by one, negotiating sessions ended in failure as the two sides discovered they were far apart on key issues. To the many union leaders, Hyundai did not recognize the need for substantive change, whereas to Hyundai executives the unions demanded nothing short of a radical social and economic revolution. Neither side saw much chance for compromise. On one occasion, union leaders began a fistfight when Hyundai managers refused to make pay raises retroactive for the previous six months. Following repeated incidents of violence and property damage, police began arresting labor organizers, but this only made matters worse. Then, a union organizer was kidnapped in downtown Seoul, apparently on the orders of a Hyundai executive. When Chung found out about the kidnapping, he reportedly was furious. Chung would always fight hard for what he believed in, but he would not condone what he considered dishonorable behavior. The company issued a public apology for the kidnapping and noted, in a change of heart, that "the existence of unions will benefit the company in the long run."[29] As one militant union leader commented at the time, "After finding out the facts, Chung Ju Yung tried to settle everything."[30]

Again, however, industrial peace proved elusive. By the spring of 1988, workers across Korea were again demanding significant wage increases. Again Hyundai, as a major heavy industry, was particularly hard hit. More than three thousand workers struck Hyundai Precision, seizing the company chairman and holding him for five days. Then, Hyundai Engine & Machinery was struck by two thousand workers.[31] At Hyundai Motor Company, twenty-thousand workers went out on strike and demanded a 48 percent pay raise. Hyundai responded with a plantwide lockout. After 26 days, the union president publicly apologized for the strike, and Hyundai agreed to a 28 percent pay raise but rejected the union's demand to be paid during the strike.[32] The strike cost HMC $500 million in lost sales of over 70,000 vehicles, including 40,000 for export to North America. The loss came at the worst possible time for HMC's efforts to ship new product to its U.S. markets. All told, the 1988 strikes were estimated to have cost Hyundai and its subcontractors over $1.2 billion.[33] It was the largest setback ever for any Korean company.

In contrast to the 1987 strikes, however, many of the 1988 conflicts were between various union factions. Some factions wanted to strike specifically to enhance pay and benefits; others had a larger political agenda. Some wanted to bring down the government or at least influence it to liberalize Korea's labor laws. During these conflicts, two workers committed suicide in separate incidents in Inchon and Kuro. The government seemed unprepared for the intensity of the turmoil. It continued to assume that both sides of any labor-management conflict would desire to return to a harmonious partnership as soon as possible. They failed to understand that for many labor leaders, harmony did not serve their political interests. They required continual conflict to achieve their political ends. Korean corporations served as a convenient target in this struggle. No matter how much companies offered, union leaders demanded more. Strikes continued into 1989, when both HHI and Hyundai Electrical Engineering were again struck by workers demanding 100 percent increases in their annual bonuses. With no compromise in sight, Hyundai responded by locking out 22,000 workers until they significantly reduced their demands.

THE NEW INDUSTRIAL ORDER

The industrial conflicts at Hyundai and elsewhere cost the Korean economy dearly. Results of the strikes led to major pay increases across broad segments of the work force. In 1987, the average pay increase in the industrial sector was 22 percent. This was followed in 1988 by an additional 15 percent average pay raise. Hence, in two years alone, national wage rates rose 37 percent, even before considering fringe benefits.[34] Within a three-year period, between 1987 and 1989, average hourly industrial wages in Korea rose from $1.59 to $3.71.[35] In 1991, South Korea gained full membership in the International Labor Organization (ILO). The number of strikes began to subside as wages and working conditions continued to improve.[36] Real wages on a national level were now increasing an average of 15 percent *per year*, well ahead of productivity increases.

Beyond the financial costs of the labor strife, social costs were also accruing. In particular, the rise in labor's power saw a concomitant decline in Confucian beliefs about the traditional role of one's employer. The psychological

TABLE 9-2

CHANGES IN WORK ATTITUDES AMONG KOREAN INDUSTRIAL WORKERS: 1979–1991

	1979	1991
Extent to which workers agree with supervisor's opinions	77%	41%
Extent to which workers will obey supervisor's directions	91	65
Extent to which workers view the company as a second family	94	59

Source: Adapted from Yoo-Keun Shin and Heung-Gook Kim, "Individualism and Collectivism in Korean Industry," in Gene Yoon and Sang-Chin Choi (Eds.), *Psychology of the Korean People: Collectivism and Individualism* (Seoul: Dong-A, 1994), pp. 189–208.

contract between employees and employers was changing. Evidence of this change can be seen in the increasing independence sought by workers from management and corporate directives, as shown in Table 9-2. Workers began transferring their allegiance from companies to the unions, as would be expected under such circumstances.

Strikes persisted intermittently at Hyundai. Some strikes again turned violent, and riot police were called in to reestablish order. In December 1991, a major strike erupted in HMC over management's refusal to give an extra month-and-a-half bonus on top of the six-month bonus already guaranteed the workers. When HMC argued that they could not afford an additional bonus because of lost revenues, workers balked. To some workers, the company's refusal was one more sign of its lack of respect for workers in general. Over 1,000 workers again seized the factory, chasing management out of the plant. Inside, they smashed 2,000 new cars, as well as factory computers and machines. Soon, close to 200,000 workers, including many working for Hyundai suppliers, were idled.

This time, however, Korean public sentiment turned against the strikers. Salaries of HMC workers, including bonuses, had increased dramatically over the past two years and now averaged $1,400 a month, well above the salary of the typical Korean worker. Moreover, the strike was jeopardizing exports and thus the national economy. The workers were being too selfish, many felt. In late January 1992, police were called in to clear the factory. Alerted before their arrival, and recognizing a lack of public sentiment, the strikers slipped away into the night. It was later discovered that only a small fraction of the HMC workers actually supported the strike; most stayed away from work for fear of union retaliation if they supported the company.

Strikes and slowdowns erupted again during the summer of 1993. This time, public reaction was even less supportive. Even Korea's new democratically elected president, Kim Young Sam, publicly criticized the strikers, saying they "have to realize that if they go to the extremes of selfishness, they will damage not only their firms but also the national economy, eventually doing harm to their own interests." Kim publicly wondered "if Hyundai workers are deep in egocentrism."[37] With an ailing economy, Korea could not afford a long strike. President Kim then followed the example of several U.S. presidents faced with similar crises. He simultaneously sent troops to surround the Hyundai factory and demanded that both sides reach an agreement within 48 hours. After long hours of bargaining, an agreement was finally reached, ending the 36-day strike. HMC workers would received a 5 percent pay raise, bonuses of 650 percent of monthly pay (up from 600 percent), a housing fund, and a guaranteed one-week paid vacation. When voted on by the union, the proposal passed with only a 1 percent margin. Other strikes erupted at HHI, Hyundai Precision, and Hyundai Pipe. Each conflict, however, seemed to bring both sides less satisfaction; no one was winning. By the end of 1993, much of the labor strife had subsided.

Out of the chaos and conflict, some felt that a new order was slowly emerging following the cathartic effects of the prolonged dispute. Both sides seemed to have learned something. Henceforth, Hyundai management would become more cognizant of union concerns. Working hours would be reduced, pay would be increased, and all workers would receive a six-month bonus. Workers would also receive time and one-half for overtime work. But perhaps most important, both sides learned that they needed each other. The time had come for management to accept workers and labor unions as an integral part of the Hyundai family and to listen to their opinions. The time had also come for unions to accept responsibility for corporate success. A new psychological contract had evolved to complement the new wage and benefits contracts.

Nationwide, both trade unions and corporations had come to the realization that the labor strife of the previous era had been detrimental to both corporate profits and employee welfare. Slowly, a fragile partnership began to develop between the opposing sides, and a new, albeit uneasy, labor-management consensus emerged.[38] In 1993, the Korean Employers' Confederation and the Federation of Korean Trade Unions for the first time reached an historic agreement limiting wage increases to between 4 and 9 percent. Again in 1994, the KEF and FKTU reached another agreement limiting wage increases to between 5 and 8 percent. Strike activity subsided dramatically (see Table 9-3). And Korea's notoriously long work week declined from a pre-strike average of around 2,800 hours per year to around 2,300 hours by 1994,

TABLE 9-3

UNION MEMBERSHIP, LABOR DISPUTES, AND PRODUCTION LOSS IN KOREA: 1987–1994

YEAR	NUMBER OF TRADE UNIONS	UNION MEMBERSHIP	NUMBER OF DISPUTES	WORK DAYS LOST	AVERAGE WAGE INCREASE	AVERAGE PRODUCTIVITY INCREASE
1987	2,658	1,036,000	3,749	6,947,000	10.1%	10.1%
1988	4,068	1,267,000	1,873	5,401,000	15.5	14.8
1989	6,142	1,707,000	1,616	6,351,000	21.1	7.6
1990	7,882	1,932,000	322	4,487,000	18.7	16.4
1991	7,698	1,887,000	234	3,258,000	17.5	16.3
1992	7,637	1,803,000	235	1,520,000	15.2	9.3
1993	7,527	1,667,000	144	1,308,000	12.2	8.3
1994	7,147	1,668,000	121	1,484,000	12.7	10.9

Source: Based on data supplied by the Economic Planning Board, Korean Ministry of Labor. Adapted from Gerardo R. Ungson, Richard M. Steers, and Seung-Ho Park, *Korean Enterprise: The Quest for Globalization* (Boston: Harvard Business School Press, 1997), p. 180.

with two weeks' paid vacation annually (see Figure 9-1). Although this was still high compared to other industrialized Asian nations, the Korean work force had come a long way toward true industrial democracy.

The new labor accords led to the signing of the 1995 Declaration for Industrial Peace, which called for sincere efforts by both sides to reach early wage settlements, avoid labor strikes, and reduce the wage gaps between large and small firms. Among the features included in this declaration were calls to increase both productivity and the quality of working life, eliminate unfair labor practices, increase dialog between management and labor, enhance job security, improve job training, and increase information sharing by both sides. This declaration was greeted with enthusiasm among diverse sectors of Korea's economy; within one month of its signing, over 1,500 companies and their workers had signed pacts of mutual cooperation. It was hoped that a new era of harmony had arrived on the labor scene.

After nearly two years of relative calm, however, a new problem arose as a result of the economic crisis that began in late 1997. As both financing and

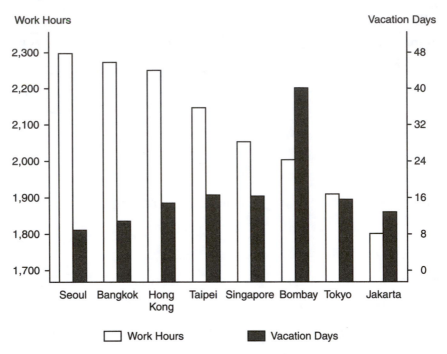

Figure 9-1   *Work Hours and Vacation Days in Eight Asian Cities: 1994*

Source: Based on data reported in "Among Cities, Seoul Residents Work Longer," *Korea Economic Weekly*, November 7, 1994, p. 2.

markets for their products evaporated overnight, many companies faced the choice of downsizing or bankruptcy. Pressures mounted on the government to rescind a decade-old prohibition against layoffs by companies that were still solvent. Companies argued that without the ability to lay off surplus workers, new bankruptcies would surely follow, thereby exacerbating an already difficult economic situation. Union leaders countered that widespread layoffs would have catastrophic results, because Korea had no safety net for displaced workers. Unions insisted that companies bear the brunt of the economic crisis. In February 1998, in return for corporate pledges to reorganize and streamline their business operations, as well as increase the transparency of their corporate finances, the government reluctantly changed the law to allow greater flexibility in worker layoffs. But neither side seemed happy with the compromise resolution. As both sides faced an increasingly uncertain economic future, the stage was set for possible future labor disputes.

CHAPTER 10

OLYMPIC PURSUITS

"If there is an economic need, politics will follow."

—CHUNG JU YUNG[1]

By the mid-1980s, Chung Ju Yung and his company had accomplished more than most successful entrepreneurs do in an entire lifetime. Hyundai had well over $10 billion in annual sales and was successfully engaged in a wide array of business enterprises. Perhaps most gratifying to Chung, Hyundai had climbed from nowhere to be ranked as Korea's number one firm (see Table 10-1). He had much to be proud of as he approached his seventieth birthday. But Chung was far from through. Retirement was out of the question; he remained a man of ideas and dreams.

Chung always saw his mission as building both his company and his country. Although Hyundai and Korea had made unrivaled economic progress by the mid-1980s, the country was politically isolated by a divided world and by Korea's unenviable role as a centerpiece in the Cold War. The Korean peninsula remained a hostile place, with frequent violent conflicts erupting along the DMZ and periodic terrorist attacks in downtown Seoul. Although most nations were sympathetic to the plight of South Korea, many, including Japan and much of Western Europe, shunned the country to avoid jeopardizing their political or economic relations with either the Soviet Union or mainland China. Though not overtly hostile toward South Korea, these nations keep a respectable distance for fear of alienating the Communist bloc.

As Chung considered this situation, he concluded that there might be a role for his own extensive business experience in helping to advance the diplomatic cause of his country. As Chung saw it, it was high time that South Korea be recognized for its accomplishments in the industrialized world. It

153

TABLE 10-1

RANKINGS OF KOREA'S MAJOR FIRMS: 1965–1985

RANK[a]	1965	1975	1985	AVERAGE ANNUAL GROWTH RATE, 1970–1985
1	Samsung	Samsung	**Hyundai**	**38%**
2	Samho	Lucky-Goldstar	Samsung	18
3	Lucky-Goldstar	**Hyundai**	Daewoo	54
4	Tai Han	Hanjin	Lucky-Goldstar	17
5	Gaipoong	Ssangyong	Ssangyong	17
6	Samyang	Sunkyong	Sunkyong	37
7	Ssangyong	Hanwha	Hanwha	12
8	Hwashin	Dainong	Hanjin	33
9	Panbon	Dong Ah	Kukje	19
10	Dongyang	Hanil	Daelim	32

[a]Rank based on total assets.

Source: Based on data presented in Byung-Nak Song, *The Rise of the Korean Economy* (Hong Kong, Oxford University Press, 1990); Eun Mee Kim, *Big Business, Strong State* (Albany, State University of New York Press, 1997); *Korea's Economy: 1997* (Washington, D.C.: Korea Economic Institute of America, 1997).

was also high time to seek a rapprochement with several of its hostile neighbors. Here was a chance—however remote—for Chung to make a diplomatic contribution to his nation, a chance for him to give something back. Chung embraced the opportunity with open arms and began a series of crusades that would help bring South Korea the international recognition and the opportunity for peace that it had desperately sought.

He set to work on four new and related challenges—all considered nearly impossible by friend and foe alike. First, he would play a leading role in bringing the 1988 Olympics to Seoul, against what many thought to be impossible odds. Then he would take the lead in opening up trade and political relations with Korea's former enemy, the Soviet Union. He would travel to the People's Republic of China—another enemy at the time—to begin discussions about a thaw in China's relations with South Korea. Finally, he would become the first Korean businessman to visit North Korea in an effort to build political and commercial ties that could eventually lead to a peaceful reconciliation between the warring halves of his country.

By the time he was through, Chung's diplomatic accomplishments would bring him public recognition from several corners of the world. He would extend Korea's political and diplomatic boundaries in ways that offered hope and promise to everyday Koreans. He would also make his own government quite anxious about a businessman who seemed to be gaining too much political clout. Even so, as he noted in his autobiography, his life would be full of many challenges, but he would not tolerate failures. Once he set his mind on a goal, little could dissuade him.

THE SEOUL OLYMPICS

By the 1980s, Korea had succeeded in becoming an export leader around the world. Now, it needed world recognition that it had truly become a member of the industrialized world. It had moved from the Third World to the First. Nothing accomplished this more than the 1988 Seoul Olympics. Hosting the Olympics erased many of the self-doubts Koreans had about who they were. They now constituted an important nation, worthy of international respect. Indeed, a 1988 headline in the *Korea Times* read: "Seoul Olympics Prove Koreans Can Accomplish Anything."[2] To some extent, it was true.

Planning for the Olympics was long in coming. Just before his death, President Park identified securing the Olympics as a national goal. In October 1979, just three weeks after Park's assassination, the mayor of Seoul reiterated this goal and formally announced that Seoul would bid for the 1988 Olympics. The response among the reporters at the press conference was mixed. Many government officials, including the all-powerful Economic Planning Board, opposed the bid. Korea was experiencing an economic downturn and it was well known that massive investments would be required to make the Games a success. Even the mayor had second thoughts when he realized the magnitude of the responsibility for successfully hosting such an event. After President Chun assumed power, he briefly considered canceling Seoul's bid but quickly realized that this might be interpreted as a sign of weakness—something the Korean government would never do. The bid had been set irretrievably in motion and would go forward.

The Korean government found itself in a serious dilemma. It had publicly made a bid for the Olympics. If it lost the bid to another country, like Japan, it would lose face. But if it won the bid, most officials now concluded that their country probably lacked the ability to deliver. Either way, Seoul would be embarrassed. At the first organizational meeting called by the government just four months prior to the site decision, only one government official and one low-ranking city employee attended. Many of the important players had strategically withdrawn so as not to jeopardize their own personal reputations by being associated with what many considered to be the coming debacle.

It was traditional for the city mayor to lead the campaign to host the Olympics. Seoul's mayor, however, quickly distanced himself from such efforts and instead publicly requested that a successful business leader like Chung Ju Yung, then chairman of FKI, lead the effort. Chung was trapped. He was soon appointed chairman of the Olympic Bidding Committee.[3] Now, *his* reputation would be on the line (see the timeline in Table 10-2).

In typical Korean fashion, the assumption was that by accepting the chairmanship of the committee, however unwillingly, Chung was agreeing to cover most of the costs of the venture out of his own pocket. The city of Seoul would save its money. But instead of viewing the campaign for the Olympics as a burden or an obligation, Chung saw it as a challenge. Here, finally, if only they could succeed, was an opportunity to showcase modern Korea, culturally as well as technologically. And Chung was determined to succeed. As one of the members of the Korean invitation committee later recalled: "Chung Ju Yung spent several million dollars, but he never wanted to profit from the Olympics. He just did it out of patriotism."[4]

At the outset, Chung identified several goals to guide his thinking. A successful Seoul Olympics would help foster peace in the region by bringing hostile neighbors together under the Olympic banner. It could create circumstances that would lead to new or improved diplomatic relations between South Korea and its neighbors. It might even further the cause of Korean reunification. The Olympics would also showcase both Korea's national economic development and its national strength to foreigners around the world. It represented an important step in being recognized among the world's leading nations. Finally, the Olympics would help to solidify a sense of Korea's national spirit among its people. After many years of living in poverty and obscurity, here was a chance to take pride in being Korean.

Chung also had a specific vision of how the Olympics could help reinvigorate Korea's stagnating economy. He drew up a development plan in his head that included constructing a new Olympic Village on the south side of the Han River. A new high-rise apartment complex would be built to house the athletes. Adjacent to the apartments would be a new Olympic stadium and other world-class sports facilities. After the Olympics, the apartments would be sold to pay for their construction and to help meet Seoul's chronic housing shortage; the sports complex would serve future generations of athletes. Local university sports centers also would be renovated in support of the Games.

TABLE 10-2

TIMELINE: THE SEOUL OLYMPICS AND BUSINESS ENDEAVORS
IN THE SOVIET UNION, CHINA, AND NORTH KOREA

DATE	EVENT
1981	Chung appointed to chair Korea's Bidding Committee for Seoul Olympics bid.
	International Olympic Committee selects Seoul for 1988 Olympics.
1988	Successful Olympics held in Seoul.
1989	Chung becomes first Korean businessman to travel to Soviet Union to meet political leaders.
	Chung becomes first Korean businessman to travel to North Korea to discuss closer ties and possible business ventures.
1990	Chung returns to Soviet Union.
	Chung becomes first Korean businessman to travel to China.
	Hyundai Resource Development Corporation established to sponsor ventures in Soviet Union.
	Svetlaya Company established to initiate wood products ventures with Russia.
	Hyundai opens offices in China.
1991	Hyundai opens offices in Moscow and Vladivostok.
1995	Hyundai Precision opens a container plant in China.
	Hyundai Electronics opens a semiconductor plant in Shanghai.
1997	Hyundai opens Vladivostok Business Center and Hotel in Russia.
1998	Chung Ju Yung receives the Olympic Order medal from the IOC at the 1998 Nagano Winter Olympics in recognition of his contributions to the Olympic games.

When the eighty-fourth session of the International Olympic Committee (IOC) met in Baden-Baden, Germany, in September 1981, the choice for the 1988 Games quickly narrowed to either Seoul or Nagoya, Japan. It was widely assumed prior to the meeting that Japan would walk away with the Games.

Korea still was seen as a relatively backward country, possibly incapable of successfully hosting such a major event. Even cosmopolitan Montreal had lost over $1 billion on its 1976 Games. Questions of personal safety in Korea were also on people's minds. What if the North Koreans used the occasion to invade the South or to send terrorists to disrupt the Games, as had happened at the 1972 Munich Games? Japan, by contrast, had proved itself to be one of the world's more accomplished organizers. It was also safe. The Japanese representatives to the meeting were so confident of success that they scheduled their victory banquet before the vote was even taken. Instead of selling the committee on the virtues of Nagoya, they spent much of their time disparaging Seoul—clearly a tactical error in any international gathering.

The Japanese representatives even tried to sabotage Korea's bid by secretly planting questions about Korea's ability to host the Games through Yuri Titov, the Soviet president of the International Gymnastics Federation and a supporter of Japan's bid. Specifically, Titov asked if Korea was sufficiently stable financially to host the Games given that the Koreans continued to receive massive capital infusions from other countries. Fortunately, Korea had included Yoo Chang Soon, the former deputy prime minister for economic planning, as one of the six Korean members of the invitation committee. Yoo was able to point out that such funds were intended for economic development and that many countries, including Japan, had received such funds. As one insider observed, "The answer was devastating to the Japanese, who were clearly exposed not only as having planted the question (which would probably never have occurred to the individual who posed it) but to have done so for the specific purpose of trying to embarrass the Koreans, rather than advancing the Japanese bid on its own merits."[5]

Despite such efforts, Chung and his colleagues developed what they believed to be a clear strategy for victory. Chung assumed command of the enterprise as though he were building the *Atlantic Baron* or Jubail Harbor all over again. He rented three stately houses in Baden-Baden to serve as a base of operations. Here they would live and work. The staff of Hyundai's Frankfurt office were pressed into the campaign. Five former Miss Koreas and a dozen Korea Air flight attendants also accompanied the entourage. Personal dossiers were compiled on each of the IOC delegates, and, over the next ten days, Chung met with each delegate. He personally lobbied representatives from less-developed nations to support one of their own, Korea. He then lobbied representatives from the developed nations to support an up-and-coming underdog—again, Korea. He emphasized to all that, because of the Korean government's effective long-range planning efforts, Seoul's facilities were already 60 percent complete, whereas Nagoya's plans were still on the drawing board. Throughout Chung's efforts, one theme was clear: not only could Korea masterfully organize and host the 1988 Olympics, but it was Korea's rightful turn. Japan, after all, had hosted the 1961 Olympics.

When the Japanese representatives presented expensive watches to all of the IOC members, Chung correctly concluded that such extravagant gifts might be seen by some delegates as an attempt to exert undue influence on the decision. Instead, he had fresh flowers delivered each morning to each IOC member's room, with a personal note of appreciation. The softer approach seemed to have the desired impact on the delegates.[6] Gradually, the tide turned toward Korea. When the final vote was taken, Seoul was selected by a sizable 52–27 vote margin. Chung jokingly referred to it as the "miracle of Baden-Baden."

The victory gave South Koreans a new national goal, one that would contribute to their national pride. The 1988 Olympics would be Korea's coming-out party, and it would be a memorable one. It would also coincide with President Chun's promise to step down as president following Korea's first truly open election, scheduled for 1987. To Chung, while winning the Games was important, so too was beating Japan.

Following the contract signing, North Korea's representative to the IOC proposed that the 1988 Olympics be shared between North and South Korea and called, simply, the Korean Olympics. Secret negotiations, led by IOC President Juan Samaranch, dragged on for several years as efforts were made to accommodate the North's demands. North Korea repeatedly pointed out that "Seoul is an insecure city where the danger of war is constantly lurking."[7] Sharing the Olympics would serve to ensure peace in the peninsula, they claimed. The IOC responded that they had already signed a legally binding contract with South Korea and that they had little room to maneuver. For its part, South Korea repeatedly offered the North a minor role in the Games, which the North refused for lack of parity. Chung, in particular, opposed joint sponsorship of the games after North Korea's murderous attack on South Korean government officials in Burma in October 1983. As he noted in a 1984 letter to IOC President Samaranch, just six months after the massacre, "It was not only a crime against compatriots who shared the same blood and all other peace loving peoples of the world, but also constituted a flagrant violation of the Olympic spirit, which pursues peace and the unity of all mankind."[8] Eventually, the North realized that intimidation would not accomplish their goal, and they withdrew from further negotiations and, instead, boycotted the Games.

Efforts then turned to making the Seoul Olympics the best Games ever. The Seoul Organizing Committee in charge of hosting the Games had a staff of over 900. It is estimated that Korea spent close to $6 billion on the facilities and related infrastructure.[9] Magnificent sports stadiums, athletic facilities, and housing all were constructed in record time. A new subway system was built, in large part by Hyundai. A major highway called the Olympic Expressway was also constructed, again by Hyundai. The Han River was cleaned up, and new parks were built along the riverfront. The south side of the river, or Kangnam, was opened to development and quickly became Seoul's most expensive high-status real estate.

The Chun government, never a popular one, was marked by intermittent student riots. As the Games approached, the Chun government determined to put its political house in order to match Korea's emerging economic status in the world. Following tumultuous negotiations and a chaotic national election, Major General Roh Tae Woo was elected president in what most outside observers considered a relatively fair and open process. Perhaps the final irony in this election was that the opposition candidates, who based their campaign on charges of antidemocratic government behavior, themselves lost the election in large measure because of their failure to learn the first lesson of democracy: compromise. The opposition candidates refused to cooperate, thereby splitting the vote and allowing Rho to emerge victorious with only one-third of the popular vote.

The opening of the Games under its first democratically elected government was a signal event for Koreans. Carrying the Olympic torch into the packed stadium on September 17, 1988, was the elderly Son Ki Jung, who, half a century earlier, had won the marathon in the 1936 Berlin Olympics. Then, he had been required to participate as a member of the Japanese team because of Korea's colonial status. Now he proudly sprinted across the track wearing Korean colors. Army commandos parachuted from the sky and landed to form the multicolor Olympic rings. Hundreds of taekwondo masters lined up on the field in formation and smashed boards in unison. The crowd roared its approval. The largest Olympics in history had begun. Over 150,000 visitors attended the Games. So did athletes from 161 countries, including China and the Soviet Union, both staunch enemies of South Korea at the time. Former communist foes were warmly welcomed by a new Korean government anxious to expand diplomatic ties. South Korea was now a power to be reckoned with.

EMERGING OPPORTUNITIES IN RUSSIA AND CHINA

In 1983, a Soviet fighter plane under orders from the Soviet high military command shot down Korean Air Lines flight #007, killing all 269 passengers and crew aboard. The Soviets accused the airliner of intentionally entering Soviet air space without permission and flying over Sakhalin Island, a high-security military base, to spy for the Americans. While not denying the plane

Chung Ju Yung meeting with U.S. President Ronald Reagan in the White House (1987).

Chung and his son, Chung Mong Joon, meeting with British Prime Minister Margaret Thatcher (1987).

Korean headlines celebrating the official opening of the 1988 Seoul Olympics. Headlines read: "Festival of Mankind Begins."

Opening ceremonies for 1988 Seoul Olympics.

Asan Medical Center, completed by Hyundai in 1989, is Korea's largest private hospital and medical research facility.

Chung Ju Yung standing in front of his birthplace in Asan village, North Korea, during his historic 1989 visit.

Chung's current home in the Chungwundong district of Seoul, built in 1958. (Photograph taken by the author in 1998.)

The living room of Chung's home, filled with oriental art and numerous books. Note the large picture of Chung's mother in the far corner. (Photograph taken by the author in 1998.)

Family breakfast in the Chung house usually began at 6:00 A.M.

Chung Ju Yung, shown here with several of his sons in 1992, walked to work for over thirty years.

Aerial view of Hyundai Heavy Industries in Ulsan, containing the world's largest shipyard. (Company-built employee apartments are shown in upper left.)

Weighing 45,000 tons, the *Exxon Harmony* offshore platform "jacket" is towed from Ulsan to its permanent location near Santa Barbara, California (1989).

Completion of a new Moss-type LNG carrier by Hyundai Heavy Industries (1993).

Display board at HHI reminding workers of the cost of each supply they use, including bolts, rubber gloves, adhesives, and lubricants. (Photograph shows author, left, with HHI executive vice president Park Seung Kyun.)

Hyundai Accents awaiting shipment to the U.S. from Hyundai Motor Company's Ulsan facility (1998).

Chung Ju Yung in traditional Korean dress at the ceremony of Confucian scholars (1991).

Chung Ju Yung on the campaign trail during his 1992 presidential campaign.

Chung waves his party's flag during a campaign appearance.

Hyundai's magnetic levitation (maglev) vehicle on display at the 1993 Taejon Expo, Korea.

Chung Ju Yung meeting with former Soviet president Mikhail Gorbachev in Moscow in 1994.

Chinese President Jiang Zemin during a 1995 visit to Hyundai's Ulsan industrial complex (Chung Ju Yung is standing second from left in back row, while his brother, Se Yung, is on the far right).

Honorary Chairman Chung at Hyundai's 1995 New Year's celebration dinner, Lotte Hotel, Seoul.

Singapore's Suntec City, completed in 1997 by Hyundai Engineering and Construction Company.

Chung Ju Yung receiving the Olympic Order medal from IOC President Juan Samaranch during the 1998 Nagano Olympics in Japan for his contributions to international athletic competition.

Chung Ju Yung, honorary chairman of Hyundai Group, poses for the crowd with a cow wearing a wreath at Imjingak, a pavilion near the DMZ, before entering the truce village of Panmunjom on June 16, 1998

Trucks carrying cows to be given to North Korea cross the Military Demarcation Line at Panmunjom on June 16, 1998.

crossed into Soviet territory, the Korean government claimed that the plane was off course as a result of a computer programming error. It was not the first time the Russians had forced down a South Korean plane. In April 1977, Soviet planes had forced another KAL airplane to land in a frozen lake bed deep inside Soviet territory. Then, too, the Soviets had accused the plane of being on a spy mission for the West. Since the end of the Korean War, South Korea and the Soviet Union had remained bitter ideological enemies; each used the other as a political sparring partner in an effort to maintain security and stability at home.

By the late 1980s, however, a thaw was occurring in Soviet-Korean relations. With the advent of the 1988 Seoul Olympics, South Korea was trying desperately to gain international recognition as a sovereign nation of global importance; it no longer wanted to be seen as U.S. pawn. At the same time, the Soviet Union was splintering into several independent republics, no longer under the tight control of a Communist regime in Moscow. With the loss of its eastern European allies, and with the fall of communism as an ideological and economic mantra, the faltering Soviet empire was seeking new directions and new friends. Both sides came early to the conclusion that they could help each other. For South Korea, security in a tinderbox area of the world was of central concern; for the new Russia, access to technical expertise was the principal goal.

Chung's interest in the Soviet Union was twofold. First, the area was rich in natural resources, including timber, oil, and minerals. Chung was convinced that with Korean technology and investment and Russian labor, Siberia could grow into a prosperous economic region from which Korea could obtain much needed resources for its own development. Second, the Soviet government had the potential to influence the pace of reunification talks with North Korea. After all, the Soviet Union had for decades been North Korea's staunchest supporter, politically and financially. Perhaps their influence could be used to further lasting peace in the region.

Always sensitive to new business opportunities, Chung clearly saw the Soviet Union as a potential bonanza in trade. In this endeavor, Hyundai could easily undersell the Japanese or any other foreign competitors in securing Russian business. Above all else, they knew how to compete. In the process, Hyundai would help develop mutually beneficial political ties between South Korea and Russia that would reinforce Korea's national security. In this, Chung saw himself as both a businessman and a statesman. Once again, the state and the company would share the same destiny.

In January 6, 1989, just four months after the Seoul Olympics, Chung became the first South Korean businessman to visit what was then still the Soviet Union. The invitation came from the chairman of the Soviet Union's

Chamber of Commerce and was aimed at initiating preliminary discussions concerning potential trade relations between the two nations. Chung's initial idea was to develop a $5 billion petrochemical facility in the Ural Mountains in western Siberia. Both partners would invest heavily in the venture. Rumors leaked out that the Soviet government had also asked Hyundai about other potential ventures. These included requests for cost estimates for an HMC-designed automobile assembly plant, three oil tankers and six bulk carriers from HHI, and a feasibility study for an oil pipeline running from Siberia across North Korea into South Korea. Business opportunities seemed to be everywhere, and Hyundai managers worked around the clock on feasibility studies and logistics. Indeed, their new Russian friends were amazed at the perseverance of Hyundai employees. One Soviet worker recruited to work for Hyundai commented that the Korean workers did not understand words like "no" or "impossible." "They never sleep."[10]

However, negotiations with the Russians proceeded very slowly. Chung thought to himself that "seventy years of communist thinking would pose great difficulties in understanding the market-driven approach to business operations."[11] Hyundai would have to be the teacher if progress was to be made. Even so, Chung remained committed to ultimate success. He returned to Moscow in 1990 and 1991 at the invitation of Mikhail Gorbachev to continue negotiations. He met personally with Gorbachev and several of his economic planners, and he officiated at the opening of corporate offices for the Hyundai Corporation, the company's trading arm, in both Moscow and Vladivostok. Hyundai also established a new Hyundai Resources Development Corporation that was specifically charged with securing Soviet business. Hyundai had staked its claim.

In his role as self-appointed trade ambassador for his government, Chung told the press that South Korea and Russia needed each other economically and that "if there is an economic need, politics will follow."[12] Soon, the Soviet and Korean governments would establish formal diplomatic ties and negotiate over $1 billion in long-term loans from Korea. As a senior news correspondent for the *Los Angeles Times* observed at the time, Chung had done more than anyone else to persuade Moscow to establish economic and political ties with Korea.[13] It was one more example of individuals accomplishing more than governments.

Chung's second visit to Moscow, in 1990, was followed by another coup. Chung would become the first South Korean businessman to visit Beijing, another former enemy. As in the situation with the Soviet Union, the Seoul Olympics provided entrée. At the time, China was actively seeking new technologies with which to expand its economic enterprises and was most impressed with what Korea had to offer. Toward this end, Chinese President

Jiang Zemin made a formal visit to South Korea, including an inspection tour of Hyundai Heavy Industries in Ulsan. For its part, South Korea saw China, like the Soviet Union, as a potential friend and trading partner. It was commonly believed that China's consumer market would ultimately become the largest in the world, and this represented an ideal opportunity to get in on the ground floor. Peaceful relations with China also might pay dividends in South Korea's quest for reunification with the North.

Chung received an invitation to visit Beijing directly from the Chinese government and arrived for his first visit in September 1990. During his visit, he emphasized the need for trilateral business ventures between China, Korea, and the Soviet Union. Proposals were discussed for $100 million in investments, including a steel mill and zinc and copper mines. Chung Se Yung also traveled to Beijing on behalf of Hyundai Motor Company to discuss possible alliances in the automobile industry. A short time later, Hyundai opened corporate offices in China's principal business centers, Beijing, Shanghai, Guangzhou, and Dalian. Hyundai would again be first to rise to an opportunity, and the Chinese government welcomed the new efforts. By August 1992, South Korea had normalized relations with China and severed its long-standing ties with Taiwan. Soon, several joint ventures with the Chinese opened for business, including a manufacturing plant for cargo containers with Hyundai Precision, a venture to produce naphtha with Hyundai Petrochemicals, and a fabrication plant for semiconductors with Hyundai Electronics Industries. Long-term business prospects looked good.

Meanwhile, trouble was brewing back in Moscow. The Soviet Union was entering a tumultuous period of economic and political transformation that would snare Hyundai for several years to come. The sudden breakup of the Soviet Union led to a major power shift in 1992. With no hard currency to pay its bills, Russia's new leaders simply refused to honor many of their former agreements, including several with Hyundai. Hyundai's oil and gas complex planned for western Siberia had to be postponed. Even so, other Russian ventures were explored, including a feasibility study for a possible joint Hyundai-Samsung-Daewoo consortium to help Russia develop a natural gas field in Yakutsk. But progress would be slow.

Then more troubles emerged. In 1990, Hyundai had signed a thirty-year joint-venture agreement with the Soviet government to harvest spruce trees in Siberia for export and processing in Japan and Korea. A new company, the Svetlaya Company, was formed to employ Russian and Chinese workers to harvest 437,000 cubic yards of trees annually, enough to fill seven barges. In Korea, the logs went to Hyundai Wood Industries Company to be made into office and home furniture under Hyundai's own brand name, LivArt. Plans called for Russia to invest $60 million to help Hyundai establish a processing plant in Siberia, but the Russians lacked the funds to initiate the venture. Under the new government, however, export duties were imposed on the trees destined for Japan and Korea, adding a considerable unexpected cost to the venture. Then, the government began limiting the size of the harvests to less than the agreed on quota. Local residents began complaining that too many trees were being cut, including some soft pine groves that provided habitat for the endangered Amur tiger that roamed the area. Finally, Russia's Supreme Court stepped in and suspended the logging operation altogether pending a formal investigation of the legality of the original agreement with the former Soviet authorities. The Svetlaya Company had to seek alternative sources of wood but was unable to match the quality or quantity found in the forests around Svetlaya. In the end, only 20 percent of their needs were being met, and much of Hyundai's state-of-the-art equipment sat idle for lack of raw materials. Hyundai would turn to Chile and New Zealand for the logs they required.

Time after time, Russian authorities refused to honor previous agreements. They always cited a lack of hard currency. A planned business complex in Vladivostok had to be delayed, as did plans for oil exploration in the southern region of Kalmyk and coal mine explorations in the Far East. Despite repeated disappointments and setbacks, however, Hyundai remained optimistic about the long-term future of Korean-Russian economic relations. To make their point, the company committed $97 million of their own money for the new hotel and business center in Vladivostok in 1995. This project was completed and officially opened by the eighty-one-year-old Chung Ju Yung himself during a visit in August 1997. Hyundai would not be deterred. If they could make money in the scorching desert sands of the Persian Gulf, they were determined to succeed in the frozen wastelands of Siberia, as well as elsewhere in Russia.

GOING HOME: NORTH KOREAN ODYSSEY

When Chung Ju Yung left Asan village for the last time in the late 1940s to build his fortune in the South, he had no idea that unforeseen circumstances would prevent him from returning for four decades. Asan village was located in what had become North Korea, and, like other Koreans separated from family members by the war, Chung could neither return nor even communicate with his relatives who were stranded in the North. All that was to change in 1989. The South Korean government used the Seoul Olympics to try to improve relations with the North. Although the effort failed to bring concrete results, a small opening had been achieved. Chung saw this brief thaw in North-South relations as an opportunity to play an instrumental role in helping to heal decades of mistrust and conflict and to lay the foundation for future reunification. This was a national cause worth risking everything for. With the coming demise of the Soviet Union, North Korea was losing its major trading partner—and financier—and was $10 billion in debt. It needed friends, and Chung felt his North Korean origins might give him the credibility needed to gain entry. To the north lay untapped resources and business opportunities, and Chung felt that Hyundai had the technical capabilities to exploit them. This was an opportunity not to be missed.

Three months after the successful Seoul Olympics, Chung was formally invited to visit North Korea to discuss trade and investment. The invitation came from Huh Dam, a ranking member of the politburo of the Workers' Party and chairman of the North Korean Committee for the Peaceful Reunification of the Fatherland. Both Chung and President Roh saw this as the opportunity they were waiting for, and the South Korean government, long opposed to its people traveling north, immediately approved the visit. The visit—the first by a South Korean dignitary since the end of the Korean War—was scheduled for January 23, 1989. Chung brought three Hyundai associates with him on the historic journey.

The trip from Seoul to Pyongyang would have taken about four hours by car, if driving were an option. It was not. Instead, Chung flew first from Seoul to Tokyo, then to Beijing, then finally to Pyongyang. In Beijing, he was met by several North Korean representatives who said they would personally escort him to Pyongyang. After several hours' delay, he was escorted onto a North Korean plane for the flight. He immediately observed that there were almost no other passengers on the plane other than the flight crew, a flight attendant, and his own party. Chung recalls being apprehensive that his North Korean hosts might not let him return to the South. It would be all too easy for the North simply to announce that Chung had decided to remain in his home village for the rest of his life. There would be little the South could do to rescue him. But Chung tried to convince himself that his new status as South Korea's unofficial liaison with the Soviet Union would provide him with some protection against kidnapping.

The plane lifted off from Beijing at 5:30 P.M. for the one-and-a-half-hour flight to Pyongyang. On arrival in Pyongyang, Chung was greeted by officials of the ruling party. In attendance also were about forty of his long-lost relatives from his hometown. It was apparent that all of them had been given new clothes just prior to his arrival; the women's clothes were all identical. Following a short welcoming ceremony, Chung and each of his aides were driven in separate Mercedes Benz limousines to their hotel.

Throughout Chung's visit, the official North Korean news agency provided extensive coverage and treated it as a major historical event. In fact, Chung's picture was splashed across the front pages of newspapers on both sides of the border. Chung spent the next ten days in the North, seeing the sights and meeting with various North Korean government officials. From the moment of his arrival, Chung set to work.

During his visit, Chung was offered the opportunity to return to his birthplace, Asan village. He was driven from Pyongyang to Asan, followed by several truckloads of gifts that he had brought from Seoul for his relatives. Over three hundred people greeted him as he entered Tongchon district. When he finally arrived in Asan, he was met by an official delegation headed by an elder cousin, along with about sixty relatives and many classmates from his elementary school. Chung would later observe that he had never heard of most of the "relatives."[14] Even so, everyone feasted on rice cakes and red wine, luxuries normally unavailable in the North. Chung distributed presents to his relatives and the local schoolchildren. The villagers reciprocated with gifts of wild honey and ginseng.

Chung spent two nights in Asan. Wherever he went, he was followed by over forty officials who ensured that none of the villagers could talk privately with him. He noted that his birthplace was still there: "Our house was a small straw house before, but they lifted the roof off and replaced it with tile. Otherwise, nothing had changed in fifty years....My sixth aunt was still living in our house. Late one night, I tried to talk with her about her life in the North. She quickly responded: "Don't ask anything, don't say anything. And leave early." When I tried to ask her why, she covered my mouth. We never talked again."[15]

Chung's government hosts provided him with a helicopter so he could survey the Tongchon region for possible tourism or industrial sites. People on both sides of the DMZ wanted to know what he thought about the prospects for development. After touring the area, Chung proposed to the North Korean government that Hyundai be given authority to develop Mount Keumkang (Diamond Mountain) into a major tourist attraction with a ski resort, a golf course, a luxury hotel, and several shopping areas. Much to the amazement of his hosts, Chung wrote out some cost estimates for the project on the spot. The development would give North Korea valued hard currency that could be used for economic development within the impoverished nation. Chung also believed, privately, that such a resort would bring an influx of tourists who would help introduce capitalist and democratic influences into this Communist-controlled land, thereby subtly opening up the country to closer ties with the South. Chung also proposed the development of several possible industrial plants, including a major ship repair facility and a rolling stock plant.

The North Korean government applauded Chung's plans, saying they would "strengthen cooperation between North and South and promote the peaceful reunification of the country," according to North Korea's Central News Agency.[16] In a news conference in Pyongyang, a jubilant Chung announced that he would seek South Korean government approval for the Keumkang venture and would return in the spring with a team of twenty surveyors and planners. As a token of his sincerity, Chung tried to make a gift of several million dollars worth of trucks, bulldozers, construction equipment, and cars to the North Koreans, but this effort was rebuffed by the North Korean government.

Chung returned to Seoul a hero. The influential newspaper *Hankook Ilbo* proclaimed that he "has brought back an ever-fresh hope to those desiring a thaw to South-North relations and free travel to and from the North."[17] According to the article, Chung had accomplished what neither government could have done "due mainly to their own political strategies."[18] The Diamond Mountain venture would allow tourists from the South to make sightseeing visits to the beautiful mountain retreat by ship or by bus. In addition to the tourism opportunities, the South Korean newspapers also praised Chung for opening possible trade agreements and joint ventures. *Hankook Ilbo* observed that his visit was "a big step toward opening doors for wide cooperative ties in economic and industrial fields for the first time in over four decades."[19] A new era in North-South relations seemed imminent. But it was not to be.

Almost immediately upon Chung's return, things began to come apart. First notice of this came when he returned from the North after only ten days of a planned sixteen-day itinerary. No reason was given for the early return. In addition, Chung was never allowed to meet with Kim Il Sung, even though he had announced before the trip that he would make a courtesy visit. Some observers suggested that Chung's ostentatious and imperious style— including bringing presents to his impoverished North Korean relatives— might have offended North Korean leaders. Others blamed the Team Spirit war games that were jointly conducted in South Korea by the U.S. and South Korean military shortly after Chung's visit. Still others blamed the fallout on Chung's reluctance to share Hyundai's lucrative new stake in Siberian timber projects with North Korea. Whatever the reason, Huh Dam, Chung's host for the visit, was soon purged, and Chung's historic visit was never again mentioned in the North. In the South, despite the much-ballyhooed triumph of diplomacy, government officials began arresting a string of South Korean religious leaders who visited North Korea in the year following Chung's visit. One by one, either the North or the South blocked each accord. South Korea refused to approve any investments by South Korean firms unless North Korea allowed for unlimited inspections of its alleged nuclear reprocessing facilities. North Korea refused and demanded that they be allowed to inspect U.S. military bases in the South for nuclear weapons. In the end, none of the agreements signed by Chung were allowed to be implemented.

Even so, it was a useful beginning, the kind that could be made only by someone with Chung Ju Yung's indomitable spirit. For three years, the two governments jockeyed for political advantage. During this time, North Korea's economy steadily worsened, as Russia and then China reduced their support for the Communist regime. Instead, both countries were racing against each other to form lucrative partnerships with North Korea's most bitter rival, South Korea. Eventually, the North Korean government was pushed beyond its breaking point. It had to try once again to establish contact with the South for economic survival. This time, in January 1992, it invited Daewoo Chairman Kim Woo-Choong to Pyongyang for discussions. Kim remained in the North for two weeks and was well received. Like Chung before him, Kim returned to Seoul amid an atmosphere of excitement and anticipation. "Trade with North Korea is much different from that with the Soviet Union, East Europe, or China," he noted. "It should be based on mutual understanding and cooperation."[20]

During the three years following Chung's visit, both North and South learned more about each other and both came to recognize that a potential opportunity was emerging that could easily be destroyed by continued political maneuvering. At the same time, both sides came to realize that Chung's plans for rapid industrialization through the development of heavy industry—the way Hyundai got its start—were probably too ambitious for the backward Communist North. A more modest effort, such as light industries, was more likely to succeed. Nine companies were proposed to produce such products as clothing, shoes, cotton yarn, and toys. These products required less capital investment than heavy industry and would be easier for the North Koreans to master. The products were also more consistent with North Korea's immediate needs.[21] The combination of South Korea's technology with North Korea's cheap labor seemed to be a winning one for both sides. One more small step had been taken toward building mutual trust.

In April 1992, the North Korean government invited 120 foreign technical experts and journalists—including 18 from South Korea—to visit a newly established free trade zone located in the far north near their border with Russia. This time, the South Korean government approved the visit. The North Korean hosts tried to portray their country as being open for business. But foreign visitors were shocked to see how primitive the port facilities and industrial complex were. The newly designated free port had actually been built by the Japanese in the 1930s, and the industrial complex had been built by the Russians in the 1950s. Rust was everywhere, and visitors saw little in the way of serious productive activity. It was all a show for Western eyes.

In July 1992, Kim Dal Hyon, reportedly a close relative of Kim Il Sung, made a historic one-week visit to South Korea. He visited numerous factories, including Hyundai Heavy Industries in Ulsan, and lobbied to secure South Korean government approval of the proposed light-industry venture. With tacit government approval, the new venture forged ahead in the North. Almost immediately, however, people began to question the value of trading with the North. North Korea's GNP in 1992 was estimated to be less than one-tenth that of the South and was actually shrinking in size.[22] Rumors circulated that the North was unable to pay for any foreign goods or services. There were clearly better business opportunities to pursue elsewhere. Hyundai's Chairman Chung was now advising colleagues to refrain from additional ventures in the North until the two troublesome issues of nuclear inspection and family reunion were satisfactorily settled. Trade was important, but not at the cost of national security. There would be a pause in the race for North Korea. Besides, as Chung predicted in 1996: "How can a society like that survive without coming to ruin? I think it [North Korea] will be in total ruins in three years."[23] In fact, it would occur even sooner.

As it turned out, the 1980s was a decade of diplomacy for Chung. In addition to beginning several new businesses, Chung managed to open promising dialogues with three former enemies. Two of these efforts led to tangible results in terms of establishing diplomatic relations and trade. Russia and China would soon emerge as two of South Korea's strongest trading partners. The third effort—to improve relations with North Korea—served at the very least to lay the foundation for future progress. Chung also led Korea's successful efforts to secure international recognition and respect by hosting the 1988 Olympic Games. These games have often been cited as one of the best-organized and most successful events in Olympic history. In all four of these signal efforts, Chung was motivated by patriotism, not profits. Indeed, none of these ventures served to enhance Hyundai's financial standing, and most cost him dearly. Rather, Chung saw himself as fulfilling his traditional responsibility to help build his country. He saw himself as a patriot. In this endeavor, he made effective use of his status and position to further Korea's national drive for global recognition, enhanced national security, and improved international relations. In doing so, he made a permanent change in the geopolitical map of the region.

PASSING THE TORCH

"Diligence will overcome all difficulties."

—Wall hanging in Chung Ju Yung's living room

To understand Chung Ju Yung, it is necessary to understand the role of the family in Korean culture. Although most Koreans work long hours, they remain devoted to their families. Families define who you are and where you belong in society. Above all, family members stick together and support one another, and Chung is no exception. From the outset, Chung viewed Hyundai as a family enterprise. He brought his brothers into the business when he was just getting started. When he married, his wife contributed to the enterprise. And when his children began growing up, it was assumed that they, too, would enter the business. Everyone had a role to play, and, although it was clear who was in charge, it was also clear that everyone would benefit.

ALL IN THE FAMILY

Chung Ju Yung had grown up with five brothers and one sister. In his own way, he would take care of all of them. Then, he would look to the next generation of Hyundai owners/managers. Oldest among Chung's siblings is Chung In Yung, born in 1920 (see Table 11-1). As noted earlier, brother In Yung began his career with Hyundai Construction, where he focused mainly on identifying business opportunities both at home and abroad. In 1962, while still working for the Hyundai Group, In Yung established his own company, Hyundai International, to manufacture plant machinery and equipment. By 1976, however, as Hyundai was beginning to enter the Middle East, he decided he wanted more independence from his older brother and left to set out on his own. He established the Halla Business Group, named for the tallest mountain on Cheju Island, and generated much of his income as a sub-contractor to Hyundai Motor Company. Halla specializes in automotive parts and industrial equipment but is also involved with cement, pulp and paper, shipbuilding, and shipping. It currently ranks as Korea's twelfth largest company, with 10,000 employees.[1] Unfortunately, Halla was one of the many companies trapped by Korea's economic crisis of 1997, but the company continues and observers are optimistic about its future. Today, In Yung is wheelchair-bound as a result of a stroke he suffered in 1989. His son Chung Mong-Won is currently chairman of the group. Still, the elder Chung continues to travel the world in search of new business for his company. "A businessman must live in the field," he notes. "Although it is uncomfortable to move around in a wheelchair, I feel at ease working in the field."[2]

Chung Soon Yung, born in 1922, began working for his oldest brother during the Korean War. He served for a time as vice president of Hyundai Construction. In 1969, however, Chung Ju Yung spun off Hyundai Cement from his construction company into a separate firm and installed his younger brother as president. With a ready customer in Hyundai Construction, Hyundai Cement continued to prosper, and in 1990 Soon Yung used it as the basis for establishing his own conglomerate, the Sungwoo Group. Today, Sungwoo is a widely diversified company involved in precision industry, construction, metal products, shipping, and electronics, in addition to its cement business.

Chung Hee Yung, Ju Yung's only sister, was born in 1925. She is married to Kim Yung Ju, president of Korea Flange. Mrs. Chung—Korean women retain their maiden names after marriage—remains an active participant in the family business, albeit somewhat in the background.

Chung Se Yung, born in 1928, is possibly the closest to Ju Yung and is certainly his most avid supporter. Thirteen years younger than the chairman, Se Yung is in many ways everything Ju Yung is not. He is easy-going, unassuming, approachable, and cool-headed. Thanks to financial support from Ju Yung, he is also highly educated, a graduate first of prestigious Korea University and also of Miami University in Oxford, Ohio, in 1957. His elder brother takes great pride in Se Yung's academic accomplishments, and Se Yung reciprocates by supporting his brother's decisions without question. Early on, Se Yung was given control over Hyundai's automobile business, and he has dedicated his life to making Hyundai Motors one of the largest and best car manufacturers in the world.

Most unfortunate among Chung Ju Yung's siblings was Shin Yung, the fifth brother in the clan. Born in 1931, Shin Yung was graduated with honors in law from Seoul National University but spurned a business career in favor of the life of a reporter, working for *Dong-A Ilbo (East Asia Daily)*, one of Korea's leading newspapers. He later moved to Hamburg, Germany, to pursue a doctoral

TABLE 11-1

THE CHUNG FAMILY

NAME	DATE OF BIRTH	RELATIONSHIP TO CHUNG JU YUNG	CURRENT POSITION
Chung In Yung	1920	Brother	Honorary chairman, Halla Group
Chung Soon Yung	1922	Brother	Honorary chairman, Sungwoo Group
Chung Hee Yung	1925	Sister	Married to Kim Yung Ju, chairman, Korea Flange
Chung Se Yung	1928	Brother	Honorary chairman, Hyundai Motor Company
Chung Shin Yung	1931	Brother	Former journalist; died in 1962
Chung Sang Yung	1936	Brother	Chairman, KCC Group
Chung Mong Pil	1936	Son	Former president, Inchon Iron & Steel; died in 1982
Chung Mong Koo	1938	Son	Chairman, Hyundai Motor Service, Hyundai Precision & Industry, Hyundai Industrial Development, and Inchon Iron & Steel
Chung Mong Keun	1942	Son	Chairman, Keumkang Development Industrial Company
Chung Kyung Hee	1944	Daughter	Married to Chung Hee Yung, president, Seonjin Shipping
Chung Mong Woo	1945	Son	Former chairman, Hyundai Aluminum; died in 1990
Chung Mong Hun	1948	Son	Chairman, Hyundai Electronic Industries, Hyundai Engineering & Construction, Hyundai Corporation, and Hyundai Engineering
Chung Mong Joon	1951	Son	Former chairman, Hyundai Heavy Industries; currently a member of Korea's National Assembly
Chung Mong Yun	1955	Son	Chairman, Hyundai Financial Service

NAME	DATE OF BIRTH	RELATIONSHIP TO CHUNG JU YUNG	CURRENT POSITION
Chung Mong Il	1959	Son	Chairman, Hyundai International Merchant Bank
Chung Mong Hyuk	1961	Nephew	President, Hyundai Petrochemical Company and Hyundai Oil Refinery
Chung Mong Kyu	1962	Nephew	Chairman, Hyundai Motor Company

degree in economics. There he suffered a ruptured spleen and died unexpectedly in 1962. It was a sad and ironic end for a bright young man whose middle name (Yung), shared by all of his brothers, means "forever" in Korean. Following Confucian tradition and family obligation, eldest brother Chung Ju Yung immediately took Shin Yung's young son, Chung Mong Hyuk, under his wing and treated him as his own son. In memory of his younger brother, he established the Shin Yung Foundation, which supports Korean journalists conducting research abroad. In times of peril as well as prosperity, the family came first.

Youngest brother Sang Yung, born in 1936, grew up to attend Dongkuk University, a well-established Buddhist institution. Ironically, he was born in the same year as Chung Ju Yung's oldest son, and the two attended university together. Upon graduation, Sang Yung joined Hyundai, where he worked his way up to become a senior vice president of HMC. Later, he would be appointed president of Korea Chemical and would use this company to begin his own business group, called the KCC Group, which is involved in chemicals, construction, and the leisure industry.

THE HONORARY CHAIRMAN

In February 1987, at the age of seventy-two, Chung Ju Yung announced that he would officially step down as chairman of the Hyundai Business Group. He would retire and assume the title of "honorary chairman." Chung Se Yung, his brother and long-time chairman of Hyundai Motor Company, was selected to replace him as group chairman. It had been a long road for Chung, from his early days in the late 1940s starting the Hyundai Construction Company to the creation of one of the world's largest conglomerates. By any measure, his lifelong dream had become a reality. Now a billionaire several times over, Chung could at last retire in peace. In addition to wealth, he had also earned the respect of a nation and had created a family dynasty to continue the company he had built with so much of his own sweat.

To those who knew him, however, it was clear that the new honorary chairman had no intention of retiring. He was just changing titles. Indeed, he had a full agenda of new plans and challenges he intended to pursue. In many ways, his retirement was a sign that he had just begun. He would not actually retire from the day-to-day operations of the firm until 1991, when he was seventy-six.

When Se Yung assumed the chairmanship of the Hyundai group in 1987, at the age of fifty-nine, it was clear that he was only standing in until one of the founder's sons was ready to assume control. Even so, Se Yung proved himself to be a very able administrator in his own right. Se Yung had run Hyundai Motor Company since 1967 and had grown the company into a major global player in automobiles. Compared to the outspoken and hard-driving founder, Se Yung was more reflective in style. He frequently describes himself as more of a "listener" and a "committeeman" than his elder brother. At times, he even seemed uncomfortable in his new position. Well into his group chairmanship, he continued to use business cards that listed him as chairman of Hyundai Motor Company.[3]

Se Yung continually praised his eldest brother for his leadership, ingenuity, and hard work. Referring to Ju Yung, he noted, "He says a man who claims he does not have time to do something is a lazy man." Thinking for a moment, Se Yung then continued, "I must be lazier than him."[4] Throughout his chairmanship, Se Yung prided himself on his connections in the United States. Unlike his elder brother, Se Yung is fluent in English and relishes talking with visitors from English-speaking countries. He once observed that when he ran HMC, "I bought tires, glass, and carpets from America. If I were not educated in the U.S., I wouldn't have thought about it."[5]

UNDER NEW MANAGEMENT

Confucian filial piety required Chung Ju Yung, as the eldest son, to oversee the welfare of his parents, his brothers and sisters, and his children. This he did. As long as his parents lived, he supported them. He also looked after his brothers and sisters and their children. But nowhere does his sense of responsibility show more clearly than in his support for his children. In all, he had eight sons and one daughter (see Table 11-1 on pages 172–173). All of Chung's sons (and nephews) shared the same middle name, Mong, Korean for "dream." In a sense, it was the living trademark of the firm.

Chung Mong Pil, Chung's eldest son, was born in 1936 to obviously proud parents. After Dongkuk University, Mong Pil began training to assume con-

trol eventually over the entire Hyundai empire. He served for a time in a
small metals subsidiary but was soon made president of Inchon Iron and
Steel. Hyundai had acquired this small, unprofitable steel mill from President
Park's government in 1978 as a consolation prize when Park refused to allow
Hyundai to build a massive new integrated steel mill. Instead, Park wanted
government-owned Pohang Iron and Steel (POSCO) to control state-of-the-
art steel manufacturing in Korea. By all accounts, Mong Pil worked hard to
get the money-losing mill into the black. Hyundai saw Inchon Iron and Steel
as a first step toward becoming a world-class player in this important industry.
Soon, however, tragedy would intervene. In April 1982, Mong Pil and his
chauffeur left Ulsan late one night for the long drive back to Seoul. En route,
their car was struck by a truck on the Kyungbu Expressway—built by
Hyundai twelve years earlier—and both passengers were killed instantly.
Several years later, Mong Pil's wife died of cancer, leaving two young daughters, who were raised in the house next to the chairman's.

The second son, Chung Mong Koo, was born in 1938. After graduating
from Hanyang University with a degree in industrial management, he joined
Hyundai Construction. In 1974, Mong Koo was appointed president and later
chairman of Hyundai Motor Service Company, the principal distributor for
Hyundai cars in Korea. By 1992, he had acquired five additional chairman-
ships, including Hyundai Precision and Industry, Hyundai Pipe, Inchon Iron
and Steel, Hyundai Housing and Industrial Development, and Hyundai
Construction Equipment Industrial Company. These five companies were
referred to as the MK Group. Mong Koo is credited with establishing
Hyundai Pipe and Hyundai Precision and building them into two of the
group's most successful firms. Hyundai Pipe soon became Korea's largest
pipe manufacturer; Hyundai Precision introduced Korea's best-selling four-
wheel-drive vehicle, the Mitsubishi-designed Galloper. Hyundai Precision
also became the world's largest producer of cargo containers and, in addition,
built trains, tanks, and even a few helicopters under license from Kawasaki
Heavy Industries. In 1993, under the leadership of Mong Koo, Hyundai Precision reached an agreement to become the lead Korean manufacturer of the
French-designed *Train a Grande Vitesse* (TGV), the speed train the government planned to build between Seoul and Pusan.

In January 1996, Mong Koo was appointed group chairman for the
Hyundai Business Group to replace the retiring Chung Se Yung. When interviewed in April 1997, he pointed out that he intended to follow his father's
precepts for running the company. Hyundai would strive to be the best in
whatever venture it pursued.[6]

Like all of Chung Ju Yung's children, Mong Koo also understands the
importance of public service. Indeed, his father insisted that all of his sons

become actively involved in public affairs. Mong Koo currently serves as vice chairman of the Federation of Korean Industries, where his father served earlier, and is also chairman of the Korea-Russian Economic Association, honorary president of the Korean Archery Association, and honorary chairman of the Asian Archery Association.

Third son Chung Mong Keun was born in 1942. Like his older brother, he attended Hanyang University, where he majored in civil engineering. Also like his brother, Mong Keun joined Hyundai Construction after graduation. By 1974, he was ready for his first executive assignment and was appointed president of Keumkang Development Company. Keumkang runs three top-of-the-line department stores in some of the trendiest areas of Seoul, as well as several other stores throughout Korea. In 1992, Keumkang opened a five-star hotel, Hyundai Hotel, in the ancient Silla capital of Kyongju, north of Ulsan. The hotel's ambiance and location overlooking a lush green valley frequently attracted members of the Chung family, referred to behind their backs as the "royal family."

Chung Kyung Hee, Chung's only daughter, was born in 1944. She was graduated from the prestigious Ewha Women's University in Seoul, where she majored in art. She is married to Chung Hee Yung, president of Seonjin Shipping Company, and has one son and two daughters. Like her mother, Kyung Hee is active in numerous charities throughout Korea.

Chung's fourth son, Mong Woo, was born in 1945. After his graduation from Chungang University in economics, Mong Woo joined Hyundai Construction and later moved to Hankook Pavement. His performance as a manager was solid, but he had never been tested under pressure. In 1987, Mong Woo got his chance when he was appointed chairman of Hyundai Aluminum. This was a small company, but it offered him a chance to prove himself at the executive level. Mong Woo set about his new assignment with enthusiasm, but pressures on him mounted. He continually worried that he would not measure up in the competitive world of business. Subject to bouts of depression, Mong Woo was soon over his head and had to be removed in 1989. He was replaced temporarily by his younger brother, Mong Il. A short time later, in April 1990, Mong Woo committed suicide by taking an overdose of pills.

The fifth son, Chung Mong Hun, was born in 1948. He was graduated from Yonsei with a major in Korean literature and then earned an MBA from Yonsei University. To gain overseas experience, Mong Hun then enrolled in Fairleigh Dickinson University in New Jersey, where he earned a second MBA in 1983. Soon after, he was appointed president of both Hyundai Electronics Industries and Hyundai Merchant Marine. In 1992, he was promoted to chairman of HEI. In 1996, he became vice chairman of the Hyundai Business Group, as well as chairman of Hyundai Engineering and Construction

Hyundai Engineering, and Diamond Ad, one of Korea's largest advertising firms. In 1997, he added another chairmanship to his portfolio, Hyundai Corporation. He is also the owner of Hyundai's professional baseball team, the Unicorns. Recently, as a result of a 1998 reorganization, Mong Hun was appointed co-chairman of the Hyundai Business Group. He and brother Mong Koo divided the business group into two spheres so the progress of the fifty-odd subsidiary companies could be monitored more closely. Mong Hun was given principal responsibility for exports, overseas construction, and overseas investments.

Chung's sixth son chose a different path from the others. Born in 1951, Chung Mong Joon studied economics at the prestigious Seoul National University before going to MIT to receive a master's degree in business from the Sloan School of Management in 1980. He then returned to work for Hyundai Heavy Industries. In 1982, he was appointed president of HHI. In this capacity, "MJ," as he is popularly known, wrote what became a signal policy piece for the company, entitled "Status of the Korean Shipbuilding Industry." In his report, he argued persuasively that the government should support industry-led economic development efforts, not the other way around. "Industrial policy is a process for making industry more adaptable and dynamic," he argued. "What is required for successful industrial policy, whether for automobiles, shipbuilding or whatever, is coordination and integration of government programs and policies and careful analysis of world market trends and sources of competitive advantage, rather than the pin-pointing of an industry as a 'winning' industry by government."[7] He was appointed chairman of HHI in 1987, only to leave in 1989 to run successfully for the National Assembly. MJ also ran his father's unsuccessful bid for the presidency of Korea (see chapter 12). Later, he returned to Johns Hopkins University, to complete a Ph.D. in economics in 1993. Today, he is enjoying his third term as an elected member of the National Assembly.

In 1996, MJ led the committee that successfully secured Korea as the co-host for the 2002 World Cup Soccer Championships. This was not unlike what his father had done earlier for the Seoul Olympics. Reportedly, his father was pleased that Korea would again host a major world sporting event but was unhappy about having to share these honors with Japan.[8] MJ currently serves as chairman of the Korean Football Association. Unlike his other brothers, MJ seems well suited for the life of a public servant. Indeed, he is sometimes referred to as the scholar of the family. Rumors abound that MJ may be a candidate for the Korean presidency in the future; perhaps he will win where his father could not.[9]

Chung Mong Yun, Chung's seventh son, was born in 1955 and attended the University of Oregon for three years before returning to Korea to be married. Following the wedding, Mong Yun transferred to San Francisco State

University and completed both his bachelor's degree in business in 1984 and his MBA in 1985. Returning to Korea, he was soon appointed senior vice president of Hyundai Marine and Fire Insurance Company. In 1988, he became company president. In 1996, he was appointed chairman of Hyundai Financial Service Company.

Chung's youngest son, Mong Il, was born in 1959. He was graduated in business from Yonsei University in 1982 and received an MBA from George Washington University in 1989. Mong Il joined Hyundai International Merchant Bank and rose through the ranks to become president in 1994.

From an early age, Chung demanded excellence from all of his sons. As Phillip Grub, a long-time American friend of Chung, notes, "He felt a responsibility for himself and his immediate family."[10] It was clear from the beginning that Chung was determined that his sons would take charge of Hyundai after his retirement. In contrast to Samsung, where the founder forced his two eldest sons out of the way and chose his third son to run the company, or Daewoo, where the founder decided that none of his children would be allowed to enter the business, Chung wanted to create a family dynasty in the Confucian tradition. Throughout, he was a hard taskmaster—instructing, correcting, nurturing, and sometimes lambasting his children. Under this harsh guidance, however, they grew and learned the business. As Grub observes, Chung "demands so much of his children. They respect the old man. They're afraid of him. He expects highest performance and highest everything."[11] Looking back, Grub considers Chung to be "a great man," although he was not sure he could survive actually working for him.[12]

It is interesting to note here that, despite his strong Confucian beliefs concerning business matters, Chung never interfered in the marriages of his sons and daughter. Traditionally, Korean parents play a dominant role in selecting wives and husbands for their children. Indeed, using the marriage of a son or daughter to solidify a business alliance remains a common practice to this day, even among some of Korea's most illustrious business families. Not so with Chung. "Chairman Chung did not make his children marry famous people," noted a long-time aide, Lee Byung Kyu.[13] "He is one of the most modern people. His way of thinking is very reasonable. All of his children married without his introduction." In a country where most marriages are still arranged under parental guidance, and where many brides and grooms have met their future spouses only two or three times prior to the marriage ceremony, Chung again stands out as a paradox. He controlled his businesses very tightly. He controlled his children very tightly. Yet he did not interfere in his children's personal lives. The choice of a spouse had to be their decision, not his. Such behavior would likely be applauded by many sons and daughters—as well as sons-in-law and daughters-in-law—in the West.

In addition to his sons and daughter and his brothers and sister, Chung also looked after two nephews. Under Chung Ju Yung's guidance, Chung Mong Hyuk, deceased brother Shin Yung's only son, pursued a successful career within the Hyundai group. For many years, the Chung family and its relatives had owned a 50 percent share in the Kukdong Oil Company, a small oil-refining firm. Following an unsuccessful takeover bid by British Petroleum in 1988, Hyundai moved to assume tighter financial control over Kukdong. In a joint partnership with Kukdong, Hyundai created Hyundai Petrochemical Company. Plans were drawn up to develop one of Korea's foremost petro-chemical facilities adjacent to Kukdong Oil at Taesan, on Korea's west coast just north of Chung's beloved Seosan farm. By 1993, over $3 billion had been invested in the project, including the construction of a new naphtha-cracking plant and a hydro-cracking plant. Also in 1993, Hyundai completed its takeover of Kukdong and renamed it Hyundai Oil Refinery Company. In 1994, a $1.25 billion expansion of the refinery began, and service stations across Korea began sprouting up with Hyundai's Oilbank brand name.

Chung Mong Hyuk, a 1989 UCLA graduate, was appointed senior vice president of Hyundai Petrochemical in October 1991. The following year, he traveled to Beijing to convince the Chinese government to sell naphtha to Hyundai for its cracking plant. In return, the Chinese agreed to purchase naphtha products from the company. This opened a new market for Hyundai, while at the same time relieving them of exclusive reliance on Kuwait and Saudi Arabia for raw materials. Today, he is president of Hyundai Petrochem-ical, which currently boasts annual sales of $700 million and is actively expanding overseas. In 1996, he was also made president of Hyundai Oil Refinery Company. Discussing future plans, he recently noted: "We will make Asia a stronghold of our offshore production. Our strategy calls for pursuing joint ventures or technology transfers of manufacturing technologies in the field of general chemicals to China and Southeast Asian countries."[14]

Chung's other nephew who remains active in the Group is Chung Mong Kyu, son of HMC (and later Group) Chairman Chung Se Yung. Mong Kyu attended Korea University, like his father, and then went on for graduate studies at Oxford University in England before returning to work for his father at HMC in 1988. Clearly his father's protégé at HMC, Mong Kyu today is making his mark as the new chairman of Hyundai Motor Company.

AT HOME WITH CHAIRMAN CHUNG

Since 1958, Chung Ju Yung and his wife have lived in a simple two-story, seven-room house built from surplus construction materials on a hill in the Chungwundong district of Seoul, near the ancient Kyongbok Palace. Though large by Korean standards, the 3,000-square-foot house is modest in comparison to those of other Korean entrepreneurs and would be considered solidly middle class in the United States. Visitors are struck by its simplicity and warmth; this is a house for living, not entertaining. Indeed, many visitors have difficulty remembering that this is the home of one of the world's wealthiest families.

Guests enter the Chung home through a simple sliding glass door opening into a large entry room that doubles as a dining room. The family dining table stands in the center of the room in front of a door leading to the kitchen. To the right is a small sewing room, used by Chung's wife. To the left is a sizable living room that comfortably seats a dozen people on two sets of well-worn sofas and chairs resting on a plain carpet. The living room serves as the principal family meeting place. Behind Chung's favorite chair is a painting of his mother and several photographs of his family. Books on topics ranging from art to philosophy to business line bookshelves along most of two walls. A piano sits prominently against one wall. Beautifully painted vases and other pieces of Asian art are scattered around the room. The walls are hung with several classical Korean paintings and two framed verses painted in traditional Chinese calligraphy. The first verse, which translates as "Simplicity, Integrity, Diligence," was painted by Park Chung Hee as a present for Chung. The second wall hanging was painted by Chung himself and is reportedly his favorite Confucian verse. It says simply, "Diligence will overcome all difficulties," and sums up the fundamental philosophy of both Chairman Chung and his wife. Upstairs is a small bedroom for the parents and one large bedroom for all of the children.

Despite Korea's hot, humid summers, the house has no central air conditioning but relies on several wall cooling units strategically placed throughout the house. Outside on the lawn, several dogs and numerous chickens roam free. The house manager notes that the chickens just showed up one day and decided to remain. That suited Chung fine.

While he remained active in the company, Chung rose every morning at 4:00 A.M. without fail. He immediately set about his morning exercises using some old equipment crammed into a small upstairs room. He then dressed for work and read a variety of newspapers and company reports delivered by his dutiful staff. Information—facts and figures—was always important to Chung. With enough information, he could get ahead of the competition. Throughout his career, he was known to be a stickler for details and demanded that his staff be able to defend every estimate or expenditure they made. At times, he also would receive visitors in these early hours before he became distracted by the numerous activities of the day. Chung also used this time to receive phone calls from project managers in local and overseas branches. Every detail was important to Chung. Supervisors who oversaw projects that were of keen interest to him, like his Seosan rice farm, were instructed to phone the chairman every morning at a certain time to report. In this way, he kept in daily contact with all of the pressing issues in his business empire around the world. It was also an ideal time for him to call people in Seoul to issue instructions; at 4:30 or 5:00 in the morning, he knew where they would be.

At 6:00 A.M., Chung's sons and their wives would arrive for a traditional breakfast of soup, rice, and fresh fruit. Chung never drank coffee or tea, and he considered smoking a waste of money. Typically, the sons and father would discuss recent developments in the business, while the wives met in the adjacent room to discuss family issues. Chung taught his sons never to arrive late; promptness was important. Each son understood that if he was tardy for breakfast, his father would instruct him to move his family into one of five small houses Chung owned near his own. There he would remain for a year under the protective eye of his father. No one was ever late.

At 7:00 sharp, Chung would gather his sons and lead them out of the house. They would then silently walk the two and one-half miles to the Hyundai headquarters building at 140-2 Kye-dong in downtown Seoul. This was a ritual Chung followed for nearly thirty years, until his retirement from the firm in 1991. Ritual, routine, and ceremony were important to this leader.

Even in his eighties, long after his formal retirement from the group, Chung would arrive in his office promptly at 7:00 each morning to conduct business for about three hours before returning home. Now, however, he takes his car and spends his afternoons following his own schedule, which includes golf, tennis, reading, and travel. He also enjoys watching television, a pleasure he never had time for throughout his busy career. His favorite program? "I like to watch the news," he responds.[15]

Throughout Chung's long career, his wife, Byun Joong Suk, remained by his side. While Chung concentrated on business, Byun took care of his family and raised the children. Chung was very strict with his children. He gave them a very small allowance, which his wife would frequently secretly supplement. He would not allow them to be driven to school in family cars; they had to use the bus like everyone else. "Only if one experiences the inconvenience of a jam-packed bus when young will one be able to feel the happiness of riding in an automobile bought with one's own efforts."[16] He continually reminded them of the importance of being frugal and working hard. And, until they entered the company, Chung's business obligations made it difficult to spend much time with his children except at breakfast. For balance, Byun provided a softer side. As she noted in an interview: "The Chairman always came home late. Therefore, the sole responsibility for the children was mine. I was soft to my children as a counterbalance for the Chairman's being strict and strong. The hardest time was when they were preparing for university entrance examinations—I went through it nine times."[17]

Throughout her life, Byun eschewed money and property. She lived frugally on a small allowance to run the house, but even out of this she managed to save money to buy presents for her children and daughters-in-law. Until her recent illness, she did her own shopping at a wholesale grocery store. She seldom used the car her husband provided for her. She was also a regular contributor to various charities. Her husband used to say that she would spend all of her money on others if allowed, "even if I gave you several million won a day."[18] "That's true," she responded, "He doesn't trust me with money."[19] Byun's simplicity leaves no room for jewelry, not even a watch. Her daughters-in-law wear no makeup when they come for visits out of respect for her simple style of living. She sews *han-boks* (traditional Korean costumes) in her spare time. Indeed, her Korean War-vintage sewing machine is a prized possession. Like her husband, Byun Joong Suk sets an example for frugality and simplicity wherever she goes.

One night many years ago, two thieves broke into the house. They entered Byun's room, tied her up, put a quilt over her head, and demanded that she give them all of her valuables. Byun calmly threw off the quilt and said: "You seem to know whose house you are breaking into. I am not going to make any noise so let's talk and try and find a compromise." On hearing this, the thieves became less agitated. She then gave them a watch that she had intended to give to her son for his wedding and a small amount of cash that she had saved. The thieves looked at their paltry take and demanded to see all of the U.S. dollars she had hidden away. They also demanded to see the golden rice bowls they believed she had. Byun calmly replied that she had never seen any dollars in the house and that she knew of no one in Korea who ate out of golden rice bowls. Frustrated, the thieves left. After their departure, Byun calmly went into the next room and awakened her husband. She had concealed his presence in the house and had probably saved his life.

One of Byun's fondest memories of her long married life with Chung dates back to when they were young. She and her husband had packed a lunch for a day trip to the Han River. Chung rented a boat for a short ride but was so clumsy in rowing that the boat capsized and both of them were thrown into the river and nearly drowned. Looking back on the incident, she wondered how a person who couldn't manage a rowboat could build the world's largest shipyard.[20]

INTO THE POLITICAL MAELSTROM

"He [Chung Ju Yung] considered it to be his sacred duty to use his energies to bring about political and economic reform."

—PARK SE YONG, PRESIDENT, HYUNDAI CORPORATION[1]

When President Roh Tae Woo assumed the reins of command from Chun Doo Hwan in early 1988, the Korean economy was booming. The success of the Seoul Olympics had put South Korea on the geopolitical map, not as one of many Asian tigers but as *the* Asian tiger. Alice Amsden's influential 1989 book on the Korean economic miracle was entitled, simply, *Asia's Next Giant*.[2] Korea was clearly on the road to becoming the next Japan. It was now enjoying a trade surplus for the first time in its existence, and it was rapidly building both political and economic ties with several countries formerly considered its worst enemies, notably China and the Soviet Union.

Despite such unbridled economic success, or perhaps because of it, President Roh soon hit Korean companies in 1989 with three back-to-back policy shifts that immediately changed the rules of doing business in Korea (see the timeline in Table 12-1). Roh was determined to make his mark as Korea's new president, and to do so he assumed what many considered to be a largely antibusiness posture. He would be the president for the common people. Roh's first policy change focused on government subsidies to companies that conducted business overseas, a mainstay of both President Park's and Chun's economic development strategies. Because of Korea's recent economic success, Roh concluded that it was no longer necessary for the government to continue to provide these subsidies to companies. Henceforth, they should seek their own capital for overseas ventures, at significantly higher interest rates. Needless to say, this was not a popular move among Korea's business leaders.

TABLE 12-1

TIMELINE: POLITICAL TRIALS AND TRIBULATIONS

DATE	EVENT
1989	President Roh Tae Woo begins campaign to curb power of Korean companies.
1991	Chung Ju Yung speaks out against the excesses of Roh's government policies. Roh retaliates with charges of tax evasion against Chung.
1992	Roh again attacks Hyundai on tax charges.
	Hyundai sues government for nonpayment of bills.
	Chung announces his candidacy for president of Korea at the age of 76 (January 10); creates United People's Party (UPP).
	UPP wins 31 seats in National Assembly election (March).
	Kim Yong Sam elected president (December).
1993	President Kim retaliates against Chung for entering political race by charging illegal campaign financing (January 15).
	President Kim launches his globalization *(segyehwa)* campaign for Korea but limits credit for corporate overseas expansion.
1994	President Kim launches attacks against several company and institute presidents, including the Bank of Korea, POSCO, Korea Development Institute, and SK Group, for not supporting his presidency.
1995	Former Korean presidents Chun and Roh jailed for corruption.
	President Kim retaliates against Samsung's President Lee for criticizing his government.
1996	President Kim charges Daewoo President Kim with corruption and bribery after Daewoo fails to support his government.
1997	President Kim's son indicted and later convicted of tax evasion and extortion.
	Numerous bankruptcies cripple Korea; IMF called in to rescue economy.
	President Kim's popularity falls from 97 percent in 1993 to 7 percent in 1997.
	Kim Dae Jung wins presidential election (December 18) against ruling party.
	D. J. Kim pledges an end to political retaliations and corruption; calls for national unification.
	Former presidents Chun and Roh pardoned.
1998	D. J. Kim assumes presidency (February 25). New era of relative political calm begins.

At the same time, Roh began curbing real estate speculation by many of the larger companies. In an effort to ease a significant housing shortage, Roh had made a campaign promise to "build two million houses" (really high-rise condominiums) in the burgeoning Seoul metropolitan area. On hearing this, many companies began buying up Seoul real estate for speculation, thereby driving up the costs of the government projects. Roh demanded that the companies divest themselves of all properties that were not specifically slated for immediate factory or commercial development. The government offered a social justification for its action. As one journalist noted at the time, "Excessive concentration of real estate in the hands of the upper crust has conspicuously deepened the disparity between rich and poor and threatens to ignite angry antigovernment outbursts among laborers in particular."[3] Even President Park Chung Hee had warned against the concentration of real estate holdings in the hands of the wealthy back in the 1970s.[4] As a result of this government order, many companies had to sell off land at significant losses. Samsung and LG were particularly hard hit because of their vast land holdings, but Hyundai also suffered. Indeed, Hyundai had to divest itself of land holdings it was keeping for long-term office development. In the late 1990s, when it finally sought to build two high-rise office buildings for a new corporate complex in Kangnam, on the south side of the Han River, it had to purchase new lands at grossly inflated prices over its previous holdings.

Finally, Roh tried—unsuccessfully, as it turned out—to force all Korean companies to narrow the breadth of their operations. Specifically, he compelled each conglomerate to identify three subsidiary companies that would be exempt from government credit regulations; credit would then be restricted to all other companies within each group. This policy was designed to force the chaebols to rein in their expansive operations and focus their limited resources on developing strategic niches in which they could best compete. In theory, each company would compete on the basis of its strengths. Roh and his economic planners worried that Korean companies had grown not just too large but also too unwieldy. They were engaged in too many diverse and unrelated businesses, often competing with one another for business instead of competing against the Americans or the Japanese.

However laudable the government's three policies might have been, Hyundai and other companies began to see the Roh government as increasingly antibusiness or, at the very least, ignorant of sound business practices. The government was engaging in activities that were limiting the ability of Korean companies to compete just at a time when global competitive forces were on the rise. Indeed, shortly after Roh's election, Korea's once magnificent economy began to sag under the weight of increasingly noncompetitive wage hikes, combined with increased government regulation. Consumer prices and inflation began to climb.

Soon, as so often occurs when governments attempt to regulate businesses, companies discovered ways to get around Roh's directives. Hyundai selected cars, electronics, and petrochemicals for its three "core companies." Like other companies, however, Hyundai proceeded to secure government-backed loans for these three "core" businesses and then transferred the funds throughout the company to those businesses in need of cash. Nothing could be easier, and it was a fitting response to a bad government policy. To Roh and his advisors, however, it was a challenge to government's right to make policy. Both sides to the conflict began asking who was really in charge of Korean economic development: the government or business?

TAKING ON THE GOVERNMENT

Chung Ju Yung grew increasingly concerned about mounting government intervention in business. He felt he had an obligation to speak out against government practices he felt were jeopardizing future economic growth. He had repeatedly criticized the Roh government for its inept handling of the economy. In doing so, Chung invited the scrutiny of government bureaucrats determined to penalize him and his company for their outspoken opposition to and criticism of the incumbents. Before a meeting of business leaders in 1991, Chung observed that "things were good under the rules of Park Chung Hee and Chun Doo Hwan."[5] Chung went on to suggest that "if I were the chief of construction for Seoul, I would clear up the traffic problem at once," referring to Seoul's notorious traffic snarls.[6] Chung argued that Roh's proposal to build a high-speed train between Seoul and Pusan was too expensive in relation to the expected benefits, especially in view of Korea's financial crisis. On another occasion, Chung stated, "There are no credible political leaders in this country."[7] In a speech commemorating the twelfth anniversary of Park Chung Hee's assassination, Chung said that Korea lacked leadership and direction under the Roh administration.[8]

Roh was outraged at Chung's repeated attacks. No one could confront Korea's national president in this insulting way and get away with it. Roh also understood that Chung might possibly enter politics and run against the ruling party in the upcoming 1992 presidential elections. He could not afford to let Chung gain political advantage at this crucial time. Had Chung remained silent and acquiesced to government policies as many other chaebol leaders had done, he would have likely remained safe from attack. As it was, he actually seemed to invite it.

When Chung reorganized his financial empire in the late 1980s, he hoped to enhance both accountability and efficiency throughout his operations. As part of this reorganization, stocks were traded across and between various subsidiary companies. This was a common practice in Korea among the major firms. But Roh's government, seizing on this as an opportunity for revenge, charged Chung with tax evasion. Specifically, they charged that Chung had used stock transfers to distribute his estate among his children before his death in order to free them from paying subsequent inheritance taxes. The government sought several hundred million dollars in back taxes. What was unusual about the government charges was that what Chung had done was common practice in Korea. Many chaebol leaders had done the same thing without government recrimination.[9] At first, Chung refused to pay. He argued against the technicalities of the tax code, but to no avail. "The tax is not acceptable," Chung argued.[10]

Roh's government began a public campaign against Chung. They called for decisive action to collect all taxes legitimately due the government from patricians like Chung. Roh threatened to have the government-controlled Korea Exchange Bank limit further credit to Hyundai, thus effectively cutting off future loans for expansion. Because most Korean companies were heavily leveraged and did business on a "grow-or-die" principle, this would lead to disaster for the company. Remembering the plight of the bankrupt Kukje Group several years earlier, in November 1991, Chung eventually bowed to government pressure and agreed to pay $181 million in transfer taxes on his estate. (Later, however, the judgment against Hyundai was overturned on appeal and the money was returned to Chung.)

Quickly following up on their victory, Roh's government struck again in April 1992. This time, they went after several executives from Hyundai Merchant Marine (HMM), including its chairman, on charges of tax evasion. Allegedly, company executives had transferred $27 million in company funds from HMM to a secret fund, in violation of Korea's foreign exchange control regulations. The government asserted that the funds were to be used by Chung Ju Yung to begin his political campaign against the incumbent government. In court, Hyundai argued that they had simply followed common practice in putting funds aside for rebates to valued customers. At most, HMM might be guilty of sloppy bookkeeping, but not fraud. They denied the funds were designated for political purposes.

In the end, the judge of the Seoul District Criminal Court took a middle course. He found several Hyundai executives guilty of tax evasion, but all were given suspended sentences. Hyundai was fined $46 million in penalties. To many, the Hyundai executives who had spent four months in jail awaiting trial emerged as heroes for standing firm against an increasingly autocratic president. Even the presiding judge seemed to recognize the politics underlying the trial. In announcing his decision, he noted that the Korean courts were now being used as an instrument of the government's political agenda.

After the conviction, Roh's government pressured various banks to withhold future loans to Hyundai. The government asserted that the money from such loans might find its way into Chung Ju Yung's campaign coffers. To avoid this possibility, they said, corporate loans should be stopped altogether. As a result, Hyundai was denied access to $500 million in loans that were to be used for expansion and research and development. Instead, it sought to borrow part of this money from foreign banks, outside the control of the Korean government. The resulting loss in added plant capacity, combined with the loss of crucial research, served to curb Hyundai's growth rate—and Korea's. Korea's economic stability was now being jeopardized as Roh's government pursued its political vendetta against Hyundai and other business leaders.

RUNNING FOR PRESIDENT

To Chung Ju Yung, these latest attacks by the government were the last straw. As he saw it, Roh's government was now persecuting him personally because of his outspoken opposition to government policies with which he disagreed. Chung now vowed to enter the political arena and offer the Korean people an alternative to government as usual. The generals had ruled long enough, he reasoned. Now it was time for businessmen to step in and show some leadership and fiscal responsibility.

In an initial act of retaliation—and in an overt effort to embarrass President Roh—Hyundai sued the government for nonpayment of $30 million for additions and renovations to Roh's presidential palace, the Blue House. The message was clear: If Roh was such a good public administrator, why was he spending huge amounts of public money to enhance his own personal comfort? And why wasn't he paying his bills? Chung followed this lawsuit with a series of accusations of government favoritism in granting government contracts and of government wiretapping of political opponents. As it turned out, his accusations proved to be correct. Roh's government was indeed awarding contracts based on favoritism. A multi-billion-dollar mobile telephone contract went to a company whose chairman was the new father-in-law of Roh's only daughter. Indeed, Roh later would be jailed for personally amassing over $600 million in secret bribes from such deals.[11] And several police units publicly acknowledged conducting police surveillance on political opponents of the Roh government. Finally, in August 1992, just four months before the presidential election, the government lifted its sanctions against bank loans to Hyundai. Roh did not want another campaign issue to damage his party's chances in the December election.

Chung formally announced his candidacy for president of Korea at a news conference in his home on January 10, 1992. Chung commented that "we have a pessimistic future with the present economy, and I have to do something about it."[12] Chung went on to say that he was very critical of the present regime and noted that "the last regime at least could control prices."[13] To support his campaign, he founded the Tongil Kukmindang, or United People's Party (UPP). Almost immediately, a veritable army of Hyundai employees joined UPP and began working for his campaign. At least one high-ranking executive resigned from Hyundai to run for the National Assembly under Chung's banner but returned after losing the election.[14] At the age of seventy-six, Chung Ju Yung was preparing for a bruising campaign.

In a recent interview, Chung looked back on his decision to run:

> The principal reason I entered the political world was to help Korea recover from its economic stagnation and to put it on a secure economic footing for the future. I had observed that the ambitions of many companies were being stifled by poor government policies and a disruptive political culture. I determined to try to correct these practices. As you know, I have devoted my life to Korea's economic development, so I thought it was my duty to do what I could for the mother country and its people.[15]

Park Se Yong, president of Hyundai Corporation and the group's highest ranking non-family member, added, "He considered it to be his sacred duty to use his energies to bring about political and economic reform."[16]

Chung compared the administration of a country to running a business. Sound business practices would lead Korea back to prosperity. What Korea needed was good long-range planning, efficient management of government bureaucracies, rational decision making and allocation of scarce resources, tight controls on government spending, and open communication with various stakeholders. All of this should be coordinated through effective leadership—his leadership. Indeed, Chung was confident that he could resolve Korea's economic problems within his five-year term, if given a chance by the voters. Chung also vowed to eliminate government corruption and the somewhat common practice of corporate shakedowns by high government officials. Political life, Chung thought, should be a higher calling that attracted young people of the best moral character to get involved and to seek an improved way of life for future generations. He felt confident that he could play a role in this endeavor.

Chung campaigned tirelessly, crisscrossing Korea in his helicopter and making speeches to any group that invited him. His campaign was based on the assertion that government had grown too large and was out of touch with the common people. Government was interfering too much in business; as a result, prices for everything consumers needed were rising at an alarming rate. The government had lost control of the economy and was bankrupt of new ideas for recovery. Chung argued that Roh's "unreasonable economic policies have caused the current ailing economy...and greatly diminished the international competitiveness of our economy....I believe the abilities that enabled me to build Hyundai can help set the government in a new direction," he concluded.[17] In many ways, the campaign was reminiscent of H. Ross Perot's 1992 presidential campaign in the United States, although Chung himself steadfastly rejected any comparisons.

In the December election, Chung would run against two principal opponents: Kim Young Sam, leader of the recently reorganized Democratic Liberal Party, which included President Roh's political faction, and Kim Dae Jung, leader of the Democratic Party. Kim Dae Jung was well respected in the West as a long-time advocate for democracy in South Korea. He had been jailed for six years by Park Chung Hee for opposing Park's increasingly authoritarian regime. Released in 1982, Kim immediately flew to the United States to seek political asylum, only to return in 1985 to continue his struggle for democracy. Although the liberal Kim and the conservative Chung were at opposite ends of the political spectrum, they shared the same sense of outrage over recent scandals and corruption in the current government. Chung and D. J. Kim (as he was called) both saw the upcoming presidential election in terms of a class struggle, an effort to return the government to the common people, not unlike H. Ross Perot's campaign in the United States. Like Perot, Chung was a billionaire capitalist. And, also like Perot, he found a large following among common citizens frustrated by an unresponsive big government.

To Chung, the Roh government was not just corrupt; it was inept. Chung had always believed in a strong, even autocratic, government. Such a government, however, had a responsibility to support strong businesses in a partnership for the benefit of the country. In Chung's eyes, President Roh had broken that partnership, first by supporting the labor unions in their quest for significantly higher wages and later by attempting to curb the growth and economic power of the chaebols themselves. As Chung saw it, Roh had failed to understand economics. Chung campaigned on the principle that running a government was no different than running a company—again, the same platform used by Perot. What counted most to Chung was the sincerity of the people running the government. As credentials he offered the fact that he had experience, understood economics, and had met a payroll.

Chung concluded early that D. J. Kim could not win the election.

Although he had considerable popular sympathy as a long-suffering advocate for democracy, the majority of South Koreans saw him as too liberal. Kim also came from the Cholla region in the south of Korea, and many people from Seoul (not including Chung) were somewhat suspicious of people from this region. No one from Cholla had ever been elected to a significant political office. During the campaign, Chung correctly identified Kim Young Sam as the principal contender and focused his attacks on him. Y. S. Kim, as he was called, had formed a coalition with his former enemy, Roh Tae Woo, and was strongly endorsed by the incumbent government. In Chung's view, Y. S. Kim had sold out; he had made a politically expedient compromise unworthy of a true leader. He was also repeatedly accused of being incompetent to run the government. Chung frequently referred to Y. S. Kim as a "stonehead," an epithet he reserved for people who couldn't do a job properly. Chung also accused Kim of secretly receiving $384 million from the Bank of Korea to finance his campaign. Further, Kim's party was accused of spying on UPP party workers. When Seoul's leading newspaper, *Choson Ilbo*, publicly supported Y. S. Kim, Chung accused them of biased coverage and withdrew all future advertising from the newspaper.

In the March 1992 National Assembly election prior to the December presidential election, the UPP won 31 seats out of 299, not a bad showing for an entirely new party. Meanwhile, the government was hard pressed to retain its previous membership in the assembly. Despite polls showing he could not possibly win, Chung marched on. As Chung saw it, Roh's problems stemmed from the fact that he would not listen to the experience of business leaders like himself—the people who were most responsible for building modern Korea. Roh's government had curtailed the money supply used by Korean firms to expand. His new policy of granting credit to only three core areas was particularly dysfunctional, according to Chung. How can you expand into overseas markets without adequate money and credit? Chung believed that Y. S. Kim would merely continue Roh's failed antibusiness policies, leading the country into greater despair.

By contrast, Chung proposed economic policies that were decidedly pro-business and fiscally conservative, mirroring the Republican party platform in the United States. In a policy statement issued by his UPP party shortly before the election, Chung promised that "we will introduce policies to lower the interest rate to the level of those of international competitors and adopt policies to draw manpower from service industries into the manufacturing sector....We will support industries which voluntarily develop innovative technologies."[18] The policy statement continued: "We will pursue an economy led by the private sector. We will minimize the government's intervention, adopting the theme of a small government, leaving the economic operation to free market play."[19] Banks would be privatized. The use of fictitious names on bank accounts and land titles—a commonly used method to keep properties off the tax rolls—also would be banned.

On the political side, Chung supported continuing the current troop strength of U.S. forces in Korea to ensure South Korean security. He called on North Korea to comply with UN directives for open inspection of all nuclear facilities. Koreans should have greater freedom to speak their minds; they should not be afraid of new ideas. However, he would resist U.S. pressure to open Korea's closed markets. Chung reasoned that the current Korean economy was too fragile for wholesale market liberalization; the impact would cripple it. Besides, the United States now had a trade surplus with Korea.

In July, Chung was still going strong and remained optimistic. To gain more room for his expanding campaign staff, he ordered that his campaign headquarters be moved from one Hyundai building to another nearer the center of Seoul. In typical Hyundai fashion, the move was completed in less than two days. (One wonders how long it would take for a similar move by the Republican or Democratic National Committee in the United States.) Chung's autobiography, *Ordeals, But No Failures*, was released and became an immediate best-seller. It told the story of Chung's rise from an impoverished childhood to his current status as a billionaire entrepreneur and philanthropist.

Despite Chung's best efforts, the results of the election were decisively negative. Even with heavy campaigning involving thousands of Hyundai volunteers and millions of dollars, Chung received only 16 percent of the Korean vote. (Curiously, H. Ross Perot received roughly the same percentage in his losing bid for the White House.) Kim Young Sam won the election with 42 percent of the vote, and Kim Dae Jung came in second with 34 percent. In a formal statement the next morning, Chung noted: "I accept the results of the election and give thanks for the support I have received despite the hardships we faced. I am sending a congratulatory message to Kim Young Sam." Chung had lost one of the few fights of his career. Even so, he felt he had made an important point.

Many people have speculated as to why Chung lost the election. Some believe that average Koreans were distrustful of business executives or entrepreneurs as political leaders and, despite their public protestations to the contrary, were more comfortable voting for professional politicians. The same rationale has been offered to explain the defeat of H. Ross Perot. Others believe that rank-and-file employees of competing chaebols voted en masse against Chung to prevent his victory. By doing so, they would deny Hyundai any possible competitive advantages in future government relations. Still others believe that many Koreans simply were not ready for another "take-charge" leader after their experiences with Chun and Roh but instead preferred a leader who appeared less threatening. Y. S. Kim, after all, had built his campaign on calls for democracy, whereas Chung had built his on calls for efficiency. Whatever the reason, available evidence shows that Chung accepted his loss and was determined to return to business and to work with the new government, whoever it was.

PAYING THE PRICE

Y. S. Kim's election in December 1992 was considered by many to be a watershed event for Korea. His election marked an end to decades of military rule that were characterized by civil war, the demise of South Korea's first republic headed by Rhee Syngman, and the authoritative rule of the "three generals," Park Chung Hee, Chun Doo Hwan, and Roh Tae Woo. Once dismissed as a war-torn agrarian economy, Korea had now become one of the most successful late industrializers, with the third largest economy in Asia, after Japan and China. Its economic presence was seen in worldwide recognition of several fast-growing household names, like Samsung, Goldstar, Daewoo, and Hyundai. It was a significant player at the technological edge of the semiconductor and consumer electronics industry. Indeed, in 1995, Korea became the world's largest manufacturer of DRAM chips, surpassing even the Japanese manufacturers that had dominated the market for the previous two decades. And Korea's acceptance in the Organization of Economic Cooperation and Development (OECD)—open only to the richest nations in the world—further enhanced its reputation among the world's leading industrial nations. Korea had definitely arrived.

Shortly after his election, President Kim issued a challenge to his countrymen to embark on a new cultural revolution. In what he referred to as the Sydney Declaration, President Kim articulated a new national goal for Korea: globalization, or *segyehwa* in Korean. As initially envisioned by Kim, segyehwa was not limited to business and economics but incorporated all segments of society, including politics, economics, culture and the arts, education, and mass communication.[20] Its purpose was not to copy foreign models but to "raise Korean standards in all these areas to the levels of the world's advanced economies."[21] Although the intended transformation commenced with the administration of President Kim, it was expected to last for several decades. It was an ambitious program that sought to develop all sectors of Korean life in harmony. Soon, segyehwa became a rallying cry of many Korean politicians in anticipation of the mounting challenges they would face in the twenty-first century.

When President Kim issued his challenge to globalize, he tapped into a nation's need to be recognized for its accomplishments. As a construct, segyehwa—the drive to achieve excellence and economic parity with the world's most advanced nations—was deeply rooted in Korea's consciousness. Many Koreans based their modern sense of identity on the country's economic growth rate.[22] Koreans from many different walks of life took considerable pride in how much they had achieved in a relatively short time. As a result, President Kim's call for globalization recognized publicly what had long been a commonly held goal for most Koreans: to join the world's elite countries on an equal basis.

President Kim enjoyed the international limelight with his call for Koreans to abandon their traditional ways and embrace the global environment, but many businessmen were more skeptical. To Chung Ju Yung in particular, Kim's new endeavor was little more than a recognition by the current government of what many Korean companies had been doing for decades. Globalization had been a hallmark of Hyundai and several other Korean firms since the 1960s. Indeed, the drive to learn from abroad and conduct business globally had begun with the presidency of Park Chung Hee. Even presidents Chun and Roh had supported efforts to internationalize Korean society. President Kim's campaign for segyehwa was dismissed by many executives as little more than a public relations stunt. Nonetheless, Kim's campaign received favorable international attention, and he became a popular political figure in foreign capitals around the world, including Moscow, Beijing, and Washington, DC.

But despite Y. S. Kim's claim that he was building a new Korea, the old politics of personal attacks and retribution remained as strong as ever. For Chung Ju Yung, his loss at the polls was a clear signal that more troubles were on the horizon. During the campaign, Chung had criticized the victorious Kim and his Democratic Liberal Party for not reducing Korea's trade deficit and for interfering with business operations. In retaliation, immediately after winning the December election, President Kim initiated a tax audit of Hyundai and its founder. Kim reportedly told brother Chung Se Yung after the election that the government would not forgive the involvement of business leaders in government. Now he would prove his point. Kim charged that Chung Ju Yung had broken Korean law by using Hyundai Heavy Industries corporate funds to support his campaign. On January 15, 1993, Chung was summoned to the prosecutor's office and interrogated for 12 hours. He was finally released in time to catch a plane to attend President Clinton's inauguration in Washington, DC. By February 1, he was back in Seoul, where he promised to clear up the conflict with Kim's government. Chung explained that a subordinate had channeled corporate funds into UPP coffers "out of loyalty."

In the Kim government's view, Chung had broken the laws governing campaign financing. But as Chung saw it, he had simply used his corporate funds—he owned HHI, after all—to support his campaign needs. In any case, Chung acknowledged that he had violated government rules on campaign financing and agreed to repay the $65 million the government accused him of secretly channeling into the campaign. Chung and his family promptly sold 3.2 million Hyundai shares to repay HHI. But on February 6, the government formally charged Chung and over two hundred other Hyundai executives. This occurred just before President Kim's inauguration, however, and, perhaps fearing a public backlash, the government declined to put Chung in jail pending the trial. In not insisting on immediate incarceration, the court cited Chung's advancing age, his status as an opposition leader, and his contributions to national economic progress.

Chung resigned from the leadership in the UPP on February 9 and, in keeping with Korean custom, apologized to President Kim for launching personal attacks against him during the campaign. For its part, Hyundai issued a public notice saying it would "join the new government in the campaign against corruption."[23] Chairman Chung Se Yung declared, "We will never again be involved in a political storm.... [We will] help the nation join the ranks of advanced nations."[24] After several postponements, Chung's trial began in November 1993 and ran on for months. Finally, following a lengthy appeal process, the appellate court upheld Chung's conviction for making illegal campaign contributions from his company to his presidential campaign. He was given a three-year suspended sentence. At long last, the trail was over.

As journalist Mark Clifford commented at the time: "In reality, Chung's trial was one of the more remarkable events in Korea in the past thirty years. The founder and the chairman of the Hyundai group, one of the world's biggest corporations, sat in a Seoul courtroom in late 1993 because he dared to challenge the established order in Korea, one that held that government mandarins should rule the affairs of business and workers."[25] Clifford, a long-time observer of Korea, continued: "Chung Ju Yung was a businessman but he was also a revolutionary, for this former peasant wanted nothing more than to pull down the old order, to change the twisted Confucian rules of Korea, Inc., which decreed that business exists to serve the government."[26]

President Kim's wrath was not reserved solely for Chung Ju Yung and Hyundai, however. Cho Soon, the well-respected governor of the Bank of Korea, was unceremoniously dismissed by Y. S. Kim for failing to support the government's unrelenting attack on Chung and Hyundai. Park Tae Joon, the highly respected founder and long-time chairman of Pohang Iron and Steel—one of Korea's real success stories—was driven out of the country by President Kim.

While the government's charges against Park involved tax evasion—the most commonly used allegations in Korea—his real crime, like Chung's, had been to challenge Kim in the presidential election.[27] And Song Hee Yoon, president of the government-run Korea Development Institute—perhaps Korea's most prestigious economic think tank—was removed from office after criticizing the government's economic stimulus program. A short while later, after Chairman Chey Jong-Hyon of SK Group also criticized the government's economic policies, Kim began an investigation of his finances until Chey recanted his position. And Samsung's chairman, Lee Kun Hee, was also punished in 1995 by President Kim's government when he publicly criticized the Korean government as being "third class."[28] In response to Chairman Lee's public statement, the government immediately stopped all government-sponsored or guaranteed loans to Samsung, blocked a public fund-raising initiative, and temporarily derailed Samsung's high-profile bid to buy controlling interest in the U.S. computer firm AST Research.[29] Finally, Kim Woo Choong, chairman of Daewoo, was convicted in 1996 of giving $43 million in bribes to both President Chun and Roh.[30] It seemed that no one was immune from President Kim's wrath.

Ironically, by 1997, as President Kim prepared to complete his term, several scandals broke over corruption in his own government. Both Hanbo Steel and the Sammi Group filed for bankruptcy after receiving massive and unjustified loans from Kim's government. In May, Kim's eldest son, Kim Hyun Chul, was arrested and later convicted of tax evasion and extorting money from several companies. In all, Kim's son was accused of accepting over 90 bribes totaling $4 million.[31] In October 1997, he was given a three-year prison term.[32] Although President Kim disclaimed any knowledge of such bribes and summarily disowned his favorite son, he nonetheless suffered the fate of a disgraced politician. His public approval rating dropped from 97 percent when first elected to 7 percent at the close of his term. Indeed, a public opinion poll taken in mid-1997 revealed that Kim had lost any respect he might have had when he entered office in 1993. The respected *Dong-A Ilbo* published the results of one poll showing that Koreans had rediscovered Park Chung Hee as an effective leader. Despite Park's autocratic ways, 76 percent of those polled felt he had been Korea's most effective leader; only 4 percent named Kim Young Sam. Worse still, a Korea University poll of the world's most admired people was topped by Mother Theresa, followed by Kim Ku (a leader of Korea's independence movement against Japan) and Park Chung Hee. Where was Kim Young Sam? Dead last, behind even Adolph Hitler.[33]

The final insult for Kim Young Sam came in the closing weeks of his administration, in late 1997, when his government was finally forced by an increasingly deteriorating economic situation to admit that its economic policies were in shambles. Preoccupied with punishing his political foes, Kim failed to implement key economic reforms that would have provided financial stability in a turbulent world. He failed to take a tough stand against both big business and big labor. Instead, he and his ministers pressured Korean banks into making massive and unsecured loans to friendly companies, like Hanbo and Kia, even though they were clearly in deep financial trouble. In the case of Kia, the government ordered the Korea Development Bank to convert Kia's sizable debts into an equity position in the company. As journalist Mark Clifford observed at the time, "It's almost as if Korea is turning back the clock, reverting to the days of state capitalism rather than continuing with liberalization."[34] By the end of year, there had been ten major bankruptcies, and Korean banks held $52 billion in bad loans—17 percent of their total loans.[35] Currency traders began selling the Korean won, driving its value down by almost by 20 percent in just two months. On November 21, Kim's government officially sought help from the International Monetary Fund to prop up the troubled Korean economy.[36]

In the final analysis, it is ironic that the steps Y. S. Kim failed to take to solidify Korea's economic gains were the same ones proposed by Chung five years earlier during his presidential campaign. Kim had looked for a political solution, whereas Chung was demanding an economic one. Had Chung succeeded in his presidential campaign and actually implemented the economic reforms he advocated in 1992, perhaps Korea's economic future would have continued on a brighter track.

THE NEW POLITICAL LANDSCAPE

On December 18, 1997, Koreans went to the polls to elect a new leader. Of the seven candidates who crowded the election, three emerged as serious candidates. Kim Young Sam's ruling party chose Lee Hoi Chang, a former Supreme Court judge, as its candidate. Long known for his honesty and integrity, Lee offered a platform that appealed principally to the business community. This included calls for restraints on labor's increasing power and reductions in government-controlled interest rates. Lee also offered continuity in a land characterized by chaos and turmoil in the light of the IMF's recent mandates for economic change. Nipping at his heels, however, was the revelation that both of his sons apparently had escaped compulsory military service by going on crash diets that left them too thin to be inducted. In a country characterized by a strong sense of obligation, this tarnished Lee's "Mr. Clean" image to a degree. Lee also had another problem. He represented the ruling party, and many in Korea wanted nothing to do with Y. S. Kim or his party. As one voter told the *Asian Wall Street Journal* just prior to the election: "The most important issue is changing governments. It's unthinkable that I would vote for the ruling party."[37]

A second ruling party member, Rhee In Je, bolted from the party after they rejected him in favor of Lee and ran on his own ticket. Rhee based his campaign on calls for government reform and increased efficiency. In a tribute to the late Park Chung Hee, whom Rhee both admired and resembled, he changed his hair style to look even more like the slain former president and tried unsuccessfully to assume his mantle. From the beginning, however, Rhee suffered because of his relative youth (he was 49 years old) in a culture that revered age. He also suffered from a lack of campaign funds.

The third candidate was 73-year-old Kim Dae Jung, who had nearly defeated Park Chung Hee for president in 1971. Soon after, however, Park had had Kim arrested and jailed on subversion charges. Later, Kim escaped to Japan but was soon kidnapped from his Tokyo hotel room by KCIA agents in 1973, returned to Korea, and jailed for a time. In 1980, Kim was charged with complicity by then-President Chun in connection with the Kwang-ju riots. Originally sentenced to death, he was eventually released and exiled to the United States. He returned to Korea in 1985 and challenged Roh Tae Woo in the 1987 presidential election. However, he and Y. S. Kim, also a candidate, split the popular reform vote, giving the election to Roh. D. J. Kim again ran for president in 1992 against Y. S. Kim and Chung Ju Yung. He was earning a reputation as a perennial candidate, so many considered it a bit of a joke when the elderly Kim again announced his candidacy for 1997. Making matters worse, he chose as his running mate the founder of the KCIA that had hounded Kim for so much of his life and a member of the original coup that ushered in nearly three decades of military rule in 1961.

D. J. Kim ran on an ambiguous platform and seemed to change his positions routinely. He first embraced the mandated IMF reforms but soon implied that he would refuse to implement several of the more stringent requirements if elected. When challenged on this point, Kim back-pedaled and reaffirmed his support for the reforms. Many considered his platform to be pro-labor. For example, Kim resisted any changes in government policies that might lead to union layoffs or downsizing. Still, Kim portrayed himself as a reform candidate who was capable of rebuilding a troubled Korea through the application of democratic principles. Many saw him as having the best chance of making progress on improving relations with North Korea. And Kim was well respected in the West as a political reformer and advocate for democracy. When Kim fell behind in the polls the week before the election, he surprised everyone by sponsoring a live telethon featuring pop star Michael Jackson and billionaire financier George Soros, both of whom urged public support for his candidacy.

On the eve of the election, public opinion was cautious, if not confused. An editorial in *The Economist* observed: "In their televised debates and on the hustings, the three serious presidential candidates have failed to grapple persuasively with the issues. All three claim to favor deregulation, but none sounds convincing.... Kim Dae Jung wins no plaudits for his economic manifesto. He promises, if elected, to encourage job-sharing, to ensure that no workers are sacked for at least six months, and to raise GNP per person from $10,000 to $30,000 in a single five-year term. This would be wizardry indeed."[38]

The campaign ran smoothly and included the obligatory speeches and campaign rallies, as well as several U.S.-style televised debates. Even so, Korea's recent economic collapse and the IMF mandates clearly cast a pall over the electoral process. Most Koreans, depressed and worried about their country's—and their families'—immediate future, sought out the candidate who offered the most security. In the end, D. J. Kim emerged the winner with 40.3 percent of the votes, compared to 38.7 percent for Lee.[39] Many felt that Rhee's candidacy, which drew 19.2 percent of the vote, had served as a spoiler, denying the election to Lee. In any event, Kim Dae Jung won by a 1.6 percent margin and assumed the presidency of South Korea on February 25, 1998. For the first time in Korean history, an opposition candidate had won. Even before his inauguration, however, Kim arranged to have former Presidents Chun and Roh pardoned and released from jail as a gesture of reconciliation. Once in office, Kim began the arduous task of meeting Korea's international obligations and rebuilding its economic infrastructure. Indeed, Korea was now facing a new political landscape.

DEVELOPING THE HYUNDAI SPIRIT

"I worked sixteen hours a day, seven days a week, for sixteen years. No holidays. If the Chairman was working, so were we. We didn't mind, however. We learned from the Chairman; we respected him. He was always very demanding, but he was a good teacher."

—A SENIOR HYUNDAI EXECUTIVE[1]

When Chung Ju Yung set about building Korea's largest and most modern medical facility in the late 1980s, nothing could stop him. The new hospital would be the best his country had to offer in medical care and research. It would be a showpiece for the new Korea. Chung was personally financing it, and Hyundai was the prime contractor. Midway through construction, however, Chung learned that a rival company not only was building a similar hospital in Seoul but was actually ahead of his own construction schedule. The rival hospital would be completed first. To Chung, this was unacceptable; he had to finish first. He called a meeting of his project supervisors and announced that Hyundai's construction schedule would need to be cut by a full six months. They would not be upstaged by a competitor.

Upon hearing this, the supervisors all bowed their heads and stared intensely at the floor. They knew the chairman's orders were impossible to achieve. The schedule was already compressed in the typical Hyundai fashion, and shortening it by six months was technically impossible. Too much work remained to be done. But everyone remained silent except for one earnest young engineer. The young man took a deep breath and timidly addressed the chairman, saying that, with respect, he had studied the plans very carefully and was convinced that shortening the construction schedule by so much time simply could not be done. Chung fired him on the spot. He then asked if anyone else disagreed with his assessment. Again, silence. Everyone returned to work and redoubled their efforts. In the end, the building was completed six months ahead of schedule, and the grand opening was held several weeks prior to that of their rival, just as Chung had said it would be. Hyundai would prevail.

Ruthless dedication to success at all costs—this is the essence of the Hyundai spirit. Failure is unacceptable. Employees either learn and enact this spirit, or they leave. As seen throughout this book, Hyundai's history is replete with examples of stunning successes that almost defy logic, from the launching of the *Atlantic Baron* to the construction of the Jubail Harbor facility in Saudi Arabia to the creation of Seosan farm. Few examples can be found of company failures, however small.

But success can only be sustained through the development of human capital—a company's valued human resources. Indeed, it is widely recognized that the quality of a company's employees is a principal ingredient in determining its long-term chances for survival and success. Hyundai is no exception. For many years, the company has invested heavily in its people. At the same time, however, it has demanded a significant return on that investment. Being a Hyundai "salaryman" (or white-collar worker—*bong-gueb-jaeng-ee* in Korean) is one of the most challenging jobs in the world. What is surprising to many outsiders is that, for all of their long hours and time away from home and family, Hyundai salarymen genuinely seem to enjoy their work and exhibit a commitment to the company that most Western executives would envy.

Over the years, Hyundai's human resource management practices have been influenced by two principal forces. The first derives from the Confucian tradition that permeates Korean society (see Chapter 2). Here we see the origins of Korea's emphasis on such values as hard work, dedication, seniority, and absolute loyalty to the company. Paternalistic leadership and top-down decision making remain hallmarks of most Korean companies today. The second and more recent influence on HRM practices is the contemporary push to use "modern," typically Western, approaches to management and employee development. Here, the company is concerned with making improvements in such practices as employee recruitment, employee training, performance appraisals, and so forth.[2] This increasing tendency toward newer approaches has been facilitated by executive decisions to make their HRM policies more "scientific." Cho Nam-Hong, vice chairman of the Federation of Korean Industries, refers to this new approach as a *capability-based* human resource management system.[3] Hyundai is clearly a leader in implementing this approach. Even so, it must be recognized that HRM practices in Korea remain quite distinct from those of the West. Korea is modernizing by seeking its own model of management that blends Eastern and Western business philosophies; it has no intention of blindly copying the practices of its U.S. and European competitors.

THE ORIGINAL ROAD WARRIORS

From the earliest days until he retired, Chung took a personal interest in the selection and development of his white-collar employees. Indeed, he frequently participated in interviewing even the most junior management trainees. Through this commitment of time and attention, he created a formidable competitive force in support of his enterprise. Highly motivated, highly skilled, unquestioning in their obedience, and unyielding in their determination, these employees are the frontline troops that carry out the chairman's orders around the world. Indeed, if Hyundai has anything approaching a "secret weapon" in its international business endeavors, this is it. Hyundai salarymen are the original "road warriors" in every sense of the word.

Prospective job applicants to Hyundai must pass through a grueling series of personal and intellectual hurdles to prove that they are worthy of joining the Hyundai team. They must pass a company-sponsored entrance examination that includes English-language proficiency as well as technical and management skills. Good university grades are also important in selection. In addition, applicants must pass through extensive personal interviews and reference checks. Personal interviews are becoming increasingly important in determining who gets hired.[4] A recent survey found that 78 percent of Korea's HRM managers believe that personal interviews are the most important screening tool.[5] Hyundai has even begun to experiment with "blind interviews," in which interviewers are not given any prior information on the applicants so as not to bias their judgments.

In hiring decisions, new college graduates are preferred over people with experience. After a period of training and indoctrination, they are typically assigned to such core departments as planning, finance, and accounting. This contrasts with the typical American recruiting practice in which previous work experience is more highly valued and new employees are typically assigned to a functional department based on their specialty. It also contrasts somewhat with the practice of Japanese companies, where new employees are more likely to begin their jobs in the field rather than at corporate headquarters.

A recent study sought to identify how major Korean companies describe the ideal manager.[6] What are the keys to managerial success and how do companies identify these characteristics when hiring new employees? The ideal young candidate for most companies was both smart and highly motivated.

He—95 percent of all Korean line managers are male—exhibited a strong work ethic and a positive attitude toward hard work for company and country. Personal initiative was important. He had a good character and background and was willing to learn. He presented himself well and was comfortable to be around. Some companies also indicated that the ideal candidate was a risk taker who had the capacity to make rapid, incisive decisions under pressure.

For his part, Chung Ju Yung was recently asked what he looked for in a new employee. He responded that he valued a positive human spirit over work skills. An employee who has a good heart and is earnest can easily learn the requisite work skills, Chung observed:[7]

> I think that diligence and honesty are the most important characteristics in new employees. Ambition and a creative mind are also important. I prefer a humble but ambitious person to a person who grew up in good circumstances. From my experience, humble but ambitious people try harder to overcome difficulties. In addition, I like people with good health and a strong mind. A person who is physically or mentally weak can't conduct business with energy and drive. That's why Hyundai requires Korean wrestling contests as part of our new employee training programs.[8]

Added to this is a long-standing requirement that all new Hyundai salarymen speak English; without this, globalization efforts are thought to be futile.

Once hired, all new salarymen begin their careers with a three-week indoctrination and orientation session at the group's training center in Mabuk-ri. The goals of this program are to inculcate the new recruits with Hyundai's corporate culture and values and to begin the socialization process so that every new employee genuinely feels that he belongs. Following this, most Hyundai subsidiary companies (e.g., Hyundai Motor Company, Hyundai Electronics Industries, etc.) put new hires through their own orientation sessions, typically lasting one week, that focus more specifically on the needs and goals of the subsidiary. Hyundai Motor Company, for example, introduces all new employees to the global automobile business and HMC's goals for this business. Time is also spent teaching the history and folklore of the specific subsidiary. With such knowledge, new hires are better prepared to fit in and help the firm attain its operating objectives. Hyundai Motor Company also uses a mentoring system, called "Hyundai Brothers," that assigns an experienced middle manager to each new salaryman for the first year of employment to help him assimilate into the firm.

All new hires quickly discover that working for Hyundai is not the same as working for many other Korean firms. A close examination reveals a number of reasons that working for this particular Korean company may be the most difficult job a person could have. To begin with, Hyundai demands total commitment and dedication to the firm. Other Korean firms also seek strong employee commitment, but they tend to allow employees greater freedom of thought and action. Hyundai brooks no criticism. The company's operating style bears a striking resemblance to that of a military organization. All employees are expected to follow orders without question. They are expected to think and behave in ways that are consistent with the firm's guiding philosophy and to make whatever sacrifice is required to help the firm succeed. Indeed, several employees have gone to jail for extended periods of time, not because they were guilty of any legal infraction but because explaining their plight in public might have put the company in a bad light. Colleagues become comrades, and companies become families. When asked where he works, a Hyundai employee will likely respond by saying that he is a "Hyundai man," not that he works for Hyundai. There is a big difference.

MANAGEMENT PHILOSOPHY AND CORPORATE CULTURE

Guiding a salaryman's behavior at work is the corporate philosophy of Hyundai and its founder. There are several ways to see this philosophy in action. The first and most visible is through the company *sahoon*, a phrase or slogan that embodies the company's most important values. At LG, for example, one frequently hears the word *inhwa*, or harmony, as a catch phrase of their management philosophy. At Daewoo, the sahoon is "creativity, challenge, and sacrifice." Samsung's sahoon is "respect for individual, pursuit of technology, and empowerment." Whereas American companies tend to relate their corporate values to aspects of functional and technical performance, such as customer service, innovation, and product excellence, Korean companies tend to emphasize the attitudes and behaviors that are expected of employees among themselves, toward the company, and toward society.[9] Sahoons also differ from Western company mottoes in their personalized nature. Many sahoons are derived from the family mottoes of the founders and represent what the founder thinks is important about the company. One frequently observes these sahoons framed and hung on the walls in managers' offices, and managers may note with pride that the chairman himself painted the sahoon.

At Hyundai, the sahoon captures what the company calls the "Hyundai spirit" and reads as follows:

> *Creative wisdom*
> *Unyielding will*
> *Indomitable driving force*

This sahoon reflects the founder's deeply held belief that virtually anything can be accomplished if people set their minds to it. It is a belief that is genuinely held throughout the company.

Symbolism also pervades the company logo: twin triangles superimposed one on top of the other. According to the company, the triangles symbolize the ancient pyramids of Egypt and stand for the natural order of a society (arranged hierarchically, following Confucian teachings). The logo is green on a yellow background; green represents the closeness of man to nature, and yellow represents the resilience of life.

The company handbook, never far from any salaryman, is a compendium of rules and requirements, corporate philosophy, company histories, product descriptions, maps, and important names and addresses. In the front of the handbook in boldface type is Hyundai's official management philosophy, consisting of five principal objectives:[10]

▶ Strive to become a leading corporation in the global community of the future.

▶ Value human resources and encourage the development of all employees.

▶ Pioneer new frontiers with creativity and leading-edge technology.

▶ Maximize customer satisfaction through a customer-first attitude.

▶ Contribute to the creation of a prosperous nation and the development of the global community.

In support of this corporate philosophy is a set of guiding principles that are prescribed for all employees. Salarymen are expected to take the lead and set an example by working diligently to follow these guidelines. These guiding principles are shown in Table 13-1. Underlying this set of guidelines is Chung's belief that building a company and building a nation are inextricably interwoven. As he recently noted: "I believe that only enterprise will lead the economic development of a nation. That's the spirit and mission that I planted in Hyundai and that's Hyundai's duty to the country."[11]

Organizational analysts have long argued that the real soul of a business enterprise is found in its corporate culture.[12] Nowhere is this more true than in Korean firms. Hyundai's corporate culture comprises several characteristics not unlike those of many other Korean firms, including a ruthless dedication to hard work, the importance of group harmony, a willingness to accept any challenge without question, and an ability to silently read the moods and intentions of people throughout the organization.

Perhaps the most prominent feature of Hyundai's corporate culture is an almost fatalistic preoccupation with hard work and long hours. Even after the

TABLE 13-1

HYUNDAI'S CORE VALUES

▶ Look to the future and initiate change.

▶ Practice optimistic and positive thinking.

▶ Show initiative and accept responsibility for your actions.

▶ Continuously improve through self-development.

▶ Strive to be diligent and frugal.

▶ Endeavor to be honest and courteous.

▶ Value mutual trust and cooperation.

▶ Provide world-class service to our customers.

▶ Preserve the environment.

▶ Serve our nation and society.

social revolution of the late 1980s and early 1990s, Hyundai employees continue their tradition of working extremely hard. Words frequently used by foreign observers in describing this include "diligent," "self-sacrificing," "dedicated," and "dependable." Even the Japanese frequently complain that the Koreans work too hard. Evidence of this can be seen in several areas. Consider, for example, one study in which Korean managers (including but not limited to Hyundai employees) were asked what they would do if they had enough money to live on comfortably for the rest of their lives.[13] A full 96 percent responded that they would continue to work hard despite their newfound wealth. Asked if the managers would prefer to have more time for work or for leisure, 61 percent responded that they would prefer to have more time for work; only 38 percent preferred more leisure time. Whether such behavior represents a strong work ethic or a national value of work centrality (that is, a belief that one must work hard regardless of one's degree of commitment to the organization) can be debated. From the standpoint of worker productivity and industrial competitiveness, however, it matters very little. Koreans simply work harder than most of their international counterparts.

Many observers feel that the cause of this exceptional work effort can be traced to the strong Confucian value system that pervades Korean society. With such an internal drive—especially when it is expressed collectively instead of individually as in the West—it is easy to understand why so many Hyundai managers at all levels of the organization work so hard on behalf of the company. It is also easy to understand why these managers consider the preservation of this drive so central to good management.

It is noteworthy to compare the nature of this achievement-oriented drive at Hyundai (and other Korean firms) to that found in the United States. Achievement-oriented individuals can be found in both countries, but the basis or focus of this behavior is typically quite different. In Korea, perhaps following the Confucian work ethic, an employee's work effort is primarily, though not exclusively, group oriented. It has a collective focus that emphasizes all-out effort so the group (and company) will succeed. In the United States, by contrast, following the more Western Protestant work ethic, an employee's efforts are more commonly individually oriented. It is important that he or she succeeds and stands out in the group. Thus, although employees in both countries are motivated by a work ethic, its derivation and orientation are substantially different.

A second characteristic that typifies Hyundai's work environment is the nature of the social contract that exists between and among employees. In Korea, this contract is predicated on a firm belief in preserving group harmony. Ensuring harmony among employees is a constant topic in discussions with executives and workers alike. Like work centrality, the principle of group harmony derives from Confucian thought, which stresses smooth, constructive, and conflict-free interpersonal relations at almost any cost. In a sense, it is everyone's responsibility to maintain societal equilibrium, and this responsibility typically supersedes any conception of individual rights. In fact, in Korea and other Asian countries, one hears considerable talk about one's responsibilities to company and country and little about one's rights in either domain; in the West, it is typically just the opposite. Westerners are often preoccupied with individual rights and seldom seriously consider individual responsibilities. When President John F. Kennedy said in his 1961 inaugural address, "Ask not what your country can do for you; ask what you can do for your country," it created quite a stir in the Western world and is remembered almost forty years later because of the uniqueness of the idea in U.S. society. In Korea, by contrast, such a statement by a new leader would never have received much attention; it would have been too commonplace an idea.

Third, if Koreans tend to emphasize group harmony and the West tends to emphasize individual rights, it is not surprising that in business relationships Koreans give more credence to personal contacts and relationships, whereas the West relies more on written contracts. At Hyundai, for example, it is imperative that one be connected, both inside and outside the corporation.

Considerable time is consumed in developing and nurturing these relationships, and business deals or simple favors are predicated on such relationships. For most Korean businessmen, agreements between two parties change as business conditions change. Because mutual benefit of both parties is a goal, it is frequently seen as inappropriate to hold one party to an agreement if business conditions change to his significant detriment. What is important is maintaining the personal relationship and enhancing mutual benefit, and a signed contract is simply a symbol of this. Needless to say, most managers in the West do not see it quite this way.[14] Contracts are the sine quia non of U.S. business enterprise, as exemplified by the proliferation of corporate lawyers and lawsuits. Or, as the film producer Samuel Goldwyn once observed, "A verbal contract isn't worth the paper it's written on." Personal relationships are often seen only as a means of securing a contract, but little effort is spent in nurturing them in the United States compared to Korea. This difference becomes particularly important as more foreign businesses attempt to initiate trade or joint ventures in Korea.

Fourth, relationships between superiors and subordinates at Hyundai are characterized by a high degree of paternalism. It is expected that a supervisor or manager will assume personal responsibility for the development of his subordinates and that these subordinates will respond by showing proper respect and obedience. These are mutual commitments and obligations. It is not uncommon for a Hyundai manager to take his subordinates out drinking one night a week to discuss both business and personal matters and to continue building a harmonious atmosphere. Moreover, it is expected that a manager will take an active interest in his subordinates' personal and family life by attending funerals and birthday parties, giving gifts on certain occasions, and the like. Like the Japanese, Korean companies believe in the "whole person" concept, which emphasizes the interrelationships between all parts of life. Conflict or problems at home may affect work performance and, therefore, must be monitored and resolved.

This practice stands in stark contrast with the Western norm that clearly separates work life from home life. In fact, in the United States, employers often are legally proscribed from inquiring about factors outside of the workplace. In the United States, superior-subordinate relationships tend to be more distant and less personal and are governed more by bureaucratic rules prescribing job responsibilities in detail. The original bureaucratic model of organization began in Germany in the nineteenth century and spread to other Western nations as an ideal form of organization governed by rationality and merit, not favoritism or personal relationships. Emphasis was placed on a clear specification of work rules that applied universally, employment and promotion based solely on merit and qualification, and the impersonality of office (that is, authority was vested in the office, not the individual, and office holders were expected to maintain an impersonal attitude when dealing with others). Under this system, paternalistic behavior in the West is often resented and resisted either as a form of favoritism or as too invasive of one's privacy. Individuals are seen as being responsible for taking care of themselves, and events outside of work are no one's business. Indeed, in most Western companies, employees are actively discouraged from bringing their "personal problems" to work.

A fifth dimension of Korea's corporate culture can be seen in its use of the concept of *nunch'i,* which translates roughly as "the look in someone's eyes." It is a nonverbal reaction of someone to a question, an order, or a comment, and Korean businessmen pride themselves on their ability to read someone's "face." In developing personal relationships and in other forms of social interaction, nonverbal behavior is far more important in the East than in the West, and in these interactions one's ability to read nunch'i—that is, the ability to silently understand what the other party is thinking—is basic. In fact, there is a Korean proverb that translates "one who does not have nunch'i cannot succeed." Moreover, in interpersonal interactions, most Koreans typically assume that the other party also has this capability. Thus, if a Hyundai employee asked for a favor that his supervisor either could not or would not grant, the supervisor would likely use nunch'i to signal his negative response, thereby avoiding a loss of face to either party by formally—and publicly—declining the request. In contrast to the West, what is *not* said is often far more important than what is said, and one's ability to interpret this silent language accurately is essential for career or business success.

Sixth, in more cases than Korean managers care to admit, decision making in companies remains highly centralized in the hands of top executives, who make decisions either unilaterally or in small groups after consultation with the various parties involved. Although the public image created by Hyundai stresses widespread employee participation, the reality is far more autocratic, probably again as a result of Confucian traditions. Orders typically come down the chain of command and are not to be questioned. The subordinate's responsibility is to comply at all costs, not to discuss or argue. As a result, Hyundai and most other Korean firms consist largely of followers, not leaders; soldiers, not entrepreneurs. This represents a serious problem as these companies try to prosper in today's increasingly competitive and fast-paced global business environment.

One final difference concerning decision implementation should be noted here. In the United States, a fundamental principle of "good management" is that authority must be delegated down to the same level where responsibility to carry out the decision lies. In other words, if someone is assigned responsibility to accomplish a certain task, that person must be given sufficient authority on matters that directly affect task accomplishment. At Hyundai, by contrast, it is not uncommon to observe situations in which authority is centralized but responsibility is decentralized. That is, a manager may be told, in essence: "You didn't choose this course of action, but you must make it work. If the project fails, you fail." This is all part of the "can-do" spirit for which Hyundai is so famous and can be seen in the myriad of executive decisions to enter new and risky businesses. Once a decision is made, it is not for subordinates to question it; rather, their job—and their future career—lies in making the venture successful against all odds. In contrast to the typical situation in the West, such individuals are held personally responsible for project success, not just for giving it their best effort.

The picture that emerges from this analysis is one of compromise. Hyundai's corporate culture is both strong and flexible. It is rooted in Eastern traditions, yet has learned from the West. It is both collectivist and individualistic. This paradox is clearly shown in a comparison of Hyundai's management practices with those of the typical U.S. firm (see Table 13-2). Hyundai management is perhaps best described as a blend of East and West, with a clear Eastern bias. Some argue, however, that the new realities of global competition are pushing Korean firms to move somewhat more Westward along this continuum in order to become true global corporations instead of just Korean firms doing business internationally.

A DAY IN THE LIFE OF A HYUNDAI SALARYMAN

Working for Hyundai is a major challenge and is not for the weak in spirit. Working hours are long, and salarymen often look tired and sleepy as they sit through meeting after meeting throughout the day. Things have improved, however. Before the labor strife of the late 1980s and early 1990s, many salarymen routinely worked all day long, six and sometimes seven days a week. As one senior executive described his work life in the early days, "I worked sixteen hours a day, seven days a week, for sixteen years. No holidays. If the Chairman was working, so were we."[15] And the chairman was always working. "We didn't mind, however. We learned from the Chairman; we respected him. He was always very demanding, but he was a good teacher."[16]

Today, although everyone still puts in long hours, work schedules represent an improvement over earlier times. The typical middle-level Hyundai salaryman rises about 6:00 A.M., six days each week. After a quick traditional breakfast of rice, soup, and fresh fruit, he catches a crowded subway at about 7:00 A.M. for the downtown headquarters building, where he usually arrives

TABLE 13-2

HYUNDAI'S CORPORATE CULTURE

CHARACTERISTIC	HYUNDAI	TYPICAL U.S. FIRM
Basis for business relationship	Personal relationships	Written contracts
Company loyalty	Very strong	Frequently weak
Decision-making style	Autocratic	Varies considerably
Individualism vs. group spirit	Group spirit dominates	Individualism dominates
Basis of work commitment	Confucian work ethic	Protestant work ethic
Basis of achievement	Group achievement	Individual achievement
Social contract	Harmony dominates	Individual rights dominate
Quality of vertical relationships	Highly paternalistic	Impersonal, bureaucratic
Job descriptions	Very general	Very specific
Nonverbal cues	Highly sensitive	Relatively insensitive
Employment	No guarantees	No guarantees
Mobility	Some mobility	High mobility

Source: Based on Gerardo R. Ungson, Richard M. Steers, and Seung-Ho Park, *Korean Enterprise: The Quest for Globalization* (Boston: Harvard Business School Press, 1997), pp. 168–176.

about 8:00. He spends his days at a small desk in a room filled with other small desks; he is always alert to the comings and goings of his supervisor.

Much of his work involves a team effort. Indeed, Hyundai has no individual job descriptions like those found in the West. Instead, one's assignments and areas of responsibility change and evolve depending on circumstance. On one recent occasion, for example, an entire management training class at Hyundai Motor Company was suspended for two weeks because several taxi companies announced they would make a major purchase of new cars. The instructor was sent home, and the managers were sent scurrying out to sell as many new Sonatas as they could. After achieving their goal, the managers returned to their training program to resume learning. The successful salary-man does whatever is called for. Nowhere throughout the corporation would a visitor ever hear the words, "That's not my job." Everything is his job.

While teamwork is important, so too is discipline. Indeed, the term *top-down* may represent an understatement in describing Korean management style. Instructions from above are to be followed to the letter and without question. From the earliest days, Hyundai employees, from senior executives down to the newest trainee, would carefully watch those above them for signs of impending action. Indeed, perhaps the greatest challenge for a salaryman is to figure out if the manager a notch or two above him approves of what he is doing. In some cases, this means that little is accomplished until a salaryman has received direct orders. Then, all hell breaks loose as he tries to accomplish his assignment in the least possible time. Once a task is assigned, failure to complete it is not an acceptable alternative. Although this military style of management has softened somewhat in recent years, discipline and compliance with directives remain important hallmarks of Hyundai, just as they are at other Korean firms.

Promptly at 12:00 noon, Hyundai's in-house television station begins broadcasting on monitors mounted throughout the building, providing employees with recent company news and upcoming events. This is usually a signal that it is time to leave for lunch. There are two cafeterias in the basement of the Hyundai headquarters complex, where lunch is served free of charge to all employees. There is also a private dining room reserved for managers above the rank of director (the equivalent of an upper-middle manager in the West). Many managers lunch at one of the numerous Korean restaurants that dot the narrow streets near the headquarters, especially if they have guests or clients.

After lunch, many employees of all ranks (and both genders) visit the Hyundai Sports Club, nestled between the two towers of the headquarters complex. Chung ordered it built in 1987 because of his strong belief in the importance of developing the whole person, mind and body. It is open to all employees and contains two Olympic-sized swimming pools, an aerobics room, an exercise room, an indoor track, a sauna, dressing rooms, and a barber shop. Above the two-story sports complex is a public park where employees, as well as others in the community, can enjoy a tranquil setting of grass and flowers in an otherwise concrete city—again, at Chung's orders.

On a typical day, the salaryman leaves work around 6:00 P.M. for the long subway ride home. Departure times can vary widely, however, because it is considered inappropriate—and certainly not politic—to leave the office earlier than one's supervisor. Moreover, as managers move up in the hierarchy, they are increasingly pressed into service entertaining clients at evening dinners and receptions, much as in the West. On Saturdays, most salarymen arrive at 8:00 A.M. and leave about 1:00 P.M. Some immediately head for the many golf courses in the suburbs, while others go home for time with their families.

Home, to a typical middle-level Hyundai salaryman, is a high-rise condominium in the suburbs that may cost between $200,000 and $400,000. Condominiums are paid for in cash, not thirty-year mortgages, so it is up to the employee to save or borrow the money required for the purchase. Homes are small by Western standards but generally very modern and efficiently designed. The salaryman's wife typically stays home and looks after the children (two, on average). For his efforts, he earns somewhere between $20,000 and $40,000 per year (including bonuses) and can expect to receive a promotion every four to five years, based more on seniority than performance.

Each year, he receives seven days vacation plus one additional day off for each year of service. Thus, in theory, after ten years of service, he would receive 17 days vacation, for example. In view of the press of work, however, he is invariably unable to take all of his vacation time, so the company pays him for his unused portion. He also receives one personal day off each month but seldom takes it. Twice a year, during Chinese New Year in January and the Moon Festival (*Ch'usok*) in September, all Hyundai employees get three-day weekends and are provided with gifts by the company. It is estimated that during these holidays, up to 30 million Koreans, out of a total population of 45 million, may hit the road to visit their extended families throughout Korea. After the brief holiday, the salaryman returns to work, ready to go again.

TRAINING FOR SUCCESS

MIT economist Lester Thurow recently analyzed global economic trends and industrial competitiveness around the world and concluded that in the future, successful companies—and countries—will compete, not on the basis of cheap labor or access to capital and raw materials, but rather on a combination of superior information, technology, and human resources.[17] Given the new openness of the global marketplace, Thurow argues, capital markets are open to almost everyone; they no longer represent a strategic asset. Similarly, raw materials are typically available in abundance in several parts of the world. And cheap labor is a fleeting advantage, as Korea discovered in the late 1980s. What will increasingly be in short supply—and hence provide comparative advantage—will be the control of information and advanced technology and access to well-trained and highly motivated employees. Interestingly, this is exactly where Hyundai is now trying to compete. A key ingredient in Hyundai's plan for the future lies in developing its employees to their fullest capacity.

As noted, Hyundai has long considered human resources to be the central building block of sustained corporate success, and considerable effort goes into the development of employees at all levels. In contrast to Western training techniques, however, developmental efforts focus not just on instilling new job-related knowledge or skills but also on molding current and future managers to fit into the company's corporate culture. Many Koreans believe that developing a positive attitude is more important than developing job skills because loyalty, dedication, and team spirit transcend a particular job or assignment. The central aim of most Korean firms is to develop what is generally referred as the "all-around person." The all-around person possesses general abilities; he or she is not a specialist. Commitment to the company and co-workers is unquestioned, and, above all, he or she fits into the group. Training is seen as one means of ensuring this across the corporation, and no company is more determined in the pursuit of training than Hyundai.

Chung Ju Yung strongly believed in the importance of developing human potential, and corporate training was seen as a primary means to this end. According to Chung: "People can be changed depending upon how they are educated. If a person is born without great talents but is diligent, trustworthy, and good natured, he can learn to be a good executive. Hyundai encourages all employees to pursue self-development."[18]

In 1980, Chung established the Hyundai Institute for Human Resource Development in a modern, campuslike setting in the village of Mabuk-ri in the beautiful rolling hills near Suwon, 50 miles south of Seoul. The institute is responsible for providing a strategic direction for the group's human resource development efforts. Its principal goal is to strengthen the administrative skills of Hyundai managers at all levels so they are better prepared for the challenges of global competition. A subsidiary goal is to enhance the personal development of managers in ways that build character as well as functional specialization. The director of the institute reports directly to the group chairman, a sign of the importance attributed to management development at the company. When he was active in the company, Chung was a frequent visitor to the institute, giving talks to the various training classes, especially those involving new recruits.

The general philosophy underlying the institute's training programs includes the importance of working for the further development of Korea, human resource development, international relationships, and a global orientation. In support of this philosophy, three overall training objectives have been set forth: incorporating the Hyundai spirit in the manager's daily life, developing managerial skills and capabilities, and strengthening international competitiveness. On an operational level, three implementing principles guide actual program design and implementation: the development of managerial and technical skills; the development of mental skills, including a heavy emphasis on what are termed "oriental values," such as creativity, positive thinking, tenacity, fraternity, devotion to company, and industriousness; and the development of one's physical capabilities. These three implementing principles—including the morning exercises and the pep talks from the chairman—aim to develop what the company refers to as the "Hyundai man."

Today, the institute has an annual operating budget of $50 million and a professional staff of sixteen, including three Americans. It offers over sixty different courses and programs, making it one of the largest such programs in Korea. These efforts are supported by fourteen additional Hyundai training centers that are operated by various subsidiary companies and offer specialized training to meet individual company needs. In the summer of 1998, the institute moved into a new, $80 million, campuslike training complex that is capable of housing 600 managers at a time. This state-of-the-art center combines two dozen electronic classrooms and lecture halls with extensive athletic facilities.

Through its various programs, the institute trains 12,000 managers each year. In addition to the orientation program for new recruits, its principal programs include a number of executive development programs for managers at various levels in the hierarchy that focus on developing decision-making and strategic skills, a leadership program aimed at developing team management skills, and a global competency program aimed at training Hyundai salarymen to succeed overseas in international business. In addition, the institute offers a wide array of self-improvement courses on such topics as presentation skills, creativity, leadership, business coaching, and basic human relations. The institute also operates a training program for foreign nationals working for Hyundai, as well as a language laboratory that teaches several levels of English, Japanese, and Chinese.

All managers are required to participate in training programs twice for each job classification they hold with the company. When a salaryman is promoted, he is immediately sent to the institute for relevant training. Then, about three years later—in preparation for his next promotion—he returns to the institute for additional skills training. Most training regimens combine intellectual and physical development. Most programs begin at 6:00 A.M. with morning exercise, such as calisthenics or a long hike. Breakfast is served in the cafeteria at 7:00 A.M., and classes begin at 8:00 A.M. Pedagogically, the institute combines the traditional instructional methods used by most American business schools, including lectures, case studies, simulations, and discussion groups. Afternoon exercise (such as a soccer game) is typically included, even during the hot, humid days of summer. Both physically and intellectually, Hyundai plans to be prepared for the future.

WOMEN AT WORK

A key factor in the economic success of many Korean firms has been the large pool of young, highly skilled, highly motivated—but relatively poorly paid—female workers.[19] Indeed, the offices at Hyundai headquarters, like those of other Korean companies, are staffed with legions of uniformed young women who work for several years prior to marrying and starting a family. They are hired on a basis of high school or college grades and skills tests conducted by the company. Once employed, they wear company-supplied uniforms and perform every clerical and secretarial task required to make the company function efficiently. They answer phones, type correspondence, run computers, act as receptionists for their male bosses, and serve tea. Throughout, they are expected to be gracious and subservient and to remain in the background.

For the average female Hyundai office worker, the typical work day runs from 8:00 A.M. to 5:30 P.M. For this, they receive a modest salary, not unlike the situation in the United States, plus a generous benefits package. In addition to the fringe benefits received by their male colleagues, women are entitled to one additional day's paid leave per month, plus sixty days paid maternity leave. Under current law, women can extend this leave for one additional year without pay and still keep their jobs. Annual salary increases are minimal, and promotions into the ranks of management are rare. College graduates fare somewhat better and receive about 15 percent more in salary than their high school–educated counterparts; they also have somewhat higher status within the organization. Although a small number of women are finding their way into managerial positions, primarily in the areas of personnel or translation services, Korean tradition still prefers that women be at home. Women are typically viewed by society as temporary workers and treated as such by most companies.

Despite these long-standing traditions, the role of women in Korean firms is slowly changing. The 1992 Equal Employment Act prohibited discrimination based on gender, and a number of companies have been fined for discriminatory practices. Indeed, a mild form of feminism is on the rise, as are several legal aid firms specializing in cases of gender discrimination.[20] As a result, the number of women hired into the white-collar ranks grew from 1 percent of all new hires in 1987 to 6 percent in 1992 to 11 percent in 1995.[21] Whether this trend will continue in the face of strong and persistent Confucian traditions remains to be seen.

Somewhat surprisingly, Hyundai, with its rugged, masculine, we-can-do-anything image, is actually in the forefront of this endeavor. Hyundai was the first—and only—Korean company to employ female sailors on its ships. In

March 1996, the 130,000-ton *Hyundai Spirit* set sail from Ulsan to Newcastle, Australia, with three women on board to help run the ship. "I decided on a life at sea and am very attracted to the thought of being part of the operation of a giant oceangoing carrier," observed 22-year-old Cho Kyong-Ju.[22] Hyundai made it happen. And women have worked on the automobile assembly lines at Hyundai for years, a sight never seen on Japanese automobile assembly lines. Again, Hyundai made it happen.

Back in corporate headquarters, Hyundai also has taken the lead in hiring and promoting women into the managerial ranks. Indeed, Hyundai currently has over 100 women managers in its headquarters, including two directors. Though small in comparison to those in the West, such numbers surpass those for other Korean firms. More to the point, Hyundai has been hiring women managers since Chung personally ordered it back in 1984, when even women in the United States had limited opportunities. Well in advance of other companies, Chung hired 100 female administrators that year as a social experiment to see if he could make it work. For various family reasons, however, most eventually left the company. So Chung hired more.

One woman who remained was Kwon Ae-Ja, currently the director of Hyundai's Welfare Department. Kwon is responsible for the company's extensive employee services programs, including cafeterias, hotels and ski resorts, golf courses, and condominiums, all of which are available to employees for no charge or at reduced rates. She also oversees the company's extensive bus system, which transports employees to and from work, as well as their educational support program. Kwon began at Hyundai as a secretary in 1966. After three years, she left to marry and raise her family. In 1984, she was hired back as a junior administrator in the Welfare Department, where she worked her way up to become its current director. Kwon was obviously proud that, in a country noted for male chauvinism, Hyundai offered women the same pay and promotion opportunities as their male counterparts.[23]

Kwon speaks warmly of the founder when asked what it was like to work for him in the early days. "We all loved and respected him," she says. "He is a very charming man."[24] She recalled that Chairman Chung frequently dined with secretaries, clerks, and workers. He would sometimes take a group out to the theater, where he loved to watch movies. Other times, he would take a group of workers to climb one of Korea's numerous mountains; he felt that mountain climbing built character. When asked to describe the chairman in a few words, Kwon responded with adjectives like "humorous," "candid," "inspires the best in us," "humanistic," "very strict," "frugal," "full of common sense," and "excellent memory." Chung always tried to challenge workers intellectually, Kwon said, and he liked people who drank; they had spirit. She noted that Chung always liked to tell Korean folk tales and sing folk songs. He even studied English on his various business trips so he could say a few words when meeting foreigners.

As an indication of her respect for the chairman, Kwon told a story of how he had recommended that she marry a certain Hyundai salaryman back in 1969. "He was always matchmaking in those days," she observed. Shortly afterward, she married a different man and left the company to raise her family. In 1984, when she returned—eighteen years later—Chung welcomed her back and jokingly chided her for not following his recommendation. "He remembered not only who I was but what he had said to me so long ago," she said with amazement.[25]

LESSONS FOR THE GLOBAL ENTREPRENEUR

"Two historic factors have served to slow human progress across the centuries. The first is a tendency to be overconfident about the future. The second is a tendency to underestimate the importance of the times in which we live."

—CHUNG JU YUNG[1]

Looking back on his contributions to the development of Korea, Chung Ju Yung recently observed:

To many people, Hyundai is seen as a leader in the industrialization and economic development of Korea through our efforts in heavy industries and other businesses. This makes all of us in the Hyundai family, including me, feel very proud. In addition, Hyundai played a key role in seeking new markets overseas based on our pioneering spirit and diligence. We worked under the slogan, 'Earn outside; become rich inside.'[2]

He continued:

Hyundai Engineering & Construction sought new overseas construction markets before other Korean companies. Hyundai Motor Company was the first Korean company to enter the American market and established a new sales record for imported cars in the U.S. in its first year. Hyundai Heavy Industries grew into the biggest and best shipbuilding company in the world. Hyundai Precision not only controls 40 percent of the world's container market but has also succeeded in becoming only the fourth company in the world to develop and test a mag-lev train. And Hyundai Electronics Industries was the first company in the world to develop the 1 gigabyte S-DRAM semiconductor.[3]

Chung referred to a record of performance that few companies around the world could even approach.

Why was Hyundai so successful in global markets? According to Chung, the answer is simple: "We competed with many famous foreign companies and defeated them based on our superior technology and competitive spirit. We did not avoid competition; competition only made us stronger."[4] And despite recent setbacks experienced by the Korean economy, Hyundai is well positioned to continue to grow in the future.

HYUNDAI TODAY

In 1997, Hyundai celebrated its fiftieth anniversary. It had grown into a multibillion dollar conglomerate consisting of 50 major companies involved in a wide array of divergent industries around the world. These include engineering and construction; automobiles, electronics, and information systems; shipbuilding and industrial plants; petrochemicals and oil refining; precision machinery; iron and steel; and trade and services (see Appendix A). These companies are backed up by the efforts of numerous research centers and institutes that work to keep Hyundai on the technological cutting edge (see Appendix B). Hyundai today has close to 200,000 employees worldwide and is responsible for more than 10 percent of Korea's total exports.

In May 1998, as part of a major corporate restructuring, Hyundai identified five core business arenas in which it planned to focus its principal attention for the new millenium: heavy industries and chemicals, automobiles, construction, financial services, and electronics. Several peripheral companies will be spun off so that available resources can be focused on these principal areas. At the same time, the company committed to securing an additional $8 billion in foreign investment and to reducing its debt ratio significantly so it can remain a competitive enterprise in the increasingly hostile global economy.

What sets Hyundai apart from most of its rivals, foreign or domestic, is its relentless pursuit of new frontiers. Above all else, Hyundai is a company that sets records. When it enters an industry, it consistently strives to become a dominant player. More often than not, it achieves this objective. A number of its recent achievements are shown in Table 14-1. All of these accomplishments come from just one highly entrepreneurial company. Few companies in the West can even approach Hyundai for its track record in such a wide range of diversified industries and services.

TABLE 14-1

RECENT ACCOMPLISHMENTS OF THE HYUNDAI BUSINESS GROUP

▶ Hyundai Engineering & Construction is one of the world's largest and most successful construction companies, recording its best sales volume ever in 1997.

▶ Hyundai Heavy Industries operates the world's largest shipbuilding facility.

▶ Hyundai Heavy Industries built the world's largest bulk carrier and equipped it with the world's largest ship engine, also built by Hyundai.

▶ Hyundai Heavy Industries is the most visited factory in the world, with a total of more than 11 million visitors.

▶ Hyundai Securities is one of Korea's largest securities firms.

▶ Hyundai's Mipo Dockyard is the world's largest ship repair and modification facility.

▶ Hyundai Motor Company will soon become one of the world's ten largest automobile manufacturers.

▶ Hyundai Motor Company operates the world's largest commercial vehicle plant.

▶ Hyundai Electronics Industries was the first company to develop both the 256M S-DRAM chip and the 1 gigabyte S-DRAM.

▶ Hyundai Electronics Industries currently controls 10 percent of the worldwide market for DRAM chips.

▶ Hyundai owns one of Korea's largest insurance companies.

▶ Hyundai Precision is a major manufacturer of four-wheel-drive vehicles, trains, and numeric control systems and is currently developing high-speed trains in conjunction with France's TGV.

▶ Hyundai owns Korea's largest housing construction company.

▶ Hyundai operates hotels, supermarkets, and a department store chain, as well as its own travel service.

▶ Hyundai operates an advertising agency, an entertainment and media business, and its own cable television station, the Hyundai Broadcasting System.

▶ Hyundai Corporation, the company's trading arm, is responsible for $22 billion in annual business.

▶ Hyundai Merchant Marine operates the fourth largest marine fleet in the world.

But while the Hyundai Group continues to set records in shipbuilding, electronics, automobiles, and so forth, it has never forgotten its roots in construction. It has never forgotten the importance or centrality of the "mother company." Hyundai Engineering & Construction continues to be the jewel in the crown and is widely respected throughout the company as being the initial vehicle for empire building. In its own right, too, it continues to progress. Today, Hyundai Engineering & Construction is more than twice the size of any of its Korean competitors, including Daewoo, Samsung, Daelim, and Dong-A. In 1997, it recorded its largest single year for sales, $6 billion. Of this, $4 billion came from overseas projects. In a typical year, it receives 60 percent of its business at home and 40 percent overseas. Indeed, this one construction company is now responsible for over half of all of Korea's overseas work.

Eighty percent of its current overseas work is in Southeast Asia, including an electric railroad and container terminal in Singapore, a marine terminal for a refinery in Malaysia, and a port and access channel in Indonesia. Hyundai was recently awarded a $279 million contract to construct a bridge and related outbuildings in Bangladesh and a $240 million contract to construct a 2,400 megawatt thermal power plant in Kuwait. After several years' absence, the company recently returned to Saudi Arabia to construct roads and government buildings. Other major construction projects can be found in Singapore, Indonesia, Tartarstan, Yemen, Tunisia, and Hong Kong. Among these projects is Singapore's new Suntec City, constructed by Hyundai at a cost of $635 million and the recipient of the prestigious Best Project award given by the Construction Industry Development Board. As the global construction industry continues to grow, Hyundai plans to remain in the forefront, technologically and economically, preserving its hard-earned reputation as contractor to the world.

How do outside observers rank the company today? In one recent major independent study of industrial competitiveness by Arthur D. Little, Hyundai Motor Company was rated as the eighth most competitive company in Asia—the only Korean company in the top 25.[5] Ahead of HMC were seven Japanese and one Taiwanese firms. And in the *Far Eastern Economic Review*'s 1988 survey of Asia's most respected companies, several Hyundai-affiliated subsidiaries were named among the top ten Korean companies.[6] This survey, conducted among 6,000 business executives throughout Asia, rated companies on criteria that included the quality of products and services, customer satisfaction, management vision, and respect by competitors. The results found that Hyundai Motor Company ranked in the top three firms on product quality, and Hyundai Electronics ranked in the top five in long-term management vision. At the same time, Hyundai Engineering & Construction,

Hyundai Motor, and Hyundai Heavy Industries all ranked in the top five among companies that competitors wanted to emulate. Overall, the Hyundai Business Group achieved higher ratings than any other Korean firm.

THE LEGACY OF CHUNG JU YUNG

To Chung Ju Yung, there is no such thing as miracles; there are only dreams—dreams and tireless effort. People—dedicated people—can accomplish whatever they set their hearts and minds on accomplishing. They do not need to be rich or brilliant or even well educated. But they need to have drive. Although this lesson is simple and easily understood, it is frequently overlooked by those would-be entrepreneurs who either dream but don't work or work but don't dream. As Chung said many years ago: "Some men live without thinking. Other men with positive thinking achieve ten or one hundred times as much as ordinary people."[7] In this regard, Chung's life represents an exemplary case study for entrepreneurs around the world. Chung was never reluctant to work hard. He considered his plans and strategies carefully before he began a new venture. He never sought to avoid conflict if he thought it necessary to achieve his goal. And he expected the same of his colleagues. As the American business professor Phillip Grub notes: "He is a very determined, calculating person who is very intense. He expects everyone to be the same workaholic that he is."[8]

This observation is correct. But Chung did something else. He never forgot who he was or where he was. He never forgot his people or his country. His company and Korea grew and prospered along the same path. Hyundai grew from nothing in 1947 to become one of the world's most successful corporations, with annual sales larger than all but about a dozen companies around the world. During the same time, Korea grew from an impoverished nation with an average annual household income of less than $100 to a prosperous and democratic nation with an average annual income of well over $10,000 and rising. Korea today has one of the best educated populations and one of the longest life expectancies of any nation on the globe. It is now an OECD member and a political force to be reckoned with. And none of this would have happened without the drive and determination—and creativity—of entrepreneurs like Chung and companies like Hyundai. Together with government leaders intent on developing independence and self-sufficiency and a national work force committed to sacrifice for the sake of future generations, the Korean people built a new nation that can serve as a model for others to follow. Of this accomplishment they can justifiably be very proud.

The significant legacy of Chung Ju Yung can be seen in three principal arenas: his contributions to business enterprise, his efforts in public welfare, and his lifelong commitment to build and unify his homeland. In the business arena, Chung's career is noteworthy in several respects. Chung rose from poverty to become one of the world's wealthiest billionaires. He accomplished this in a country that was first occupied by a foreign power, then racked by civil war, and then left to wallow in its own poverty by a largely indifferent world that was convinced Korea could not succeed. Korea had few resources and little usable land. It also had few friends or supporters around the world. But it was rich in human resources, and Chung knew how to capitalize on this. Chung brought ideas, drive, and tenacity—what he continually referred to as an indomitable spirit—to the task of rebuilding Korea. Begining from scratch, he built a global enterprise worthy of admiration and respect by world leaders. As Hyundai prospered, so too did its 200,000 employees. Other Korean firms, like Samsung, LG, Daewoo, and SK, also prospered. In short order, Korea emerged from poverty to become the world's thirteenth largest trading nation. It had moved from Third World to First World status in record time, a feat that clearly would have been impossible without entrepreneurs like Chung.

Chung's indomitable spirit led him to accomplish things that others with more opportunities and resources only dreamed about. He created one of the world's largest and most successful business conglomerates. In the process, he built one of the world's largest construction companies and holds several world records for engineering innovations. He built the world's largest shipyard, the world's largest commercial ship, and the world's largest commercial ship engine. He exported the first Korean-made cars to the United States and broke all import sales records in doing so. He then built one of the world's largest automobile companies, which now sells cars around the world. He built an electronics company that is rapidly proving its technological prowess on several fronts in Asia, North America, and Europe. He became Korea's biggest farmer by reclaiming a huge tract of land from the Yellow Sea and converting it for agricultural use. And he built a family dynasty to continue his efforts well into the next millennium.

Chung certainly proved himself to be one of the world's greatest entrepreneurs. But in addition to his significant business accomplishments, he also showed a willingness to confront controversies head on when he believed in a cause. He led Seoul's contentious but successful bid to host the 1988 Olympics after his own government had all but given up. He led the way in opening political and economic relations between his country and two former enemies, China and the former Soviet Union, at a time when his own government was skeptical. He was the first businessman from the South to venture into North Korea to initiate a dialogue aimed at peaceful reunification, again when his own government was timid. He was a traditional Confucian male executive who created career opportunities for women long before other Korean firms would consider it. He openly admired slain President Park Chung Hee as a nation builder at a time when most Koreans considered him to be a malevolent dictator. He was known for being ruthless and harsh, for demanding the impossible from his staff, but at the same time he commanded a respect and allegiance from his employees that most CEOs today can only envy. He fought against independent labor unions but, once he saw that change was inevitable, took the lead in building innovative worker-management partnerships. He ran for the presidency of his country on a platform of democratization, deregulation, and open competition and paid dearly for challenging the establishment. But he never gave up. "Man's potential is limitless," Chung used to say.[9] And he truly believed it.

Just as his contributions to economic and business development are significant, so too are his efforts to improve public welfare. Throughout his career, it is estimated that, including his stock contributions, Chung personally contributed the equivalent of over $1 billion to various charitable, medical, and educational ventures. Few entrepreneurs throughout history—regardless of national origin—have contributed so much. Indeed, a 1997 *Forbes* magazine survey identified only two philanthropists who have contributed more: Walter Annenberg ($1.2 billion) and George Soros ($1.1 billion).[10] Chung's personal fortune may have been smaller, but his generosity was not.

Despite his frugal image, giving back was always on Chung's agenda. When the fiftieth anniversary of Hyundai approached in 1997, senior executives went to work planning a gala extravaganza to commemorate the event. It was to be a lavish testament to the achievements of the honorary chairman and founder. No expense would be spared. When Chung learned of the plans, however, he reminded his colleagues of Korea's current economic problems and of the starvation throughout North Korea. People who had money should set an example, he reasoned. The considerably subdued celebration that went forward to mark the event saved the company almost $15 million. Chung quietly directed that the funds saved from the celebration be donated to buy food for North Korea.

The principal vehicle through which Chung has supported public welfare over the years is the Asan Foundation. Named after his birthplace, the foundation was created by Chung in 1977 with a contribution of one-half of his Hyundai stock.[11] This equity increased as the company grew and prospered. In addition, Chung frequently supplemented this with additional contributions of stock and cash for the foundation. He is also known for simply writing personal checks when he sees a worthy cause, as he did in 1995 when he surprised administrators at Johns Hopkins University with a $3 million check to express his appreciation for their granting him an honorary doctorate.

The overall goal of the Asan Foundation is to provide support for the underprivileged of Korea's society. In this endeavor, the foundation supports various social welfare programs, especially in the field of medicine. Since its founding just over twenty years ago, over $700 million has been spent to improve the welfare of Korea's less fortunate citizens. Chung refers to this contribution as "small but meaningful."[12]

Over the years, the foundation built, staffed, and continues to operate eight modern hospitals in rural communities, many of which previously lacked any hospital facilities. In addition, in 1989, Chung's foundation opened the Asan Medical Center, Seoul's largest and best-equipped medical facility, with over 3 million square feet of state-of-the-art facilities. The center has 2,200 beds and employs 900 doctors in 35 departments and 41 clinics. In an average day, the center sees 7,000 patients, including inpatients, outpatients, and emergency visits. These medical services are offered without charge to the poor. The Asan Foundation also operates nursing homes, orphanages, and facilities for the handicapped. Programs benefit single teenaged mothers, provide scholarships for indigent students to return to school, and support medical research.

Chung has also demonstrated a long-term commitment to higher education. In 1970, he used his own money to found Ulsan University to train future engineers, doctors, scientists, and business leaders. Currently, the university has over 500 faculty and 13,000 students and boasts over 25,000 alumni. How many other entrepreneurs—East or West—have invested their wealth to build an entire university? In the United States, only the Rockefeller family comes to mind. In addition to Ulsan University, Chung has personally donated funds to construct various buildings at key universities throughout Korea. The new five-story engineering building at Ewha Woman's University is illustrative of his commitment to supporting education. It is noteworthy that this particular building was constructed to help train *female* engineers, still a controversial endeavor in conservative Korean culture. At the dedication ceremony in 1996, Chung noted that his contribution was meant "to foster the development of a corps of women engineers" to cope with Korea's crucial shortage of well-educated scientists and engineers.[13]

The third arena in which Chung made significant contributions can be seen in his efforts to rebuild Korea from a war-torn Third World nation struggling to survive into a prosperous and respected member of the global economic community. Perhaps more than any other single individual, Chung deserves credit for developing Korea into an economic powerhouse to be reckoned with. He did much to build Korea's modern infrastructure, technological base, and global markets. He is clearly Korea's greatest entrepreneur.

But to Chung, rebuilding his homeland also meant rebuilding—and unifying—the entire Korean peninsula. More than anything, Chung wanted to see Korea as a unified nation once again, as it had been before the advent of the Korean War. Toward this end, he had traveled to the North in 1989 on a path-breaking mission that ultimately fell short of his intended objectives. Not to be deterred, he continued to work quietly behind the scenes to create another opportunity for dialogue and progress with the North. His time came—almost a decade later—in June 1998, when Chung was again invited to return to his birthplace. Diligence and perseverance, Hyundai's motto, had once again paid off.

On June 16, with live television coverage, including CNN, Chung led an eight-person delegation across the DMZ into North Korea at Panmunjom for the beginning of an historic eight-day visit. He thus became the first South Korean civilian to enter into North Korea through this traditionally hostile crossing. Including in his delegation were three of his brothers, Chung Soon Yung, Chung Se Yung, and Chung Sang Yung, as well as two of his sons, Chung Mong Koo and Chung Mong Hun. Chung was later joined by seven additional Hyundai executives, who had entered North Korea by way of Beijing to join the delegation.

As a gesture of friendship, Chung brought with him five hundred head of cattle that had been raised on his beloved Seosan Farm. The cattle, intended to help improve North Korea's farming, were transported on fifty trucks specially built by Hyundai for the trip. The cattle and the trucks were both intended as gifts to the North Korean people from a native son. The North Korean economy had declined for eight consecutive years—6.8 percent in 1997 alone—and flooding and famine had caused countless deaths in recent years. Chung asked that the cattle be sent to help the people of his native Tongchon district in Kangwon Province. Chung also promised to send another five hundred cattle on fifty more trucks shortly after his return. In addition, Chung donated fifty thousand tons of grain to the North to aid victims of hunger and starvation. In all, he spent $8.5 million on the venture. The people in the South referred to it as "cattle diplomacy."

For Chung, the cattle had a special symbolic meaning beyond their value in farming. Chung had always felt remorse over taking 70 won from the sale of his father's cow back in 1933 to fund one of his aborted escape attempts from the farm in Asan village. Now, sixty-five years later, here was a way to repay the debt to his father's memory. Chung would not miss this opportunity.

From Panmunjom, the delegation traveled by car to Pyongyang, North Korea's capital for high-level discussions with government officials. Foremost on Chung's agenda for these meetings was his long-cherished Keumkang

Mountain development project. Keumkang Mountain lies only 12 miles from Chung's birthplace and has always held fond memories for him. It is also widely recognized for its beauty and imposing landscape. Chung had first proposed the development to the North Koreans during his 1989 visit, but nothing came of it. Even so, he never ceased to dream about it. To Chung, Keumkang Mountain could become a world-class tourist facility, including hotels, golf courses, casinos, department stores, and other leisure facilities. People would visit from all over the world.

By the end of Chung's visit to the North, both sides had agreed to a development plan for the resort area. Plans were made to establish a cruise ship connection between Donghae in the South and Changjun in the North. Ships would bring up to one thousand tourists per day. At Changjun, the tourists would board buses for the 8-mile trip to the new Keumkang Mountain resort. Considerable new employment and tourist income would be generated from the business, which could help regional economic development as well as open dialogues between the peoples of the North and South. To Chung, it was a win-win opportunity for both sides.

Other possible joint ventures were also discussed during Chung's visit. These included proposed plans to make rolling stock for the railroads with Hyundai Precision, a salvage and ship repair business with Hyundai Heavy Industries, and an automobile assembly plant to make passenger cars for export to China and Russia with Hyundai Motor Company. Although no formal agreements were signed, both sides were optimistic about the long-term prospects for such ventures.

Chung returned from his trip physically exhausted. He was frail and in poor health. But at the age of 82, he was proud of his accomplishments and immediately announced his intentions to return to North Korea within several months. He believed strongly in person-to-person diplomacy and in the power of business to lead political relations. He remained convinced that creating business opportunities for the North—opportunities for significant economic development—remained the best route to peace and ultimate reunification. In this sense, he hoped that his visit would not be an isolated event, but rather the cornerstone of reconciliation and peace between North and South. To the people of South Korea, Chung returned a national hero once again, not unlike his first venture to the North. He had once again accomplished what governments could not: he had opened the door a bit further to peace and stability in the region. His legacy as a peace maker had been assured.

Chung Ju Yung clearly made a lasting mark in the world. He excelled in global business, public service, and serious efforts toward regional peace and reunification. But perhaps his single greatest accomplishment to date has been to demonstrate by example that Korean history teaches us valuable lessons about the future. He taught us that the Korean spirit soars when it is allowed to be truly free. Chung's ancestors invented movable type for printing, ironclad ships for warfare, rain gauges for agriculture, and scientific encyclopedias for medicine. They made early and important contributions to world civilization in areas ranging from astronomy to religion to government to military science. In their time, Koreans repulsed assaults and military invasions from China, Japan, Europe, and the United States. Also in their time, they lost military and cultural invasions from these same world powers. For most of his countrymen, Korean history is the story of conflict between rare opportunities and often insurmountable economic and geopolitical constraints. For Chung, it is only the story of opportunities.

REFLECTIONS ON AN ENTREPRENEURIAL LIFE

As long as Chung Ju Yung could remember, he had to work hard. Recalling his early days in Asan village, he observed: "I was driven to accomplish things because of the poverty I experienced as a child. I was the eldest of eight children. My father was a diligent but poor farmer. My parents both worked hard from early morning until late into the night, but they were always poor. I became determined to help both my family and my countrymen prosper."[14] Later, as a contractor building the Kyungbu Expressway from Seoul to Pusan, Chung continued his unyielding efforts. As he recalls, "Faced with a project that was so important to our nation's future, we could never rest. We worked so hard that we didn't even notice the seasons changing."[15]

But it took more than hard work to build his company. It required creativity and leadership. "People call me an idea bank," Chung observed in a recent interview. "I planted barley in a cemetery to make the fields green in the winter. I developed the 'oil tanker method' to complete a dike at Seosan farm. Ideas come to me because I spend considerable time concentrating and contemplating problems. Some people just look for quick solutions. In my view, ideas come from people's attitudes. If you are optimistic and have an affirmative attitude, you can do anything. Always look at a problem from new angles. That is the key."[16] Chung thought for a moment and then continued: "Whether you succeed or fail depends on your thoughts and attitudes. I always tried to challenge things up to the limit, and I always found pleasure in achieving what others thought was impossible."[17] Juhn Myung-Hun, president of Hyundai Motor America, agrees: "Chung Ju Yung is a very special person. He taught us that you have to make ideas flow like they are coming from a spring."[18]

At Hyundai, hard work and creativity combine with exceptional leadership skills to create an unbeatable force for accomplishment and innovation. According to Chung, leadership at Hyundai is based on the traditional Confucian principal of reciprocity among leaders and followers. Managers teach their subordinates, and subordinates do their best to meet the expectations of the superiors. Each looks out for the other. "We think of all Hyundai employees as family," Chung noted in an interview. "People say that Hyundai's culture is patriarchal. This is true, but it is also true that we lead with a warm heart. We care about the welfare of our people."[19]

His subordinates uniformly agree. Park Chong Sup, who served as Chung's personal assistant in the late 1970s and remained to become president of Hyundai Electronics America, observed: "People say he is autocratic. Well, yes and no. It is true that he is decisive and gives orders to us. But, in retrospect, I am amazed how much power he gave to each of us. He empowered us; he helped us achieve. He was a genius at knowing when and where to let us take responsibility....He was a great teacher."[20] As evidence, President Park noted that after Chung's retirement, competent managers were in place throughout the group to carry on his work. "Everyone knew what to do.... People have grown significantly under the honorary chairman," Park concluded. "He taught us that nothing is impossible."[21] In a similar vein, Lee Ik Chi, president of Hyundai Securities and a long-time associate of Chung, observed, "To me, Chung Ju Yung is more important than all the world leaders combined. He saved this country from poverty. It was a privilege to work for this man. Together, we made history and I was able to participate in these efforts. This was quite an honor for me."[22]

What drives Chung Ju Yung personally? In a 1996 newspaper interview, Chung noted: "I work because I can't relax. Working is my hobby."[23] More recently, Chung added: "I am the kind of person who lived life because of the joy that work brought me. I enjoyed working so much that my joy grew with the development of my business. Even so, I found myself being called something I disliked intensely, a 'tycoon.'"[24] Park Chong Sup adds an additional observation: "Chairman Chung has a different motivation in his life than most people. He wants to create, not just make money. He wants to provide opportunities for others."[25] Indeed, Chung lives by a code of behavior that offers many lessons to aspiring entrepreneurs, regardless of their national origin.

How does Chung feel about being the richest man in Korea? "That is a silly question," he responds. "It might not be convincing to others, but the truth is that I simply kept climbing toward the top of the mountain and happened to reach its peak before anyone else. I worked hard and took advantage of the opportunities I found. I lived like this all of my life and, one day, you can see what happened."[26] Even so, Chung does not like discussing his wealth and goes to great lengths to avoid conspicuous consumption.

Throughout his life, he was uncomfortable in opulent surroundings. "I had a feeling that I was wearing clothes that didn't fit me," he recalls.[27] He insists on being evaluated by people on the basis of his contributions to Korea's economic growth and development, not his personal wealth. "I hope people will not measure me using money as a yardstick," Chung observes.[28]

Is there anything special about Korean culture that has allowed the Koreans to succeed against all odds? According to Chung, the Korean people are diligent, honest, responsible, and intelligent. They are also enthusiastic and committed when properly motivated. In fact, when he is asked the secret to Hyundai's success, he routinely gives credit to his people. "Our people are the greatest in the world," he notes with pride. "They succeed wherever they go. Where else could people with only an elementary school education go overseas and compete successfully against foreign businesses?"[29] He attributes this success to a culture born of five thousand years of accumulated wisdom and knowledge. "The [Korean] nation's resources are limited, but human creativity is unlimited. An economy based on natural resources will falter when its resources become depleted, but growth based on human endeavor will continue regardless of natural resources. This is the lesson of Korea and the lesson of Hyundai."[30] Even so, while touting Korea, Chung believes firmly that successful entrepreneurial traits can be developed in any people or culture that is genuinely committed to accomplishing great things. "Any business or, for that matter, any culture can succeed if its leaders can instill these characteristics in their people," he notes.[31]

However, Chung shares the concerns of many Korean leaders about what awaits future generations. Since it emerged from poverty to become an industrialized nation, Korea has witnessed both a declining work ethic and an increasing consumption rate among its young people. As just one example, consider that the average wedding in Korea in 1997 cost over $83,000.[32] As Chung Ju Yung noted in a recent interview: "Whenever I see the young generation, I feel that they are growing up in happy times. Compared to my childhood, they enjoy enormous material prosperity. In my opinion, however, they have become a little selfish. Young people depend more on materialistic possessions than on their mental powers. When young people face challenges, to my sadness they tend to get frustrated easily." Chung continued: "Our education system should focus more on encouraging positive and diligent behavior and correcting shortcomings where they exist. Schools should look at the whole student, not just grades. Parents have to bring up their children more strictly and, in society, more adults should correct young people's conduct wherever they see it. Even so, as our desire for education is very high and the mental power of our people is also very high, we can overcome these problems."[33]

When Chung himself looks back over his long career, what does he see as his greatest accomplishments? Clearly, he takes considerable pride in having helped to develop a modern, prosperous nation worthy of international respect. The story of Korea's economic miracle would have been quite different without Chung. But in contributing to nation building, Chung also notes with pride some of his favorite accomplishments along the way. He is proud of his role in creating the Soyang River Dam. "The Japanese consulting firm and the Korean government both recommended a conventional concrete dam," Chung said recently. "I was against that recommendation. As you know, my choice was a zone-fill type dam made from soil and rocks that existed in profusion right on the site. It later proved that my choice was correct, and we completed the project at 30 percent below the original estimate."[34] He also beams with pride when discussing the Kyungbu Expressway. "Construction of the Kyungbu Expressway opened up our country to modernization," he observes.[35] Then, in short order, he lists several more achievements, each of which could occupy the entire lifetime of most entrepreneurs—establishing Hyundai Heavy Industries, establishing Hyundai Motor Company, building Jubail Harbor Industrial Port, securing the 1988 Olympics for Seoul, creating Seosan Farm, and so on.

Summing up, Chung's son and current group chairman Chung Mong Koo observes: "The most important achievement of my father has been to lead the economic development efforts of my country. He simultaneously built a company and a country."[36]

LESSONS FOR THE WEST

Over the past thirty years, many Korean business ventures were begun. Some succeeded, some failed. In fact, of the top ten business conglomerates in the late 1960s, only three remain today.[37] What separated the successful from the unsuccessful more often than not was the entrepreneurial drive of the group's founder. As Chung Ju Yung frequently observed, with characteristic modesty befitting a Korean elder statesman, "I am somebody who lives enthusiastically with a firm conviction and indomitable effort; I am not somebody special."[38] If Chung Ju Yung is not special, one wonders who is.

To understand the psychology underlying Hyundai's successful drive for industrial achievement, it is necessary to understand what is referred to in the company as the enterprising spirit, or the Hyundai spirit. This spirit is not just an aspect of the corporate culture but, indeed, a philosophy of operations that is embedded in the hearts and souls of Hyundai employees, regardless of their positions in the organization. Even in the depths of Korea's worst labor turmoil in the late 1980s, Hyundai workers would routinely walk the picket line or begin a demonstration singing the company song and chanting company slogans—a sight seldom if ever witnessed during U.S. or European labor disputes. Even when workers were fighting against the company, most remained committed to its philosophy, its business goals, and its founder.

Chung's significant success as an entrepreneur can be traced to several factors (see Table 14-2). These factors reflect Chung's beliefs about the keys to success in initiating new entrepreneurial ventures:

1. Throughout his career, Chung had a *clear-cut vision* of what he wanted to accomplish. Whether it was completing a construction project or building a great company, he had a picture in his mind of what it should look like. Before setting out to secure the 1988 Olympics for Seoul, he developed a mental image of what an Olympic Village would look like on the south bank of the Han River, complete with high-rise apartments for athletes, major sports facilities, shopping areas for visitors, and transportation networks. Such pictures served as road maps, guiding his financial and physical investments until he had achieved his goal.

2. Chung's visions were backed by *uncanny insight*. Many of Chung's ventures—from building ships from scratch to shipping massive steel jackets across 7,000 miles of open seas without insurance to reclaiming farmland from the Yellow Sea—appeared at first glance to be highly impractical, even foolhardy. Indeed, on many occasions, his subordinates silently wondered if Chung had simply overreached himself on many projects. Time and again, however, Chung proved to his colleagues that his instincts about what was possible were entirely correct. This is part of Chung's notion of the enterprising spirit.

3. Chung pursued his various business ventures with a *zeal* or *drive* that frequently stunned even his chief Korean rivals. Once begun, his commitment to a project or cause was absolute and unyielding. His decision to cut by six months an already tight construction schedule so his medical center would be completed before his rival's initially appeared literally impossible to everyone, but he succeeded. He would never concede defeat. As Chung himself noted, "I am considered by some to be a major international industrialist, but I have never regarded myself as a capitalist. I am only a fairly wealthy laborer who produces wealth with labor."[39]

4. Chung insisted on complete *autonomy and control* over all of his ventures. He would do things his way or not at all. In contrast to some of his competitors, Chung insisted on building new companies from scratch. He did

TABLE 14-2

CHUNG JU YUNG'S KEYS TO SUCCESS

▶ *Stay focused*. Maintain a clear vision of what you want to accomplish. Never lose sight of your primary goal.

▶ *Seek new solutions to old problems*. Study each problem in detail. Insights and inspirations frequently emerge through looking at the same problem from several different angles.

▶ *Pursue your business with a passion*. Once you begin an endeavor, commit all of your energies and resources to attaining your goal.

▶ *Maintain complete autonomy and control*. Don't get slowed down by needless entanglements with others. Swift accomplishment of your projects requires full independence.

▶ *Be frugal in all your business dealings*. Watch the pennies; save money wherever possible.

▶ *Sweat the details*. Prepare everything carefully before you begin. Organization is the key to success in all ventures.

▶ *Be honest and straightforward in working with others*. This includes investors, customers, employees—everybody.

▶ *Don't fight city hall*. Wherever possible, develop productive working relationships with bureaucrats and government officials who can affect your business. Help them do their job so you can do yours. In all things, try to build harmonious relationships.

▶ *Good fortune without adequate preparation leads to failure*. Always be on the lookout for new opportunities. However, remember that such opportunities can only be exploited if you recognize and are prepared for them.

▶ *Serve the nation*. Successful business enterprises benefit the company and the country. Strong economies support strong businesses. Always remember to give something back.

not want to take over failing firms and turn them around. Instead, he wanted each venture to be nurtured from the beginning with the Hyundai spirit. Throughout his career, he monitored even the smallest details of each firm's operations. These were his companies and he would personally manage each one.

5. In all of his business dealings, Chung was *frugal* to a fault. He placed large signs inside his factories telling his workers what each little part or supply cost. Most of these items cost only a few cents, but the point was made: don't waste anything. He nearly fired a maid who threw out his old thread-bare slippers and replaced them with a new pair. In the maid's eyes, billionaire Chung deserved better slippers, but to Chung, the old slippers had many more years of life in them. At other times, he would remind managers that they were spending "the owner's money." While he would invest millions and sometimes billions in new plants and technologies he felt would help the company, he would also fret over a supervisor's purchase of premium-grade paper goods. The first he considered an investment, the second an extravagance. As he noted recently: "I am a man who asks others to use both sides of a piece of paper so as not to waste resources. I am also a man who reprimands workers who leave even a few pieces of gravel on the ground at a construction site. Resources are too precious to be squandered."[40]

6. Everything Chung did was characterized by *order*. He rose early at the same time each morning. He followed a routine that created organization for his busy life. No time was wasted. He demanded that throughout his company everything be well organized at all times. During his frequent, unannounced inspection tours of his various factories, he expected the factory floors to be impeccably clean. If they were not, the supervisor or plant manager would certainly hear about it. Chung's reputation as the "tiger" was richly deserved.

7. Chung also demonstrated an *honesty* and *straightforwardness* in dealing with others that gained him their support when he needed it. Building open, honest, and mutually beneficial relationships with business colleagues and employees alike was something Chung saw as part of his Confucian responsibility. It was also good business. People trusted him, and this, in turn, created additional opportunities. This was a lesson he learned early as a rice broker and automobile repair shop owner. Neither of these initial ventures would have prospered had people doubted his word. As he noted in his autobiography, "trust is wealth."[41] It later proved invaluable when he needed European bankers to back his fledgling shipyard and automobile company. President Park Chung Hee trusted Chung enough to overrule his experts in the construction of both the Soyang Dam and the Kyungbu Expressway. And the Russians, Chinese, and North Koreans trusted him enough to take political risks they would not take with others.

8. In addition to his managerial skills, Chung also possessed keen *political skills* in an environment in which politics often governed business success. The government influenced financing, technology acquisition, and export licensing. On a regular basis, Chung had to convince the Korean government that his plans had merit and would support the economic development of the country. Without this key support at the highest levels of government, Hyundai never would have received the necessary approval or support for its new ventures. Chung succeeded here in large part because his goals were compatible with those of the government. In addition to being an industrialist, Chung was also a nationalist intent on improving the welfare of his countrymen. He and the government both understood this.

9. Chung's efforts were supported by a touch of *good luck*. Economic opportunities that emerged were quickly exploited, often leading to new opportunities. For example, in the mid-1980s, Korean businessmen frequently discussed the Age of the Three Lows—low oil prices, low Korean currency valuation, and low interest rates. Because of this, and because of the concomitant rise in the value of the Japanese yen, Hyundai and other Korean companies were able to move quickly into Western markets and compete head on with others. Or consider the Kyungbu Expressway. Because Chung had built a road in the jungles of Thailand, he emerged as a key player when the Korean government wanted to build a superhighway across Korea. He was in the proverbial right place at the right time. Even so, to be successful, an entrepreneur had to recognize such opportunities—preferably before his competitors—and exploit them. Chung proved to be a master at this.

10. Finally, Chung believed strongly that he should *serve the national interest*. He believed that businesses had to work in concert with the nation. Strong economies served strong businesses; strong businesses served strong economies. Chung recently noted, "I firmly believe that anyone who puts his own business interests ahead of his country's cannot succeed in the long run."[42] "My objective for Hyundai was to continuously create wealth in Korea by means of foreign marketing. With that in mind, the fact that Hyundai continues to grow makes me feel very proud."[43] Throughout his career, Chung tried to give something back to his country, whether it involved working to secure the Olympics, seeking a rapprochement with North Korea, or running for president because he felt he could do better than the career politicians. Chung always viewed himself as a nationalist in service to his country. This belief represented a powerful influence on his choice of businesses to pursue.

Industrialists like Chung Ju Yung make it clear that the Korean tradition of innovation and creativity is alive and well. In ancient times, Korea was a world leader in the development of astronomy, movable-type printing, rain gauges, spinning wheels, and ironclad ships. Today, it is a world leader in shipbuilding, construction, automobiles, home electronics, semiconductors, and telecommunications. The entrepreneurial drive continues; only the products have changed.

Some observers claim that Korea's economic success during the past thirty years resulted from a combination of good fortune and hard work. Korea learned from the earlier experiences of Japan and capitalized on the status of being a late industrializer. The Koreans combined hard work with low wages and imported technology to manufacture products the world was eager to buy. In a different age, this winning combination might not have existed, and Korea might have remained mired in poverty and isolation. In all likelihood, Chung Ju Yung would agree with this observation. But he would add, "Without persistent hard work, people miss good fortune when it arrives."[44] Luck? Yes. Hard work? Yes. But Korea's success is based on much more. It is based on what Chung calls an enterprising spirit, a dedication to diligence, tenacity, and creative thinking. Throughout history, many nations have had good luck and many have worked hard. But the ones that truly prospered also had an enterprising spirit.

As Chung himself observed over twenty years ago, "Two historic factors have served to slow human progress across the centuries. The first is a tendency to be overconfident about the future. The second is a tendency to underestimate the importance of the times in which we live."[45] His advice is equally applicable today. Seizing the moment while planning for the future may seem to some like contradictory advice, but to Chung it represents the essence of entrepreneurial success.

APPENDIX A

PRINCIPAL COMPANIES OF THE HYUNDAI BUSINESS GROUP

DATE FOUNDED	COMPANY	NUMBER OF EMPLOYEES (1998)
1947	Hyundai Engineering & Construction[a]	6,221
1953	Inchon Iron & Steel[b]	3,127
1964	Hyundai Oil Refinery[c]	1,570
1967	Hyundai Motor	46,888
	Hyundai Industrial Development & Construction	2,050
1971	Keumkang Industrial Development	4,174
1973	Aluminum of Korea	652
	Hyundai Heavy Industries[d]	27,196
1974	Hyundai Engineering	1,528
	Hyundai Motor Service	15,298
1975	Hyundai Mipo Dockyard	2,542
	Hyundai Pipe	1,265
1976	Hyundai Merchant Marine	2,697
	Korea Industrial Development	1,465
	Hyundai Corporation	704
1977	Hyundai Precision & Industry	8,531
	Hyundai Securities[e]	1,675
	Hyundai Livart[f]	993
1978	Hyundai International Merchant Bank[g]	133
1983	Hyundai Electronics Industries	19,846
	Hyundai Marine & Fire Insurance[h]	4,016
	Diamond Advertising	627
1984	Hyundai Elevator	1,429
1986	Hyundai Housing & Industrial Development	2,225
	Hyundai Research Institute	128
1987	Korea Electronic Fuel Injection (KEFICO)[i]	786
	Hyundai Aluminum Industry	637
1988	Hyundai Information Technology[j]	3,255
	Hyundai Petrochemical	1,750
	Hyundai Logistics	572
	Hyundai Investment Management	21
1989	Hyundai Construction Equipment Service	734
1990	Hyundai Resources Development	25
	Hyundai Munwha Shinmun	578
	Korea Soviet Shipping	NA

DATE FOUNDED	COMPANY	NUMBER OF EMPLOYEES (1998)
1991	Hyundai Media Systems[k]	67
1993	Hyundai Financial Services	20
1994	Hyundai Space & Aircraft	654
1995	Hyundai Oil Sales	550
1996	Hyundai Finance & Factoring	164
1997	Citizens Investment Trust Management Securities	1,124
	Hyundai Broadcasting System	261

[a]Renamed from Hyundai Construction in 1981.

[b]Originally founded in 1953; acquired and renamed by Hyundai in 1978.

[c]Originally founded as Kukdong Oil Refinery in 1964; formally integrated into the Hyundai Group in 1993.

[d]Renamed from Hyundai Shipbuilding in 1978.

[e]Originally founded in 1962; acquired and renamed by Hyundai in 1977.

[f]Formerly Hyundai Wood Industries.

[g]Originally founded in 1977 as Korea Kuwait Banking Corporation (KKBC); renamed in 1994.

[h]Originally founded in 1955; acquired and renamed by Hyundai in 1983.

[i]Joint venture between Hyundai Electronics, Bosch of Germany, and Melco of Japan. Hyundai Motor Company owns about one-third of the stock.

[j]Renamed from Hyundai Allen Bradley in 1993.

[k]Originally founded as Konic Systems in 1988; renamed by Hyundai in 1992.

APPENDIX B

HYUNDAI'S MAJOR RESEARCH CENTERS AND INSTITUTES

Asan Institute for Life Sciences. Located in Seoul's Asan Medical Center, this institute specializes in a wide variety of medical research projects.

Hyundai Central Research Institute. Focuses on developing a wide range of new products based on emergent technologies throughout the company.

Hyundai Electronics Industries Research Institute. Includes the Semiconductor Research & Development Laboratory, focusing on semiconductor development, and the Industrial Electronics R&D Laboratory, which researches multimedia computers, HDTV, advanced information systems, and satellite technologies.

Hyundai Engineering Research Institute. Specializes in the development of industrial plant engineering technologies.

Hyundai Industrial Research Institute. Focuses on improving welding technologies, material science, factory automation, robotics, sanitation industrial plant development, laser research, and environmental research.

Hyundai Institute of Eco-Management. Focuses on the development of pollution-free technologies and sustainable development.

Hyundai Institute for Human Resource Development. Seeks ways to improve human performance in work organizations and serves as the company's principal training center.

Hyundai Maritime Research Institute. Specializes in improving ship design and offshore construction.

Hyundai Motor Company R&D Institutes. Includes the Technology Research Institute, Mabuk-ri Advanced Engineering & Research Institute, Hyundai America Technical Center, and the new Namyang Technology Research Center.

Hyundai Petrochemical R&D Center. Emphasizes applied research in the development of new materials, polymers, and fine chemicals.

Hyundai Precision Research Institute. Focuses on research on improving rolling stock, four-wheel-drive vehicles, defense and aerospace systems, and mag-lev trains.

Hyundai Research Institute. Focuses on economic research, industrial development and emerging technologies, business management and financial markets, and public policy and social development.

Hyundai Light Metal Research Institute. Conducts research on material science and the development of new materials using advanced technologies.

APPENDIX C

CHRONOLOGY OF EVENTS

DATE	AGE OF FOUNDER	PERSONAL AND POLITICAL EVENTS	HYUNDAI'S ACHIEVEMENTS
1910	—	Korea occupied by Imperial Japan.	
1915	—	Chung Ju Yung born November 25 in Asan Village.	
1931	16	Chung graduates from Songjun Primary School.	
1934	19	Chung takes job at Bokheung Rice Store.	
1936	21	Chung marries Byun Joong Suk.	
1938	23	Chung establishes Kyungil Rice Store.	
1940	25	Chung begins Ado Service Garage in Seoul.	
1941	26	World War II begins; Koreans drafted into Japan's war effort.	
1943	28	Ado Service nationalized by Japan for war effort.	
1945	30	World War II ends; Japanese ousted.	
1946	31		Hyundai Auto Service founded.
1947	32		Hyundai Civil Works Company, the cornerstone of today's Hyundai Business Group, founded.
1948	33	Rhee Syngman elected president of South Korea; Kim Il Sung assumes power in North Korea.	

DATE	AGE OF FOUNDER	PERSONAL AND POLITICAL EVENTS	HYUNDAI'S ACHIEVEMENTS
1950	35	Korean War begins; South Korea invaded.	Hyundai Construction Company established by merging Hyundai Auto Service and Hyundai Civil Works.
1953	38	Korean War ends; DMZ established.	
1955			Hyundai Marine & Fire Insurance established.
1958	43		Han River Bridge rehabilitation completed.
1960	45	Korean per capita income rises to $100.	Hyundai emerges as Korea's largest construction company.
1961	46	Park Chung Hee ousts Rhee Syngman in coup.	
1962	47	Park's first five-year plan emphasizes development of country's basic infrastructure.	
1964	49	Park establishes National Export Day.	Hyundai Cement established.
1965	50		Fifty-eight-mile Thailand Highway Project begun. Hyundai initiates overseas construction projects in Guam, Papua New Guinea, Australia, Alaska, and Vietnam.
1967	52	Park's second five-year plan emphasizes modernization of industrial structure.	Hyundai Motor Company (HMC) founded. Soyang earthen dam construction begun.
1968	53	North Korea sends commandos in unsuccessful attempt to kill President Park.	Work on Seoul Pusan Expressway commences.

DATE	AGE OF FOUNDER	PERSONAL AND POLITICAL EVENTS	HYUNDAI'S ACHIEVEMENTS
		USS Pueblo captured.	HMC begins production of Ford Cortina.
1971	56		Keumkang Industrial Development Company established.
1972	57	Yushin Constitution enacted by President Park.	
		Park's third five-year plan emphasizes development of heavy and chemical industries.	
1973	58		Hyundai Heavy Industries (HHI) established.
			Aluminum of Korea established.
1974	59		260,000 DWT VLCC *Atlantic Baron* launched.
			Hyundai Engineering established.
			Hyundai Motor Service established.
1975	60	Chung awarded honorary doctorate in engineering from Kyunghee University.	Hyundai Mipo Dockyard established.
			Hyundai Pipe established.
			Hyundai moves into Middle East construction with projects in Bahrain, Saudi Arabia, and Iran.
1976	61	Chung awarded honorary doctorate in economics from Chungnam University.	Jubail Industrial Harbor Project begins in Saudi Arabia.
			HMC launches Pony subcompact car.
			Hyundai listed as an International Fortune 500 company.

DATE	AGE OF FOUNDER	PERSONAL AND POLITICAL EVENTS	HYUNDAI'S ACHIEVEMENTS
			Hyundai Corporation established as trading company.
			Hyundai Merchant Marine established.
1977	62	Park's fourth five-year plan emphasizes increased industrial competitiveness and R&D. KAL plane forced down inside Soviet Union.	Chung elected chairman of the Federation of Korean Industries. Hyundai completes first nuclear power plant. Asan Foundation established. Hyundai Precision & Industry Company established. Hyundai Securities established. Hyundai Livart established.
1978	63		Hyundai assumes control over Inchon Iron & Steel. Hyundai receives land reclamation permit for Seosan. Hyundai International Merchant Bank established.
1979	64	Park Chung Hee assassinated.	Hyundai ranked 78th on International Fortune 500.
1980	65	Chun Doo Hwan becomes president. Korean per capita income rises to $1,589. Chun moves to break power of major firms.	Hyundai forced to cede Hyundai International to government.
1981	66	Chung asked to chair Invitation Committee for the sponsorship of the 1988 Olympics.	

DATE	AGE OF FOUNDER	PERSONAL AND POLITICAL EVENTS	HYUNDAI'S ACHIEVEMENTS
1982	67	Korea's fifth five-year plan emphasizes technology improvement, price stability, and improved quality of life. Chung awarded honorary doctorate in management from George Washington University. Chung elected chairman, Korean Amateur Sports Association.	Chung begins Seosan Land Reclamation Project. Penang Bridge project in Malaysia begun.
1983	68	KAL flight #007 shot down by Soviets. President Chun begins Ilhae Foundation for private gain. North Korean terrorists kill seventeen Korean government officials in Burma.	Hyundai Electronics Industries (HEI) established. Hyundai Electronics America established. HMC Pony IIs exported to Canada. Diamond Advertising established.
1984	69		Mabuk-ri R&D Center established. Seosan seawall completed. Hyundai Elevator established.
1985	70	Chung awarded honorary doctorate in economics from Yonsei University.	Hyundai Department Store opened. HEI's Inchon semiconductor complex dedicated. Hyundai Motor America established.
1986	71	Chung awarded honorary doctorate in humanities from Ewha Women's University.	Hyundai Industrial Development & Construction Company established. Hyundai Research Institute established.

DATE	AGE OF FOUNDER	PERSONAL AND POLITICAL EVENTS	HYUNDAI'S ACHIEVEMENTS
1987	72	Sixth five-year plan emphasizes regional development, technology development, and industrial restructuring.	Excel establishes record as best-selling U.S. import car.
			Chung Ju Yung named Hyundai honorary chairman; Chung Se Yung becomes group chairman.
		Chung elected honorary president, FKI.	
		KAL flight #858 blown up in flight by North Korean terrorists.	Korea Electronic Fuel Injection Company (KEFICO) established.
1988	73	Roh Tae Woo elected president of Korea.	Hyundai Petrochemical established.
		Highly successful Seoul Olympics completed.	Hyundai Logistics established.
1989	74	Roh government tries to limit growth of chaebols; Chung resists and incurs government retaliation.	HMC achieves 1 million Excel exports.
			HMC produces total of 3 million cars.
		Chung becomes first Korean businessman to visit Soviet Union and North Korea.	HMC opens car assembly plant in Canada.
			Hyundai Aluminum Industry established.
			Hyundai Construction Equipment Service established.
1990	75	Chung becomes first Korean businessman to visit China; returns to Russia.	Hyundai opens offices in Moscow and Vladivostok.
			Hyundai Resources Development established.
		Chung awarded honorary doctorate in politics from Sogang University.	Hyundai Munwha Shinmun established.
			Korea Soviet Shipping established.
			Svetlaya Company formed in Russia.

DATE	AGE OF FOUNDER	PERSONAL AND POLITICAL EVENTS	HYUNDAI'S ACHIEVEMENTS
1991	76	Roh's government continues pressure on chaebols to comply with government directives; companies are forced to make major donations to Roh and other officials. After resistance, Hyundai is indicted for tax fraud.	Chung formally retires from Hyundai.
			Hyundai achieves $51 billion in sales.
			Hyundai ranked 11th on International Fortune 500.
			HMC's Alpha-12 gasoline engine developed.
		Chung decides to offer himself as an alternative candidate in upcoming presidential election.	HEI develops 16M DRAM and 64M DRAM.
			Magnetic levitation train developed.
			Hymex-Hyundai de Mexico container plant established.
			HHI dedicates LNG shipbuilding plant.
1992	77	Chung announces candidacy for presidency; establishes United People's Party.	HMC produces total of 5 million cars.
			Hyundai Merchant Marine begins Far East–Europe route.
		Chung awarded honorary doctorate in public service from George Washington University.	Hyundai opens offices and manufacturing facilities in China.
		Chung wins National Assembly seat on UPP slate.	
		Kim Young Sam elected president of Korea.	
		Chung receives 16 percent of votes for president.	
1993	78	After criticizing new government, Chung and other business leaders are harassed by Kim's government.	HHI develops Moss-type LNG carrier.
			Hyundai Oil Refinery established.

DATE	AGE OF FOUNDER	PERSONAL AND POLITICAL EVENTS	HYUNDAI'S ACHIEVEMENTS
		Chung resigns from UPP and National Assembly.	Hyundai Information Technology Company established.
1994	79		HMC launches Accent car.
			HEI joins GlobalStar Project.
			Hyundai Space & Aircraft established.
1995	80	Korean per capita income rises to $10,000.	HMC Chunju plant production begins.
		Total Korean GNP reaches $377 billion.	Hyundai Precision opens container plant in China.
		Chung awarded honorary doctorate from Johns Hopkins University.	HEI acquires Symbios Logic; sells in 1998.
		Chung awarded honorary doctorate in philosophy from Korea University.	Hyundai Corporation marks $10 billion in exports.
1996	81	Korea ranked 13th largest trading nation in world.	Chung Mong-Koo becomes group chairman of Hyundai.
			Hyundai Business Group has forty-five subsidiaries and sales revenues of over $77 billion.
			HEI begins construction of largest chip plant in the United States.
			HEI develops 256M DRAM.
			HMC Sports Coupe Tiburon launched.
			A 200,000 BBL refinery plant dedicated.
			HMC marks 10 million cars produced.
			HMC marks 4 million cars exported.

DATE	AGE OF FOUNDER	PERSONAL AND POLITICAL EVENTS	HYUNDAI'S ACHIEVEMENTS
			Hyundai Financial Services established.
			Hyundai Finance & Factoring established.
1997	82	North Korean economic crisis worsens; widespread starvation reported.	Hyundai marks its 50th anniversary.
		Y. S. Kim's government accused of corruption and bribery.	Hundai Broadcasting System established.
		Korea hit with major bankruptcies.	HHI marks delivery of 50 million DWT of ships.
		Economic crash; Korea seeks IMF bailout.	HEI opens semiconductor plant in Oregon.
		Kim Dae Jung elected president of Korea.	HMC launches Atos mini car.
		Former presidents Chun and Roh pardoned.	Citizen's Investment Trust Management Securities established.
			Hundai's Vladivostok Business Center and hotel opened in Russia.
1998	83	Kim Dae Jung assumes presidency.	Chung Mong Hun becomes co-chairman of Hyundai Business Group.
		Korea's economic crisis drags on.	Hyundai presents reorganization plan to cope with Korean economic crisis.
		Chung awarded Olympic Order by IOC.	
		Chung returns to North Korea to negotiate new business ventures.	

NOTES

Chapter 1

1 Chung Ju Yung, *Ordeals, But No Failures* (Seoul: Chesamgihoik, 1991), p. 6.

2 United People's Party, *An Episode: The Birth of Hyundai Heavy Industries* (Seoul: United People's Party, 1992), p. 2.

3 Chung Ju Yung, "Have a Goal!," *Hyundai Newsletter,* August 1990, p. 1.

4 Ibid., p. 1.

5 United People's Party, *An Episode,* pp. 4–5.

6 Ibid., p. 5.

7 Alice Amsden, *Asia's Next Giant: South Korea and Late Industrialization* (New York: Oxford University Press, 1989), p. 276.

8 Michael E. Porter, *The Competitive Advantage of Nations* (New York: Free Press, 1990), p. 471.

9 Ibid.

10 "The Fortune Global 500: The World's Largest Corporations," *Fortune,* August 4, 1997, p. F-2.

11 Geoff Hiscock, *Asia's Wealth Club* (London: Nicholas Brealey, 1997). The other nine wealthiest families in Asia are the sultan of Brunei; Walter, Thomas, and Raymond Kwok of Sun Hung Kai Properties of Hong Kong; Yoshiaki Tsutsumi of Seibu Railway of Japan; Kee Shaukee of Henderson Land of Hong Kong; Tsai Wan-lin of the Lin-Yuan Group of Taiwan; Li Ka-shing of Cheung Kong of Hong Kong; Rachman Halim and the Wonowidjojo family of Gudang Garam of Indonesia; Minoru and Akira Mori of the Mori Group of Japan; and the Suharto family of Indonesia. See also Kerry Dolan, "The Global Power Elite," *Forbes,* July 28, 1997, pp. 97–176.

12 Michelle Conlin, "When Billionaires Become a Dime a Dozen," *Forbes,* October 13, 1997, pp. 148–194. See also Dolan, "Global Power Elite."

13 *Time,* cited in *Hyundai Newsletter,* December 1996, vol. 20, p. 14. The other five leaders were Li Ka-shing of the Cheung Kong Group of Hong Kong, Akio Morita of Sony, Eiji Toyoda of Toyota, Robert Kuok of the Kuok Group in Malaysia, and JRD Tata of Tata and Sons in India.

14 Leslie Helm, "The Koreans Are Coming: South Korea Bets Its Future on an Export Drive Aimed at the U.S.," *Business Week,* December 23, 1985, pp. 46–52.

15 William Holstein and Laxmi Nakarmi, "Korea Headed for High Tech's Top Tier," *Business Week*, July 31, 1995, pp. 56–64.

16 Gerardo R. Ungson, Richard M. Steers, and Seung-ho Park, *Korean Enterprise: The Quest for Globalization* (Boston: Harvard Business School Press, 1997), Chapter 1; "South Korea: The End of the Miracle," *The Economist*, November 29, 1997, pp. 21–24; *International Herald Tribune*, September 1, 1997, p. 1.

17 Chung Ju Yung, *Ordeals*, p. 6.

18 For a discussion of the causes and consequences of the December 1997 economic crash, see Moon Ihlwan, "Seoul Is Still Teetering on the Edge," *Business Week*, December 29, 1997, pp. 56–58; "The Party's Over," *Business Korea*, December 1997, pp. 18–20; Andrew Sherry, Shim Jae Hoon, and Charles S. Lee, "South Korea: State of Inertia," *Far Eastern Economic Review*, December 11, 1997, pp. 16–23; Anthony Spaeth, "Biting the Bullet," *Time*, December 15, 1997, pp. 16–24; "South Korea's Meltdown," *The Economist*, December 13, 1997, pp. 33–35.

19 Chung, *Ordeals*.

20 Amsden, *Asian's Next Giant*, p. 80.

Chapter 2

1 Bruce Cumings, *Korea's Place in the Sun: A Modern History* (New York: Norton, 1997), p. 19.

2 Several excellent books can be found on the history of Korea. These include Woo-keun Han, *History of Korea* (translated from Korean by Kyung-shik Lee) (Honolulu: University of Hawaii Press, 1970); Andrew Nahm, *Introduction to Korean History and Culture* (Seoul: Hollym, 1993); Ki-baik Lee, *A New History of Korea* (Cambridge, Mass.: Harvard University Press, 1984); and Bruce Cumings, *Korea's Place in the Sun*.

3 James Gale, *History of the Korean People* (Seoul: Royal Asiatic Society, 1972), p. 93.

4 Illyon, *Samguk Yusa*, translated by Tae-hung Ha and Grafton K. Mintz (Seoul: Yonsei University Press, 1972), pp. 32–33.

5 Kim Choong Soon, *The Culture of Korean Industry: An Ethnography of the Poongsan Corporation* (Tucson: University of Arizona Press, 1992).

6 Laurel Kendall, *Shamans, Housewives, and Other Restless Spirits: Women in Korean Ritual Life* (Honolulu: University of Hawaii Press, 1985), p. 123.

7 Han, *History of Korea*.

8 Pico Iyer, "The Yin and Yang of Paradoxical, Prosperous Korea," *Smithsonian*, August 1988, pp. 47–58.

9 Nahm, *Introduction to Korean History and Culture*.

10 For a discussion of the role of Confucianism in Korean history, see Han, *History of Korea*. For a study of the influence of Confucianism on Korean corporations, see *Culture of Korean Industry*.

11 Yung-Chung Kim, *Women in Korea: A History from Ancient Times to 1945* (Seoul: Ewha Women's University Press, 1976).

12 Kae H. Chung and Hak Chong Lee, *Korean Managerial Dynamics* (New York: Praeger, 1989).

13 Young-Chul Chang, "Cultural Influences in Korean Management Practices," Working Paper, Faculty of Business Administration, National University of Singapore, Spring 1995.

14 Paul S. Crane, *Korean Patterns* (Seoul: Kwangjin Publishing Company, 1978).

15 T. K. Oh, "Understanding Managerial Values and Behavior among the Gang of Four: South Korea, Taiwan, Singapore, and Hong Kong," *Journal of Management Development*, 1991, vol. 10, no. 2, pp. 46–56.

16 Carter Eckert, *Korea Old and New: A History* (Cambridge, Mass.: Korea Institute, Harvard University, 1990).

17 "Excellence in Science and Technology," *Pacific Bridge*, January–February 1993, p. 8.

18 Richard M. Steers, "Reassessing Korea," *Register-Guard*, July 16, 1995, pp. 1B, 4B.

19 Pow-key Sohn, *Nanjung Ilgi: War Diary of Admiral Yi Sun-sin* (Seoul: Yonsei University Press, 1977); and Chong-young Lee, *Imjim Changch'o: Admiral Yi Sun-sin's Memorials to Court* (Seoul: Yonsei University Press, 1981).

20 Bank of Korea, *The Economic Yearbook*, Seoul, Korea, 1948.

21 Rabindranath Tagore, quoted in Andrew C. Nahm, *A Panorama of 5000 Years: Korean History* (Seoul: Hollym International, 1983), p. 121.

Chapter 3

1 Personal interview with Chung Ju Yung, honorary chairman, Hyundai Business Group, April 11, 1997.

2 Chung Ju Yung, *The Pony Runs*, 1987 (in Japanese), p. 182.

3 Chung Ju Yung, *Ordeals, But No Failures* (Seoul: Chesamgihoik, 1991), p. 10.

4 Personal interview with Chung Ju Yung, honorary chairman, Hyundai Business Group, April 11, 1997.

5 Chung, *Ordeals*, p. 11.

6 Chung, *The Pony Runs*, pp. 182–183.

7 Chung, *Ordeals*, p. 12.

8 Ibid., p. 12.

9 Ibid., p. 15.

10 United People's Party, *Chung Ju Yung: A New Vision to Revive the Korean Economy*, 1991, pp. 4–5.

11 Chung, *Ordeals*, p. 16.

12 Ibid., p. 17.

13 Ibid.

14 Ibid.

15 Ibid., p. 24.

16 Ibid., p. 37.

17 Ibid., p. 41.

18 Ibid., pp. 50–51.

19 Donald Kirk, *Korean Dynasty* (New York: M. E. Sharpe, 1994), p. 25.

20 Chung, *Ordeals*, p. 49.

21 Ibid., p. 52.

22 Wang Ok-Gyum, "Wife at the Top: Light in the Shadow," *Business Korea*, January 1986, p. 25.

23 Chung, *Ordeals*, p. 53.

24 Ibid.

25 Ibid.

26 Ibid., p. 54.

27 Chung Ju Yung interview with *Hankuk Kyongje Shinmun*, February 16, 1986, p. 1.

28 Personal interview with Chung Ju Yung, April 11, 1997.

29 Chung, *The Pony Runs*, Chapter 6.

30 Chung, *Ordeals*, p. 57.

31 Ibid., p. 59.

32 Ibid.

33 Hyundai Business Group, *Orientation Course for New Recruits*, 1989.

34 Chung Ju Yung, *My Conviction: Clean Government* (Seoul, United People's Party, 1992).

35 Ibid.

36 Jang Jung-Soo, "Hyundai's Chung Ju Yung: Still Driving Hard at 70," *Business Korea*, January 1986, p. 22.

37 Chung, *Ordeals*, p. 75.

38 Alice Amsden, *Asia's Next Giant* (New York: Oxford University Press, 1989), p. 232.

39 Hyundai Business Group, *Orientation Course for New Recruits*, p. 38.

40 Personal interview with Chung Ju Yung, April 11, 1997.

Chapter 4

1 Mark Clifford, *Troubled Tiger: Businessmen, Bureaucrats, and Generals in South Korea* (New York: M. E. Sharpe, 1998/1994), p. 9.

2 Ibid., p. 43.

3 Attributed to General Charles Helmick, who made the statement in February 1948. Cited in Clifford, *Troubled Tiger*, p. 29.

4 *The 1993–94 Korea Yearbook*, pp. 1–2. Seoul: *Business Korea*, 1993, pp. I1–2.

5 Ibid., p. I-1.

6 Myung Hun Kang, *The Korean Business Conglomerate: Chaebol Then and Now* (Berkeley: Institute for East Asian Studies, University of California, 1996), pp. 25–30.

7 Ibid., p. 26.

8 Ibid., p. 30.

9 Chung, *Ordeals, But No Failures* (Seoul: Chesamgihoik, 1991), p. 83.

10 Earle Whitmore, *History of the United States Army Engineer District Far East*, U.S. Army Corps of Engineers, Far East District, Seoul, 1976, p. 17.

11 Chung, *Ordeals*, p. 89.

12 Personal interview with Chung Se Yung, honorary chairman, Hyundai Motor Company, September 12, 1997.

13 Wang Ok-Gyun, "Wife at the Top: Light in the Shadow," *Business Korea*, January 1986, p. 25.

14 World Bank, *World Bank Economic Report* (Washington, DC: Author, 1957).

15 World Bank, *East Asia and the Pacific Development Review* (Washington, DC: World Bank, 1961), p. 11.

16 Donald, MacDonald, "Korea through Western Eyes," *Business Korea*, April 1989, p. 36.

17 Quoted in Clifford, *Troubled Tiger*, p. 30.

18 Park Kwon Sang, quoted in ibid., p. 31.

19 Park Tae Joon, quoted in ibid., p. 45.

20 Park Chung Hee, *Our Nation's Path* (Seoul: Dong-A Publishing Company, 1962), p. 62.

21 Hahm Chai-bong, "Confucian Tradition and Economic Reform in Korea," *Korea Focus*, May–June 1997, vol. 5, no. 3, p. 88.

22 Park, Chung Hee, *Our Nation's Path*, p. 72.

23 Bryung-Nak Song, *The Rise of the Korean Economy* (Hong Kong: Oxford University Press, 1990), p. 130.

24 *The 1993–94 Korea Handbook*, p. 46.

25 Park, *Our Nation's Path*, p. 204.

26 The government package of reforms between 1964 and 1967 included the devaluation of the won from 130 to 225 to the U.S. dollar in 1964. A unitary floating exchange rate was adopted in March 1965. The government also doubled interest rates on bank deposits and loans in 1965 in order to increase voluntary savings. *1993/94 Korea Yearbook*, pp. 1–2.

27 Clifford, *Troubled Tiger*, p. 56.

28 *1993/94 Korea Yearbook*, pp. 1-2–1-3.

29 Yang Soo Rhee, B. Ross Larsen, and G. Pursell, *Korea's Competitive Edge* (Baltimore: The Johns Hopkins University Press, 1984).

30 Personal interview with Lee Hong-Kyu, cited in Gerardo R. Ungson, Richard M. Steers, and Seung-Ho Park, *Korean Enterprise: The Quest for Globalization* (Boston: Harvard Business School Press, 1997).

31 Alice Amsden, *Asia's Next Giant: South Korea and Late Industrialization* (New York: Oxford University Press, 1989), p. 266.

32 Clifford, *Troubled Tiger*, p. 115.

33 Richard M. Steers, Yoo Keun Shin, and Gerardo R. Ungson, *The Chaebol: Korea's New Industrial Might* (New York: Harper & Row, 1989).

34 Amsden, *Asia's Next Giant*.

35 Ungson et al., *Korean Enterprise*.

36 Chung, *Ordeals*, p. 91.

37 Ibid., p. 92.

38 Personal interview with Lee Ik Chi, president, Hyundai Securities, September 5, 1997.

39 Hyundai Business Group, *Chung Ju Yung: His Life and Success* (Seoul, 1989).

40 Chung Ju Yung, *The Pony Runs* (Seoul: Hyundai Business Group, 1987, p. 61).

41 Chung, *Ordeals*, p. 98.

42 Ibid., p. 97.

43 Ibid., p. 100.

44 Jon Woronoff, *Korea's Economy: Man-Made Miracle*, (Seoul: Si-sa-yong-o-sa, 1983), p. 108.

45 Park Chung Hee, *To Build a Nation*, p. 121.

46 Ibid., p. 121.

47 Kim Chung-yum, *Policy-making on the Front Lines: Memoirs of a Korean Practitioner, 1945–79* (Washington, DC: Economic Development Institute of the World Bank, 1994), p. 107.

48 Shim Jae Hoon, "Chung's Road to Riches Leaves a Doubtful Legacy," *Far Eastern Economic Review*, December 12, 1985, p. 72.

49 Quoted in Michael Keon, *Korean Phoenix* (Englewood Cliffs, NJ: Prentice-Hall, 1977), p. 79.

50 Quoted in Clifford, *Troubled Tiger*, p. 53.

51 Interview with Chung Hoon Mok, a former Hyundai executive, October 1993, cited in ibid., p. 116.

52 Interview with unidentified government official, quoted in ibid., p. 76.

53 Ibid., p. 77.

Chapter 5

1 Quoted in Donald Kirk, *Korean Dynasty* (New York: M. E. Sharpe, 1994), p. 133.

2 Alice Amsden, *Asia's Next Giant* (New York: Oxford University Press, 1989), pp. 175–179.

3 Linsu Kim, *Imitation to Innovation: The Dynamics of Korea's Technological Learning* (Boston: Harvard Business School Press, 1997), p. 112.

4 Chung Se Yung, interview in the *Asian Wall Street Journal*, April 23, 1982, p. 1.

5 Ibid., p. 1.

6 Amsden, *Asia's Next Giant*, p. 151.

7 Quoted in Kirk, *Korean Dynasty*, p. 133.

8 Takao Eiji, *The Day Korean Cars Kick Out Japanese Cars*, 1988 (in Japanese), Working Paper, pp. 105–106.

9 United People's Party, *The Birth of Hyundai Heavy Industries*, 1992, pp. 7–8.

10 Bae, p. 23; see also Richard M. Steers, Yoo Keun Shin, and Gerardo R. Ungson, *The Chaebol: Korea's New Industrial Might* (New York: Harper & Row, 1989).

11 Kyuhan Bae, *Automobile Workers in Korea* (Seoul: Seoul National University Press, 1987), p. 23.

12 David Halberstam, *The Reckoning* (New York: William Morrow, 1986).

13 Chon Sung Won, quoted in Mark Clifford, *Troubled Tiger* (New York: M. E. Sharpe, 1994), p. 253.

14 Personal interview with Chung Se Yung, honorary chairman, Hyundai Motor Company, September 12, 1997.

15 Quoted in Clifford, *Troubled Tiger*, p. 256.

16 Personal interview with Lee Ik Chi, president, Hyundai Securities, September 5, 1997.

17 Quoted in Kirk, *Korean Dynasty*, p. 144.

18 Jim Mateja, "Cartalk," *Chicago Tribune*, January 19, 1992.

19 Richard Johnson, *Automotive News*, May 30, 1994.

20 Alice Amsden, "The South Korean Economy: Is Business-Led Growth Working?" in Donald Clark, ed., *Korea Briefing*, (Boulder, Colo.: Westview, 1992).

21 Kirk, *Korean Dynasty*, p. 166.

22 "HMC Marks Two Records," *Hyundai Newsletter*, January 1977, vol. 21, pp. 8–9.

23 Ibid., p. 8.

24 "Hyundai Dedicates World's Largest Commercial Vehicle Plant," *Hyundai Newsletter*, June 1997, vol. 21, p. 10.

25 "HMC Starts Accent Production in Indonesia," *Hyundai Newsletter*, September 1996, vol. 20, p. 2; "The World of Hyundai Motor Company" (Seoul: HMC, 1996).

26 "Hyundai Motor Advances into African Market," *Business Korea*, June 1996, p. 65.

27 "HMC to Build Car Plant in India," *Hyundai Newsletter*, January 1997, vol. 21, p. 2. See also "Hyundai Motor in India," *Business Korea*, January 1997, p. 42.

28 "Hyundai Motor's R&D Center," *Business Korea*, November 1996, p. 48.

29 Interview with Chung Mong-Kyu, cited in *Business Korea*, April 1997, pp. 50–51.

30 Personal interview with Chung Se Yung, September 11, 1997.

31 Chung Se Yung, quoted in Kirk, *Korean Dynasty*, p. 48.

32 Personal interview with Juhn Myung Hun, president and CEO, Hyundai Motor America, November 7, 1997.

33 Ibid.

34 Ibid.

35 Ibid.

Chapter 6

1 Simon Winchester, *Korea: A Walk through a Land of Miracles* (Englewood Cliffs, N.J.: Prentice-Hall, 1988), p. 6.

2 Richard M. Steers, Yoo-Keun Shin, and Gerardo R. Ungson, *The Chaebol: Korea's New Industrial Might* (New York: Harper & Row, 1989), p. 42.

3 Alice Amsden, *Asia's Next Giant* (New York: Oxford University Press, 1989), p. 288.

4 Personal interview with Kim Taik Ho, president, Hyundai Information Technology Company, and chairman, Korea Software Industry Association, September 11, 1997.

5 Chung Ju Yung, *Ordeals, But No Failures* (Seoul: Chesamgihoik Publishing Company, 1991), p. 121.

6 Although she was commonly referred to as Mrs. Park, her actual name was Yuk Young Su. Korean women do not change their names after marriage.

7 Chung Mong Joon, *Status of the Korean Shipbuilding Industry* (Seoul: Hyundai Heavy Industries, 1979), pp. 7–12.

8 Personal interviews with Kim Jung Kook, Lee Youn-Jae, C. H. Cho, K. S. Min, Park Seung Kyun, Kim Eung-Sup, and K. H. Kim, all senior executives of Hyundai Heavy Industries, January 20, 1997.

9 Alvin Meyersahm, quoted in Kirk, *Korean Dynasty* (New York: M. E. Sharpe, 1974), p. 53.

10 Ibid.

11 Winchester, *Korea*, p. 6.

12 Amsden, *Asia's Next Giant*, p. 287.

13 Ibid., p. 287.

14 Jack Kamont, quoted in Kirk, *Korean Dynasty*, p. 43.

15 Ibid.

16 Ibid.

17 Tony Robinson, quoted in ibid., p. 106.

18 Ibid.

19 *Hyundai Newsletter*, Seoul: Hyundai Business Group, June 1997, p. 9.

20 Choi Bo-Sik, personal interview with Chung Ju Yung for *Choson Magazine*, November 1996, pp. 3, 25 (English translation).

21 "Hyundai Heavy Industries," Seoul: Hyundai Heavy Industries, 1997; "Hyundai Tones Industrial Muscle," *Shipbuilding & Ship Repair*, Winter 1995, pp. 2–4.

22 "Guinness Book of Records Cites HHI Visitors," *Hyundai Newsletter*, October 1996, vol. 20, p. 9.

23 "Shipbuilding: We Build a Better Tomorrow," Seoul: Hyundai Heavy Industries, 1997.

Chapter 7

1 Personal interview with Lee Ik Chi, president, Hyundai Securities, September 5, 1997.

2 Chung Ju Yung, *Ordeals, But No Failures* (Seoul: Chesamgihoik, 1991), p. 128.

3 Personal interview with Lee Ik Chi, president, Hyundai Securities, September 5, 1997.

4 Chun Bum Sung, *The Secret Story of the Founding of Hyundai* (Seoul: Seo Moon Dangsa, 1984).

5 Ibid.

6 Ibid.

7 Chung, *Ordeals*, p. 140.

8 Personal communication, Seoul, April 1997.

9 Hyundai Group, *Chung Ju Yung: His Life and Success*, 1989, p. 13.

10 Personal communication, Seoul, April 1997.

11 Quoted in Donald Kirk, *Korean Dynasty* (New York: M. E. Sharpe, 1974), pp. 92–93.

12 Personal communication from interviews with several Hyundai executives, Seoul, Korea, February and April 1997.

13 Personal interview with Lee Ik Chi, president, Hyundai Securities, September 5, 1997.

14 Interview quoted in Kirk, *Korean Dynasty*, p. 93.

15 Eun Mee Kim, *Big Business, Strong State: Collusion and Conflict in South Korean Development, 1960–1990* (Albany: State University of New York Press, 1997), p. 153.

16 David Steinberg, *The Republic of Korea: Economic Transformation and Social Change* (Boulder, Colo.: Westview Press, 1989).

17 Quoted in Mark Clifford, *Troubled Tiger* (New York: M. E. Sharpe, 1994), p. 214.

18 Interview with Mark Clifford, cited in ibid.

19 Richard M. Steers, Yoo Kuen Shin, and Gerardo R. Ungson, *The Chaebol: Korea's New Industrial Might* (New York: Harper & Row, 1989), Chapter 3.

20 *Yonhap*, Seoul, November 10, 1988.

21 Shin Bong Seung, "King Chaebol Who Came to the Hearing: Chung Ju Yung." *Jik Jang In* [*Working Man*, in Korean], December 1988.

22 *Hankook Ilbo*, April 25, 1989.

23 Shin Bong Seung, "King Chaebol."

24 *Hankook Ilbo*, April 25, 1989.

Chapter 8

1 Personal interview with Chung Ju Yung, honorary chairman, Hyundai Business Group, April 11, 1997.

2 Ibid.

3 Quoted in Donald Kirk, *Korean Dynasty* (New York: M. E. Sharpe), p. 184.

4 Ibid., p. 185.

5 Ibid., p. 185.

6 According to the Korea Development Institute, Korean spending for R&D was only 1.91 percent of GNP in 1990, compared with 2.69 percent for Japan and 2.75 percent for the United States. In dollar amounts, Korea spent only one-eighteenth as much as Japan and one-thirty-third as much as the United States on R&D. See Korea Development Institute, *The Reality of Development of Industrial Technology and Implications of Policies* (Seoul: KDI, 1992). For more recent information on Korean investments in R&D, see Gerardo R. Ungson, Richard M. Steers, and Seung-Ho Park, *Korean Enterprise: The Quest for Globalization* (Boston: Harvard Business School Press, 1997), Chapter 7.

7 Kirk, *Korean Dynasty*, p. 215.

8 H. Garrett De Young, "Hyundai's Gambit to be a Big Player in PCs," *Electronics Business Asia*, 1993, p. 77.

9 Quoted in Kirk, *Korean Dynasty*, p. 216.

10 See Thomas R. Howell, Brent L. Bartlett, and Warren Davis, *Creating Advantage: Semiconductors and Government Policy in the 1990s* (Cupertino, Calif.: SIA Dewey Ballantine, 1992), pp. 353–355.

11 Ibid. p. 152.

12 "Samsung Electronics Forges Tie-up with Japan's NEC," *Business Korea*, March 1994.

13 Steven Brull, "Samsung's $8 Billion Gamble on Upscale Chips," *Business Week*, June 2, 1997, pp. 54–55.

14 Lucky-Goldstar. *Lucky-Goldstar* (Seoul, 1994).

15 "Personal Computers: Sleeping with the Enemy," *Business Korea*, December 1996, pp. 40–41.

16 Kirk, *Korean Dynasty*, p. 206.

17 Ibid., pp. 206–207.

18 "Breaking New Ground," *Business Korea*, May 1997, pp. 55–56; "Opening Soon: Hyundai's Engene, Oregon, Semiconductor Plant," *Business Korea*, November 1997, p. 31.

19 Joe Kidd. "Hyundai Comes to Town." *The Register-Guard*, May 22, 1995.

20 Sherri Buri, "Hyundai Starts Work on First Sample Chips," *Register-Guard*, January 2, 1997, p. A-1.

21 "Breaking New Ground," *Business Korea*, May 1997, pp. 55–56.

22 *Hyundai Electronics Industries: My Perspective*, 1994.

23 Kim Linsu, *Imitation to Innovation: The Dynamics of Korea's Technological Leaning* (Boston: Harvard Business School Press, 1997).

24 Personal interview with Kim Young Hwan, president, Hyundai Electronics Industries, September 11, 1997.

25 Ibid.

26 Nadin Washington, customer marketing engineer, Symbios Logic, quoted in *Hyundai Electronics*, 1997, p. 14.

27 Personal interview with Park Chong Sup, president, Hyundai Electronics America, November 6, 1997.

28 Quoted in *Hyundai Electronics*, 1997, p. 9.

Chapter 9

1 *The Korea Times*, June 19, 1993.

2 Kyuhan Bae, *Automobile Workers in Korea* (Seoul: Seoul National University Press, 1987), p. 44.

3 Boye deMente, *Korean Etiquette and Business Ethics* (Lincolnwood, Ill.: NTC Business Books, 1988).

4 Bae, *Automobile Workers in Korea*, p. 47.

5 Quoted in Donald Kirk, *Korean Dynasty* (New York: M. E. Sharpe, 1994), p. 45.

6 Ibid., p. 46.

7 Ibid., p. 46.

8 *Business Korea*, September 1986, p. 26.

9 Japanese Ministry of Labor, 1986; see also: T. Kang, *Is Korea the Next Japan?* (New York: Free Press, 1989).

10 Richard M. Steers, Yoo-Keun Shin, and Geraldo R. Ungson, *The Chaebol: Korea's New Industrial Might* (New York: Harper & Row, 1987), Chapters 1 and 7.

11 Ibid., p. 2.

12 Ibid.

13 Kae Chung and Harry Lie, "Labor–Management Relations in Korea." In Kae Chung and H. C. Lee, eds., *Korean Managerial Dynamics* (New York: Praeger, 1989).

14 Ibid.

15 Robert Kearney, *The Warrior Worker: The Challenge of the Korean Way of Working* (New York: Henry Holt, 1991).

16 Chung and Lie, "Labor-Management Relations."

17 J. J. Choi, *Interest Conflict and Political Control in South Korea: A Study of Labor Unions in Manufacturing Industries: 1961–1980*, Ph.D. dissertation, University of Chicago, 1983, p. 282.

18 Chung and Lie, "Labor-Management Relations."

19 Bae, *Automobile Workers in Korea*.

20 Mark Clifford, *Troubled Tiger* (New York: M. E. Sharpe, 1994), p. 279.

21 Mark Clifford, "Inoffensive Spring," *Far Eastern Economic Review*, May 23, 1991, pp. 28–31.

22 Kim Chi-sun, "Korea's Labor Legislation: Past and Present." *Korea Focus*, May–June 1995, vol. 3, no. 3, pp. 78–84.

23 Chung and Lie, "Labor-Management Relations."

24 Steers et al., *The Chaebol*.

25 Personal interview with Chung Se Yung, honorary chairman, Hyundai Motor Company, September 12, 1997.

26 "I Won't Use Temporary Remedy Even Though the Dispute Takes Time" (interview with Chung Ju Yung), *Seoul Daily*, August 8, 1987, p. 1.

27 Nancy Cooper, "South Korea: Labor Pains," *Newsweek*, August 31, 1987, pp. 20–21.

28 "Workers Rampage in Korea," *International Herald Tribune*, August 18, 1987, pp. 1–2.

29 Quoted in Kirk, *Korean Dynasty*, p. 225.

30 Ibid., p. 226.

31 "Striking at the Heart: South Korean Workers' Protests Turn Violent Again," *Far Eastern Economic Review*, March 24, 1988, p. 106.

32 *Asian Wall Street Journal*, June 24, 1988.

33 Joseph Manguno, *Asian Wall Street Journal*, April 14, 1989.

34 Ibid.

35 Kim Chong-Tae, "Falling Farther and Farther Behind," *Business Korea*, July 1997, p. 15.

36 Ibid.

37 *The Korea Times*, June 19, 1993.

38 Barry Wilkinson, *Labour and Industry in the Asia-Pacific: Lessons from the Newly-Industrialized Countries* (Berlin: Walter de Gruyter, 1994).

Chapter 10

1 Interview with Sam Jameson, *Los Angeles Times*, October 15, 1990.

2 Cited in Mark Clifford, *Troubled Tiger* (New York: M. E. Sharpe, 1994), p. 240.

3 The official invitation committee consisted of Chung Ju Yung; Park Young Soo, mayor of Seoul; Cho Sang Ho, president of the Korean Olympic Committee; Yoo Chang Soon, chairman of the Korean Trades Association and former deputy prime minister for economic planning; Lee Won Kyung, chairman of Hapdong Group; and Lee Won Hong, vice chairman of the invitation committee and president of Korea Broadcasting System.

4 Interview with Shin Yong Suk, cited in Clifford, *Troubled Tiger*, p. 289.

5 Richard W. Pound, *Five Rings over Korea* (Boston: Little, Brown, 1994), p. 6.

6 Personal interview with Chae Soo-Sam, president, Diamond Ad Ltd., September 11, 1997.

7 Direct quote from Kang Sung San, North Korea's prime minister of the state administrative council, December 10, 1984. Quoted in Pound, *Five Rings over Korea*, p. 74. For a detailed study of the secret negotiations concerning the possible inclusion of North Korea in the 1988 Olympics, see Pound's book.

8 Chung Ju Yung letter dated April 2, 1984, quoted in Pound, *Five Rings over Korea*, p. 71.

9 Kim Jong Gie, *The Impact of the Seoul Olympic Games on National Development* (Seoul: Korea Development Institute, 1990), p. 2.

10 Vladimir Orlov, "Hyundai Staff around the World," *Hyundai Newsletter*, July 1992, p. 12.

11 Chung Ju Yung, *Ordeals*, p. 231.

12 Sam Jameson, *Los Angeles Times*, October 15, 1990.

13 Ibid.

14 *The Korea Times*, February 3, 1989.

15 Choi Bo-Sik, personal interview with Chung Ju Yung, *Chosun Magazine*, November 1996, p. 22 (English translation).

16 Cited in *The Korean Herald*, February 2, 1989.

17 Cited in *The Korea Times*, February 3, 1989.

18 Ibid.

19 Ibid.

20 Quoted in Donald Kirk, *Korean Dynasty* (New York: M. E. Sharpe, 1994), p. 115.

21 *The Korean Herald*, May 29, 1992.

22 *The Korean Herald*, August 14, 1992.

23 Choi, p. 22.

Chapter 11

1 "Halla Group: Building a Better World," *Business Korea*, November 1997, pp. 46–47.

2 "Halla Chairman Chung In Yung: Beating Adversity," *Business Korea*, November 1991, p. 31.

3 Personal interview with Chung Se Yung, honorary chairman, Hyundai Motor Company, September 12, 1997.

4 Paul Ensor, "Seoul Success: Shadows over Hyundai's New Man at the Top," *Far Eastern Economic Review*, June 18, 1987, p. 91.

5 Laxmi Nakarmi, "Korea's New Corporate Bosses: Made in America," *Business Week*, February 23, 1987, p. 59.

6 Personal interview with Chung Mong Koo, chairman, Hyundai Business Group, September 11, 1997.

7 Chung Mong Joon, "Status of the Korean Shipbuilding Industry," Hyundai Heavy Industries, 1984, pp. 15–16.

8 Choi Bo-Sik, personal interview with Chung Ju Yung, *Choson Magazine*, November 1996, p. 30 (English translation).

9 Personal interview with Chung Mong Joon, member, Korean National Assembly, and former chairman, Hyundai Heavy Industries, September 12, 1997.

10 Phillip Grub, quoted in Donald Kirk, *Korean Dynasty* (New York: M. E. Sharpe, 1994), p. 40.

11 Ibid.

12 Ibid.

13 Lee Byung Kyu, quoted in Kirk, *Korean Dynasty*, p. 6.

14 "Hyundai Petrochemical Plant to Open Soon," *Business Korea*, November 1997, p. 41.

15 Choi Bo-Sik, personal interview with Chung Ju Yung, *Choson Magazine*, November 1996, p. 22 (English translation).

16 Chung Ju Yung, *Ordeals, But No Failures* (Seoul: Chesamkihae Publishing Company, 1991), p. 331.

17 Wang Ok-Gyun, "Wife at the Top: Light in the Shadow," *Business Korea*, January 1986, p. 25.

18 Ibid., p. 26.

19 Ibid., p. 26.

20 Chung, *Ordeals*, p. 328.

Chapter 12

1 Personal interview with Park Se Yong, president, Corporation and Office of Planning and Control, September 12, 1997.

2 Alice Amsden, *Asia's Next Giant: South Korea and Late Industrialization* (New York: Oxford University Press, 1989).

3 Shin Sang Kap, "The Great Land Grab," *Korea Business World*, August 1989, p. 1.

4 Park Chung Hee, *Our Nation's Path* (Seoul: Dong-A Publishing Company, 1962), p. 73.

5 *Weekly Choson*, October 20, 1991, p. 1.

6 Ibid., p. 1.

7 "Tax Office Investigates Hyundai: Government Retaliation?" *Business Korea*, November 1991, p. 14.

8 Ibid., p. 14.

9 Ibid., p. 14.

10 *Weekly Choson*, October 20, 1991, p. 1.

11 Gerardo R. Ungson, Richard M. Steers, and Seung-Ho Park, *Korean Enterprise: The Quest for Globalization* (Boston: Harvard Business School Press, 1997).

12 Quoted in Donald Kirk, *Korean Dynasty* (New York: M. E. Sharpe, 1994), p. 315.

13 Ibid., p. 315.

14 Personal interview with Lee Nae-Heun, president, Hyundai Engineering & Construction Company, September 6, 1997.

15 Personal interview with Chung Ju Jung, honorary chairman, Hyundai Business Group, April 11, 1997.

16 Personal interview with Park Se Yong, September 12, 1997.

17 Quoted in Kirk, *Korean Dynasty*, p. 317.

18 United People's Party, "Chung Ju Yung: A New Vision to Revive the Korean Economy," 1992, p. 17.

19 Ibid., p. 20.

20 Although *globalization* is not defined precisely, it generally means the deepening of all economic sectors across country borders. See M. E. Porter, *The Competitive Advantage of Nations* (New York: Free Press, 1990); George Yip, *Total Global Strategy* (Englewood Cliffs, NJ: Prentice Hall 1992); and Kenichi Ohmae, *The Borderless World* (New York: HarperCollins. 1990).

21 *1995–96 Korea Company Handbook* Seoul, 1995, pp. 111–112.

22 *Korea Business* (San Rafael, Calif.: World Trade Press, 1995), p. 22.

23 *The Korea Herald*, March 18, 1993.

24 "Hyundai's Future: Trial and Failure?," *Business Korea*, January 1993, p. 22.

25 Mark Clifford, *Troubled Tiger* (New York: M. E. Sharpe, 1994), p. 3.

26 Ibid.

27 Ibid., p. 4.

28 Steve Glain, "For South Korean Firms, Speaking Too Freely May Carry Steep Price," *Wall Street Journal*, August 18, 1995, p. 1.

29 Joe Kidd, "Hyundai's Past Haunts Future Plans," *Register-Guard*, July 22, 1995, pp. 1A, 15A.

30 "The Last Campaign of a Chaebol Warrior," *The Economist*, January 8, 1997, p. 77.

31 "Yet Another Shock to South Korea's System," *The Economist*, May 24, 1977, pp. 37–38.

32 *Far Eastern Economic Review*, October 23, 1997, p. 13.

33 Shim Jae Hoon, "Rose-Tinted Glasses," *Far Eastern Economic Review*, July 17, 1997, p. 23.

34 Mark Clifford, "Can Korea Battle Back?" *Business Week*, November 24, 1997, p. 59.

35 Ibid., pp. 58–59.

36 "South Korea Turns to IMF for Bailout," *Register-Guard*, November 21, 1997, p. 13A.

37 Michael Schuman and Namju Cho, "Kim Dae Jung Wins Presidency of South Korea," *Asian Wall Street Journal*, December 20, 1997, p. 1.

38 "Panic in South Korea," *The Economist*, December 13, 1997, pp. 15–16.

39 Shin Yong-bae, "Kim Dae Jung Wins Election," *Korea Herald*, December 19, 1997, p. 1; Sonni Efron and David Holley, "Opposition Leader Wins Presidential Race in South Korea," *Los Angeles Times*, December 19, 1997, p. A-1.

Chapter 13

1 Personal interview, 1997.

2 For a detailed examination of contemporary Korean HRM practices, see Gerardo R. Ungson, Richard M. Steers, and Seung-Ho Park, *Korean Enterprise: The Quest for Globalization* (Boston: Harvard Business School Press, 1997).

3 Nam-hong Cho, "Human Resource Management in Korean Enterprises." Paper presented at the Tenth International Industrial Relations Association World Congress, Washington, DC, 1995.

4 Lee Tae-gyu, "Revolution in Recruiting New Employees," *Korea Focus*, January–February 1995, vol. 3, no. 1, pp. 81–85.

5 Lee Yoo-Lim, "More Companies Rely on Employee Interviews," *Business Korea*, November 1994, pp. 22–23.

6 Steers, Shin, and Ungson, *The Chaebol.*

7 Interview with Chung Ju Yung by Choi Bo Sik, reported in *Choson Magazine*, November 1996, p. 21 (translated from Korean).

8 Personal interview with Chung Ju Yung, honorary chairman, Hyundai Business Group, April 11, 1997.

9 Kae Chung, Hak Chong Lee, and Ku Hyun Jung, *Korean Management: Global Strategy and Cultural Transformation* (Berlin: Walter de Gruyter, 1997).

10 Hyundai Business Group, *Company Handbook*, Seoul, p. 9 (translated from Korean).

11 Personal interview with Chung Ju Yung, honorary chairman, Hyundai Business Group, April 11, 1977.

12 Richard M. Steers and Stuart J. Black, *Organizational Behavior*, 5th edition (New York: Harper Collins, 1994).

13 Kyong-Dong Kim, "Cultural Aspects of Higher Productivity." In D. K. Kim (ed.), *Toward Higher Productivity: Experiences of the Republic of Korea* (Tokyo: Asian Productivity Association, 1985).

14 Song-Hyon Jang, *The Key to Successful Business in Korea* (Seoul: Yong Ahn, 1988).

15 Personal interview, 1997.

16 Ibid.

17 Lester Thurow, *Head-to-Head: The Coming Economic Battle among Japan, Europe, and America* (London: Nicholas Brealey, 1993).

18 Personal interview with Chung Ju Yung, honorary chairman, Hyundai Business Group, April 11, 1997.

19 Cho Hyoung and Chang Pil-wha, *Gender Division of Labor in Korea* (Seoul: Korean Women's Institute, Ewha Women's University Press, 1994).

20 "Planting the Seed of Feminism." *Business Korea*, January 1990, p. 19.

21 Lee Yoo-Lim, "Korean Companies Rely on Employee Interviews," *Business Korea*, November 1994, pp. 22–23.

22 Choi Jinni, "Women Advance in the Workplace," *Korea Economic Report*, August 1997, p. 59.

23 Personal interview with Kwon Ae-Ja, director, Welfare Department, Hyundai Engineering & Construction Company, September 4, 1997.

24 Ibid.

25 Ibid.

Chapter 14

1 Chung Ju Yung, "Requirements for a Leading Nation's Economy," speech presented at the annual meeting of the Korean Management Association, Seoul, July 26, 1977, p. 5.

2 Ibid.

3 Ibid.

4 Ibid.

5 Arthur D. Little Study, cited in *Asia, Inc.*, June 1997, p. 34.

6 John M. Leger, "Asia's Leading Companies: The Fifth Annual Review 200," *Far Eastern Economic Review*, January 1, 1998, pp. 38–90.

7 Chung Ju Yung, quoted in Donald Kirk, *Korean Dynasty* (New York: M. E. Sharpe, 1994), p. 39.

8 Phillip Grub, quoted in ibid., p. 39.

9 Chung Ju Yung, *Ordeals, But No Failures* (Seoul: Chesamkihae, 1991), p. 6.

10 Ann Marsh, "They Don't Expect to Take It with Them," *Forbes*, October 13, 1997, p. 130.

11 "Asan Foundation: Chung's Wealth Is Plowed Back," *Business Korea*, January 1986, p. 24.

12 Quoted in "Contributing to the Welfare of Society," *Hyundai Newsletter*, August 1997, p. 8.

13 "Honorary chairman Chung Donates Asan Engineering Building," *Hyundai Newsletter*, September 1996, p. 10.

14 Personal interview with Chung Ju Yung, honorary chairman, Hyundai Business Group, April 11, 1997.

15 Ibid.

16 Ibid.

17 Ibid.

18 Personal interview with Juhn Myung-Hun, president, Hyundai Motor America, November 7, 1997.

19 Chung, personal interview April 11, 1997.

20 Personal interview with Park Chong Sup, president, Hyundai Electronics America, November 6, 1997.

21 Ibid.

22 Personal interview with Lee Ik Chi, president, Hyundai Securities, September 5, 1997.

23 Chung Ju Yung interview with *Choson Magazine* conducted by Choi Bo-Sik, November 1996.

24 Chung, personal interview, April 11, 1997.

25 Park, personal interview, November 6, 1997.

26 Chung, personal interview, April 11, 1997.

27 Ibid.

28 Ibid.

29 Ibid.

30 Ibid.

31 Ibid.

32 "A Seoul Wedding: $83,3000," *The U.S.-Korea Review*, September–October 1997, p. 14.

33 Chung, personal interview, April 11, 1997.

34 Ibid.

35 Ibid.

36 Personal interview with Chung Mong Koo, group chairman, Hyundai Business Group, September 11, 1997.

37 Eun Mee Kim, *Big Business, Strong State: Collusion and Conflict in South Korean Development: 1960–1990* (Albany: State University of New York Press, 1997), p. 124.

38 Chung, *Ordeals*, p. 1.

39 Ibid., p. 7.

40 Chung, personal interview, April 11, 1997.

41 Chung, *Ordeals*, p. 55.

42 Chung, personal interview, April 11, 1997.

43 Ibid.

44 Chung Ju Yung, "Statement of Operations," Hyundai Business Group, Seoul, March 11, 1985, p. 1.

45 Chung Ju Yung, "Requirements for a Leading Nation's Economy," speech presented at the annual meeting of the Korean Management Association, Seoul, July 26, 1977, p. 5.

SELECTED REFERENCES
(In English)

Amsden, Alice. *Asia's Next Giant: South Korea and Late Industrialization*. New York: Oxford University Press, 1989.

Bank of Korea. *Annual Report: 1997*. Seoul: Bank of Korea, 1997.

Chang Chan Sup and Nahm Joo Chang. *The Korean Management System*. Westport, Conn.: Quorum Books, 1994.

Cho Lee-Jay and Kim Yoon Hyung, Eds. *Economic Systems in South and North Korea: The Agenda for Economic Integration*. Seoul: Korea Development Institute, 1995.

Chung, Kae H., and Hak Chong Lee. *Korean Managerial Dynamics*. New York: Praeger, 1989.

Chung, Kae H., Hak Chong Lee, and Ku Hyun Jung. *Korean Management: Global Strategy and Cultural Transformation*. Berlin: Walter de Gruyter, 1997.

Clifford, Mark L. *Troubled Tiger: Businessmen, Bureaucrats, and Generals in South Korea*. New York: M. E. Sharpe, 1994.

Covell, Jon Carter, and Alan Covell. *Korean Impact on Japanese Culture: Japan's Hidden History*. Seoul: Hollym, 1984.

Cumings, Bruce. *Korea's Place in the Sun: A Modern History*. New York: W. W. Norton, 1997.

Far Eastern Economic Review. *Asian Trade and Investment*. Hong Kong: Far Eastern Economic Review, 1997.

Federation of Korean Industries. *Korea's Economic Policies: 1945–1985*. Seoul: FKI, 1987.

Han Woo-keun. *The History of Korea*. Honolulu: University of Hawaii, 1971.

Janelli, Roger L. *Making Capitalism: The Social and Cultural Construction of a South Korean Conglomerate*. Stanford, Calif.: Stanford University Press, 1993.

Kang Myung Hun. *The Korean Business Conglomerate: Chaebol Then and Now*. Berkeley: Center for Korean Studies, Institute of East Asian Studies, University of California-Berkeley, 1996.

Kang, T. W. *Is Korea the Next Japan?* New York: Free Press, 1989.

Kearney, Robert. *The Warrior Worker: The History and Challenge of South Korea's Economic Miracle.* New York: Henry Holt, 1991.

Kim Choong Soon. *The Culture of Korean Industry: An Ethnography of the Poongsan Corporation.* Tucson: University of Arizona Press, 1992.

Kim Chung-yum. *Policymaking on the Front Lines: Memoirs of a Korean Practitioner, 1945–79.* Washington, DC: Economic Development Institute, World Bank, 1994.

Kim Eun Mee. *Big Business, Strong State: Collusion and Conflict in South Korean Development, 1960–1990.* Albany: State University of New York Press, 1997.

Kim Linsu. *Imitation to Innovation: The Dynamics of Korea's Technological Learning.* Boston: Harvard Business School Press, 1997.

Kirk, Donald. *Korean Dynasty: Hyundai and Chung Ju Yung.* New York: M. E. Sharpe, 1994.

Korea Development Bank. *Industry in Korea: 1997.* Seoul: Korea Development Bank, 1997.

Korea Economic Institute of America. *Korea's Economy: 1997.* Washington, D.C.: KEIA, 1997.

Lee Ki-baik. *A New History of Korea.* Cambridge, Mass.: Harvard University Press, 1984.

Lee, Peter H., and William T. de Bary, Eds. *Sources of Korean Tradition.* New York: Columbia University Press, 1997.

Nahm, Andrew C. *Introduction to Korean History and Culture.* Seoul: Hollym, 1993.

Naisbitt, John. *Megatrends Asia: Eight Asian Megatrends That Are Reshaping Our World.* New York: Simon & Schuster, 1997.

Porter, Michael. *The Competitive Advantage of Nations.* New York: Free Press, 1990.

Pound, Richard W. *Five Rings over Korea: The Secret Negotiations Behind the 1988 Olympic Games in Seoul.* Boston: Little, Brown, 1994.

Saccone, Richard. *The Business of Korean Culture.* Seoul: Hollym, 1994.

Sakong Il. *Korea in the World Economy.* Washington, D.C.: Institute for International Economics, 1993.

Sejong Institute. *Korea's Economic Diplomacy: Survival as a Trading Nation.* Seoul: Sejong Institute, 1995.

Song Byung-Nak. *The Rise of the Korean Economy.* Hong Kong: Oxford University Press, 1990.

Steers, Richard M., Yoo Keun Shin, and Gerardo R. Ungson. *The Chaebol: Korea's New Industrial Might.* New York: Harper & Row, 1989.

Stern, Joseph, Ji-hong Kim, Dwight Perkins, and Jung-ho Yoo. *Industrialization and the State: The Korean Heavy and Chemical Industry Drive.* Cambridge,

Mass.: Harvard Institute for International Development, Harvard University Press, 1995.

Ungson, Gerardo R., Richard M. Steers, and Seung-Ho Park. *Korean Enterprise: The Quest for Globalization.* Boston: Harvard Business School Press, 1997.

Vogel, Ezra F. *The Four Little Dragons: The Spread of Industrialization in East Asia.* Cambridge, Mass.: Harvard University Press, 1991.

Weisenborn, Ray E. *Korea's Amazing Century: From Kings to Satellites.* Seoul: Korea Fulbright Foundation, 1997.

Wilkenson, Barry. *Labour and Industry in the Asia-Pacific: Lessons from the Newly Industrialized Countries.* Berlin: Walter de Gruyter, 1994.

Winchester, Simon. *Korea: A Walk through the Land of Miracles.* Englewood Cliffs, NJ: Prentice-Hall, 1988.

INDEX